There's Coffee in the Fridge

One Man's Journey Through
Anxiety & Depression

James Francis

Green Heart Living Press

There's Coffee in the Fridge: *One Man's Journey Through Anxiety and Depression*
Copyright © 2023 James Francis Rinere

ISBN Paperback: 978-1-954493-31-5

Cover artwork and design: James Rinere

This is a work of nonfiction. The events are portrayed to the best of the author's memory. While all the stories in this book are true, some names and identifying details have been changed to protect the privacy of the people involved.

Dedication

To my life soulmate and partner Chris, who has been on this journey with me and who has cried, laughed, hugged, learned, evolved, and experienced everything with me. Most importantly, she has taught me what unconditional love really means, and for that, I will be eternally grateful and my future generations will be impacted in a positive way forever!

To my children, Ashley, Lyndsay, and James. You have been a driving force in my goal to be healthy and you are loved. The only thing that matters is happiness and I hope that through the work that we have all done, you follow a life path of peace and joy.

Contents

Foreword

As in the iconic holiday movie, *It's A Wonderful Life*, we all have a purpose. Jim found his purpose in writing his story to save others, to save men.

It is often difficult for one to see purpose when desperately fighting through clouds of doubt and despair. Some never know their worth, but Jim found it before it was too late.

He drove ever so close to the brink but got pulled back.

What was it that saved him?

A Godwink, his wife and kids, one last iota of inner strength?

Purpose, love, just enough caring about one's self to know that yes, you matter, even at the very last moment.

Life is messy, not a straight line, there are bumps and bruises, heartache. We weave our way through.

Men who don't often spill their guts to others over coffee, like women can do with such ease, get permission to look deeply into their life, their soul through this life lived.

Jim knows he is now a helper. He feels it deeply. His mission is to make the sun come up another day for anyone who reads his story.

PURPOSE, Pass it on.

Ann Nyberg, Emmy Nominated Broadcast Journalist, WTNH-CT, Host of NYBERG *and Founding Board of Trustees Member of The Katharine Hepburn Cultural Arts Center*

Preface

A Word From The Author

On a late Wednesday night as I was packing and organizing for my first business trip in over four years, I turned to my wife and said, "I set the alarm for 4:30 a.m. and I put some coffee in the refrigerator for the ride to the airport." I had spent 25 years of my career traveling all over the country, had taken thousands of flights, and stayed in as many hotel rooms. Despite that, I was extremely anxious about this trip.

I hadn't traveled for so long because I had left my former "business executive" life and was learning how to live a life of peace and authenticity after trying to die by suicide. Going out into the world and returning to a life where I had lived for decades with severe anxiety and depression was daunting.

The next morning, pre-dawn, my alarm awakened me. I sat up, put my feet on the floor, took a deep breath, and started to tiptoe to the bathroom. On the way to the shower, I leaned over to kiss my wife on the cheek. She turned her head and said, "There's coffee in the fridge." We both laughed, and I felt a healing chill throughout my entire being.

That simple sentence and loving "connection" gave me the strength to move forward with a big smile on my face, and it also helped to remind me of what is important and magical in the smallest of moments that occur in our daily lives. This book will challenge you to honor and heal the impact of your trauma on yourself and those you love, and to find your path to a life of connection with your soul, the place where life's magic truly begins.

I welcome you to the reading of my story and my life's work in examining myself. It is a story of pain, depression, love, peace, and everything in between. I have chosen to share some of the deepest parts of me with the world, with the goal of helping somebody that might feel that they cannot be themselves out there in what can be a fucking cruel world.

There is such a prevalence of mental and emotional pain and so much suffering resulting from the epidemic of mental illness. Yet, despite that prevalence of illness and pain and suffering, there still exists an ignorance of what mental illness is, preventing people from thinking that they can be open and honest about what they are experiencing. That ignorance leads to stigma and judgment, which prevents people from seeking help. I know this because I am one of those people.

I share this story with the hope that the stigma will start to dissipate because people like me will stand up and say, "HEY! This is *part* of who I am; it isn't *who* I am; it's just part of my experience—and, I need some fucking help!"

When I started to write this story in 2008, there was little talk of depression, anxiety, and other "mental" ailments. We might have had an occasional celebrity pop-up and admit to taking medication or going to a facility. As I write this now in 2021, and we have lived through a pandemic for the past year. There have been many more stories about celebrities, athletes, and others that have readily admitted to having struggles with depression. That is a good thing. Of course, it is not good that people experience pain and suffering. It *is* a good thing that it is becoming more commonplace to discuss it. However, it is still laced with stigma in many cultures and areas of daily life; for example, in business, where I spend most of my time, it is seen as the ultimate weakness to admit any level of vulnerability or the need for help, especially among business executives. This is the population that I want to speak with. These are people that my story could really help and allow them to drop the veil of shame that many feel about having the pain that they experience. Too often, people feel that they must shoulder the burden, and put their head down and keep their arms swinging.

My goal is for people to talk about these things and not feel like they are being victimized for asking for help. As you read this story, please keep those people in mind. And, if you are one of those people, I know that it is daunting to admit that you need help, but the world needs you, and you make a difference. You may not be able to see that today, but there could be lots of todays to come and you cannot know the impact that you can have in one of those todays.

Since my attempted suicide, my children have graduated from high school and college, one of my daughters has gotten married and the other has gotten engaged, my son has become a professional artist and my wife has celebrated the 10th anniversary of a business that she created from nothing. Yes, all great accomplishments, and all things that happened during a "today" that I would not have been here to experience.

A word of caution and some information about the language used in my story: This book was written using the language of the diseased life that I was living for many years. I have chosen to tell my story using language that is true to the story. More importantly, it provides insight into the stark contrast of living a peaceful existence, which I believe we all strive to live. Also, I grew up on Long Island, and much of the language that I use is simply the way that I talk, even in my most peaceful of states. If you are offended by harsh language, you may not choose to read on.

Our lives are the result of every choice that we have and will make. The stories that follow are all true to my memory and the people in my life. At times, my memory has been pieced together, as in the case of Chapter 1, where my recollection is an amalgam of events throughout a very foggy inpatient experience at a mental health facility. I wrote this chapter several years after it happened, and I used my journal and whatever memory I could bring back to my brain. I have chosen to change the names of almost everyone, with the exception of several people that have either given me their consent to use their name or those that I think would think that it is cool to be included.

My journey from sickness to health has taken about 15 years, so far, and it continues to be a work in progress. If that work has stopped, it will mean that I am either dead or that I have given up. Since the latter will not happen because of the commitment that I have made to my family, the work of self-examination will cease upon my death and passing into some other existence. My point here is that you will not read this book and walk away knowing all the secrets of life, have it all figured out, and be finished with whatever work you are trying to do.

I hope that this is the beginning of the continuance of an introspective part of your life. I believe that if everyone in the world could live the change and consciousness that I am trying to live we would all be a lot happier and co-exist more functionally for all.

CHAPTER 1

BREAKING DOWN
TO BREAKING THROUGH

The day was May 6, 2005. I was in my office on a beautifully clear Friday afternoon, overlooking the country's first planned town green in downtown New Haven, Connecticut. How is that for a little-known fact? I love little bullshit facts; they help my brain feel like it is being fed nutritive morsels that keep it evolving. Having information like that also helps me do the Sunday Times crossword puzzle, one of my rituals. At the time, though, I had not been able to concentrate long enough to look at a puzzle for more than a few minutes.

I was down, experiencing a depressive state as deep as any of the deepest depressive states that I had ever experienced in my life. My head was swirling in a sea of random and uncontrolled thoughts, my brain was racing out of control, and I was intermittently breaking out in cold sweats. The tremors in my hands were happening more regularly, as if they are filled with rage and anger and hate and reminded me of the dysfunction that has taken over one's life.

I was the CEO of an employee benefits brokerage firm that I created to offer something different and of value. My corner office is on the fifth floor of the former Bank of New Haven building, with a 15-foot ceiling, a solid oak door, and two large wood-framed windows that face Church Street and the town green beyond and two others that overlook the City Court House. I picked the building to house our company because I enjoyed the history and the architecture, and while the fixtures are a little old, the views of the green and Yale University are inspiring. The subconscious feeling of stability that I get when I look at Yale's staid structures and the village green helps offset the constant flux inside my head.

On that particular Friday, the value of the life that I had created, the relationships that I had developed, my career's success, and everything that I had become, seemed flimsier than ever. I felt as though I had been living a lie, and I was completely lost in a sea of whirring and endless chatter in my head. Society can do that to a person; there is so much noise bombarding us every day. For even the most grounded of people, filtering this noise can be challenging. I mean, Buddhist monks spend their entire lives practicing the ability to calm the mind—entire lives in practice—the rest of us have not got a fucking chance.

In depressive states before that day, I had experienced the phenomenon of racing thoughts, and I had learned to slow them down at times. In that episode though, the racing thoughts had gone unchecked for a month and were taking over every thought throughout the day. I could not make them stop, and it was like having 25 people in my head, all speaking simultaneously and not paying attention to each other. So, I kept my office door closed and shut out the world beyond.

I stared out the window watching the world below—cars driving by the building, birds flying from above the man who feeds them his bits of breadcrumbs by the large fountain. Yalies with books in their arms scrambled from dorms to classes. Jimmy, "The Hot Dog Guy," was preparing for the lunch crowd, and the world continues to move along as I opened and closed the window, debating whether the five-story drop would end in death or if I would end up in the hospital having failed to end this fucking pain. I felt as though I was floating above it all and was preparing to continue to float beyond my ability to return.

I had not had a solid night's sleep in over two weeks, most nights rolling over again and again and just laying still, staring out the window into the abyss of darkness while my mind ran laps around my world. I had lay there listening to my wife breathe: I occasionally pray for the guts to tell her that I am going to leave the world. Lack of sleep in my depressive states is not a usual symptom—usually, all I want to do is sleep.

My wife's brother, my best friend for many years, sat in the office next to mine; our relationship has experienced some very rough spots since we started to build this business. He is a minority owner in the company and has been with me since the beginning. His support and presence should be fun, a positive experience in building something that is growing and starting to thrive. However, I felt essentially alone in this company that I began with such high hopes of offering something different—something special. I could hear him on the phone, but I do not want to talk to him. I did not want to talk to anyone.

My office had two doors, one that opened to the office suite's main reception area and one that separated my office and my brother-in-law's office—it was an excellent setup for two brothers creating a business together. For much of the time that we have been working together, that door has remained open. It was a great way for us to communicate and interact during a typical business day and share funny stories and stuff that makes you laugh with co-workers throughout the day. The door has become a metaphor for distancing myself from my world. I had closed it in recent months, just as I had closed myself off from anyone around me. Isolation is one of my symptoms of depression and anxiety. It's a very aggressive form of exit that I use to punish myself—through confinement and separation from anyone and anything. If gone unchecked, it leads me to the belief that all I deserve is to be alone.

The phone rang. It was my wife, Chris. She chats with me about the upcoming events in the day—events that fill me with dread. I was the President of the Madison Youth Lacrosse program, and that day, I was coaching the third session of a lacrosse fundamentals clinic for about 100 second and third graders. I started to run this clinic format a couple of years ago. It was a lot of fun once I was on the field with the kids. Unfortunately, the buildup of pressure around putting together a fun program and dealing with all of the parent's needs was just too much for me.

I suffered panic attacks on Fridays when the clinic takes place. I could not manage my own need for perfection and the fact that I felt like I put my reputation as a great coach on the line every week. How's that for unmitigated ego? On top of that, Chris is running a large event for a youth organization that she co-chairs, the Madison Arts Barn. Chris is the Board President for this drug and alcohol-free teen facility in town, and she has devoted as much time to this volunteer endeavor as I have to run the lacrosse program. Today, our youngest daughter was participating in a craft fair at the Arts Barn and our oldest was playing in a lacrosse game. They both worked hard and have had fun creating jewelry and custom handbags made from old blue jeans that will be sold at the craft fair.

"How are you doing?" she asks nervously.

"Fine," I answered, ending the conversation.

Last night, Chris (to whom I have been married for almost 17 years) and I had a conversation in which I told her, without any uncertainty, that I have been having suicidal thoughts. This was the first time I had said that my suicidal thoughts are happening "right now" and in real-time. This is a departure from the normal approach that I had taken where I would say—you know, "I've had those thoughts in the past." We have had some difficult conversations throughout our relationship, as most couples have, and Chris can usually last for six or seven months at times and then just throws her hands up and cannot handle the disconnect between us.

These are conversations that we have had many times throughout our 20-year relationship. If we didn't have children, Chris would already be gone, but life changes when you have kids and others to consider in the big picture. I reveled in the miserable thoughts that I am such a loser and that I cannot and do not deserve the loving connection that this amazing person has offered to me—every day of my life.

The conversation would begin with my defensive ego fighting and pushing back hard, with Chris crying, saying that she loves me and doesn't want to live a life with an unfulfilling relationship in a marriage that is sexless, loveless, and lonely. We would do a relationship dance that would take us to an understanding that I could change, that I "wanted" to change, be engaged, and live the love that I feel for her.

It's those quiet moments that we work to, after breaking through layers of walls and obstacles that I create to prevent her from seeing me, and when those moments are achieved, there is a glimmer of hope and optimism that lasts for a bit. Unfortunately, when you're depressed, that optimism cannot be sustained. After these discussions, we would live our lives for a few months, or so, I would separate little by little with each passing day, and Chris would get to a place where she couldn't accept it any longer, and she would question me again, with increased intensity.

Those questions stemmed from her need to be loved and to be in a relationship with someone that would provide her with some happiness. All the "normal" stuff that people want when they are in a relationship with someone. Unfortunately, my model for marriage and relationship was two parents who "didn't know what they didn't know." When you add in depression and severe anxiety, it's the perfect recipe for a disconnected experience. I will add here that in my defense (and others who suffer from depression or any form of anxiety or other mental illness), my rationale for wanting that disconnect is that I felt that I was doing Chris a favor by not exposing her to the most intense and dark corners of my mind.

I wanted to protect her from my pain and darkness and thought this was the best way to do it. As I learned and will discuss later in the story, embracing the darkness, holding it like an electrified wet blanket, and suffering the burns and scars that go along with that is the way to release that pain into the Universe.

Chris had known for many years that I was not a happy person; we have discussed the lack of feeling and the numbness that I experienced in my life. I could go through a day, a fun day, like, attending a party with 50 people or an intimate dinner party with friends, tell jokes, and engage in fun behavior, seemingly happy. I could be the life of the party, the guy that tells funny stories about life, the guy's guy. I have been told by many people that I am the funniest person that they know; the irony is as thick as the black thoughts that are like magma in my mind.

After leaving a party like that, I would experience an intense feeling of emptiness and say to myself, "If that's all there is, then I'm fucking outta here." It had been hard for Chris to maintain her level of sanity while watching someone she loves fall apart emotionally before her eyes. She had learned the hard way that you cannot change a person or be responsible for their pain or joy.

Until the night before, she didn't know the depths to which my mind would take me; she just couldn't get her head around it. This was understandable. People who do not experience this type of pain and suffering, which is entirely silent on the outside and happening inside a person's mind, would never identify with it or make sense of this sponsoring thought. For Chris, who is a happy person and generally positive, the idea of living a life of chronic sadness and self-loathing is just unfathomable.

If not for her exposure to a pretty miserable husband, she wouldn't even know that depression exists—it just would not be part of her experience. We have had many of the conversations that we had the night before, but I had never taken her to the actual place of my mind's solution—death of the destructive thoughts. I had believed for many years that the only way to control those thoughts and ease the pain and suffering is the death of the entire being—body, mind, and soul.

I had carried the shame of hiding this secretive thought for many years, and now that I have shared the thought, it has opened up the real option of leaving. I would not have wanted to leave without sharing some level of acknowledgment that I have these thoughts. Chris deserved to have the knowledge that it wasn't just a spur-of-the-moment decision. In my insane mind, that conversation was the green light that it is now OK to leave—I had shared my deepest pain...now I could go.

Getting up from my chair, I realized that I must get out of the office. The tension is building in me to the point where I could no longer remain in a business environment. It is one of my triggers. So, I open the door, walk out of the office, and say to the team, without making eye contact, "Have a nice weekend."

Outside, I made my way to 900 Chapel Street, for the stairs that took me to the parking garage beneath the Omni Hotel. I had parked my 3-series BMW convertible here. The car has a beautiful silver exterior with a black top and a black leather interior. As someone whose first car was a '73 Oldsmobile Cutlass, I love this machine. I have appreciated having such a beautiful car at times, and I have worked hard to achieve it. I felt like I had arrived when I first drove this car, like all was right with the world, which is another bit of fucking irony since I had decided that I was going to kill myself in this car that day.

Isolation Wins

I got in, turned the key, felt the engine fire up, and was surrounded by pure power. I dropped the roof and headed for the exit. Soon, I was driving down the stretch of highway that ran along the Connecticut shoreline due east of New Haven. Yes, it's technically 95 North, but that road is moving due east for most of Connecticut. This thought pissed me the fuck off!

Nearing the town of Branford, I decided to make a stop at a computer store to have my laptop looked at because I've been having issues with the hard drive. This may seem odd, given my plan, but it has been my personal experience that there are always things that I am trying to do to maintain some connection to reality so that I avoid the unreal. So far, this has worked for me. I was popping in and out of life in each moment, and some small part of me was still trying to survive with some semblance of normalcy.

I wondered if I was together enough to perform this errand. I felt as numb as I have ever felt in my life, and I was having a hard time seeing specific objects in my field of view. I could tell that there were cars, road signs, gas stations, and exits, and that life was happening around me. However, all I saw were the blurs of stuff flying by me. I felt I was slipping away. I felt like dying, I felt like I had just had enough of feeling worthless and was not feeling happy to be in this life—what from the outside looked like a wonderful life. I was tired of trying to understand why some people are happy and why I was not—it provoked such a strong sense of inferiority in me. This feeling added to my self-loathing and shame, to the point of just tossing my hands up and saying, "Fuck it."

Intellectually, I knew that my life was wonderful. Emotionally, I could not accept it, couldn't feel it, and didn't believe it. I pulled into the parking lot of the computer shop and walk into the store feeling as though I am lost in some nightmare. Behind the counter is a young woman, probably 22 or 23 years old, and she asks, "How are you doing?"

My first thought was, "You haven't got enough time or the schooling to begin to understand how I am doing."

My second thought was, "When I was your age, if I knew where I was going to be 20 years later, I'd have thrown myself in front of the fucking train on the LIRR platform—kill yourself while you still have time—it's not too late!"

Ultimately, I say, "I'm good."

I didn't think that I was very convincing, but it doesn't matter anyway; I was just another customer that came in with a computer that is screwed because of some virus that has attacked the hard drive. She takes it to the back room, where I imagine a 19-year-old computer geek being interrupted from the latest version of Dungeons and Dragons. He is plugging it into a diagnostic program that produces the diagnosis—USER FUCKING ERROR!

The diagnosis is not good—the computer is fried and needs to be refurbished—the cost is about $500. The bottom line is that I am going to have to buy another computer. This is not good news. I am feeling so much financial pressure. While the company was growing, I was not taking any salary—and we are digging into our savings every month to offset the deficit in earnings vs. expenses. Every financial decision, every piece of what I perceive to be bad news, was a reminder of my shortcomings as a business manager, decision-maker, and provider for my family. *The alpha male is not allowed to show weakness of any kind; I must provide for my family. I must prove to the world that I am a Master of the Universe.* The masculine ego must be fed the line that it is good and taking care of its tribe.

As I stood there looking at this young woman, with her cheery disposition and friendly smile, hearing news that I need to buy another computer with money that I didn't have, I decided that I was done. She would be the last face that I saw in this life. Thirty years of dealing with the demons of depression have led me to this place. I told her that I would have to get back to her on the next steps, fully knowing that in 10 minutes, it won't matter anymore—the computer would be in a thousand pieces, along with my skull. In a thousand pieces on I-95 fucking East!

The sensation of looking at someone and knowing that they are the last face you will see is very surreal. I wondered if she would even remember that I was there.

I got into the car, and my hands began to shake again as I started it up and shift into first gear and drive West on Route 1. I did not want to hear any more bad news, I wanted the constant fucking noise in my head to stop for good, and I wanted to leave this place. I wanted to hit the reset button.

I travelled down Route 1, trying to establish some mental stability to see if this moment of extreme pain would pass. I was thinking about my working days in New York City, which provided me with a financial base to live here on the Connecticut shoreline. I drove through Branford, which, like most shoreline towns, is a quintessential New England suburban outpost, an "American Dream" type place. It is filled with history, character, and the "look mom, I've made it" feeling I had strived for.

In the short three-mile trip down Route 1, I decided that I needed to have an "accident" to save my children and my wife from a life of questions about why I would die by suicide. I wanted those questions and all of the other missteps in my life to be dead with me.

I headed back to the turnpike. On the entry ramp, I hit the gas hard and upshift through the gears quickly, now in fifth I can barely see the speedometer's needle as it passes 70, 80, 90, 100, and it stops moving at 110. Tears were streaming down my face as I look for a concrete embankment to impale myself on. The steel guardrails are flying by me the way clouds do when you're flying in a plane. I knew that somewhere on this stretch of road from East Haven to Madison, there was a rock outcropping or concrete barrier that I could angle into that would destroy this car.

Suicide: A Permanent Solution to Temporary Pain

A couple of years ago, a friend of ours, Dave, jumped off a mountain at Sleeping Giant State Park in Hamden, Connecticut. In talking with other friends after the funeral, the common theme was that people didn't have a clue as to how unhappy he was and the depths of the depression that he had succumbed to. I had spoken with Dave a week before he ended his life, and I knew that he wasn't happy and that he was conflicted, but I had no idea that he was on the threshold of such a permanent solution. That's what suicide is, a long-term solution to short-term problems. I repeat, PERMANENT. I wish that I had known how sad my buddy was; I wish that I had the answer to why he thought he had to end it by jumping off the side of a mountain.

However, as Chris and I sat in the church at his memorial service, a church filled with hundreds of people mourning this fun-loving and seemingly vibrant guy's death, I felt like I completely understood his need to jump off that mountain, to jump out of this world, to just fucking jump out of his body.

I remembered saying to Chris as we sat there listening to Bette Midler sing "Wind Beneath My Wings," "I can understand the need he had to end his pain."

Of course, Chris felt that his actions were extremely selfish and destructive as we watched his widow sob in the front pew, and she was absolutely spot on. On the contrary, there was no more selfless act in my tortured mind than taking yourself out of another's life if you believe that you are not a positive influence.

I didn't want Chris to experience those questions, not to have some idea of the unknown depths of the depression I have been living with. In my mind that day, sharing those thoughts the night before was enough that I had now explained myself thoroughly. Of course, as I mentioned, Chris could not even get her head around the unexplained sadness of depression, so thinking that I had explained myself to eliminate the questions of, "why suicide?" is just further evidence of my incredibly suspect understanding of the reality around the issue.

In my depressed mind, a mind driven by thoughts of self-loathing, fear of failure, fear of being able to continue the success that I had achieved, fear of parenthood, fear of intimacy, and heightened anxiety, the only solution is death. All other options would either take too long or require a prolonged path of work and medication—lots of it, and for like...like...well, forever.

Forever is too fucking long for an anxiety-ridden, manic-depressive personality. Think of a small child. They go from one thing to another, and if they want something, they want it now! There is no patience for the hedonistic desires of a child. I had the emotional development of a child, the immaturity, and the emotional IQ of a self-indulgent three-year-old. I was a model Freudian illustration of arrested development.

I began to experience the "life flashing before my eyes" moment and thought about all that I had lived through in my life. It shone a light on the contrast that was my world. My children are just an amazing accomplishment; despite my fear of being a horrible father, I think they are uniquely impressive. I had provided a beautiful home for them and my wife in Madison, Connecticut, a very tiny jewel of the Connecticut shoreline.

I thought about the days of taking the train to Manhattan at 5:30 in the morning to sell insurance to companies all over the country, the late nights entertaining clients, the grueling battle of climbing the corporate ladder here in Connecticut, the weeks and weeks of business travel away from home—leaving on a Monday and coming home on Friday, the golf junkets for business, Caribbean vacations with my family, playing lacrosse in and graduating from college, getting married, running the New York City Marathon, running miles and miles pushing my daughter in a three-wheel jogging buggy, the 4th of July pool parties at our house, the gourmet group that we started with friends, playing basketball with a bunch of 30+ year old executives three mornings a week for years, all of it—cycling through my head as I move down the path of goodbye.

Then, the horrible things that I have done in my life, the unspeakable acts of dishonesty, disconnection, destruction, drinking, and emotional exits—it overshadows the good that I have done, and a wave of shame covers me like molten lava— it was fucking suffocating.

At this moment, all I could think about is my wife, the legacy of pain that I was leaving to this person that had been nothing but good in my life, really, the "best good" that I had ever experienced for a consistent length of time. It struck me very succinctly and with tremendous power. I immediately felt that I need to hear her voice, and I reflexively reached for my cell phone and dialed her number. I think, *if she doesn't pick up, it's a sign that it's the right time to leave, and I'll just leave a message.*

The Hand of the Universe

My wife rarely answers her cell phone, especially at 3:30 in the afternoon when the kids are descending on our house from school. Chris's devotion to our children and our home and family are just a couple of the reasons why I was not already dead. Her involvement in the world was one of those signs that there is a god or some Universal Life Force—she is an incredible person. She picks up the phone on the first ring and I hear the buzzing of life in the background on the other end. My head was spinning as I made my way toward the Leete's Island exit. Time was truly standing still.

Through my sobs and in a flat, monotone voice, I said to Chris, "I'm calling to say goodbye, I can't do this anymore and want to die...now. I am on the highway, and I am looking for a place where I can drive off the road and hit something very hard that will kill me."

I was coming down the hill toward the Guilford Route 1 exit; I knew that there's a large boulder on this stretch, but I couldn't see a damn thing through my crying eyes, and I was sweating so profusely that my hands can barely grip the steering wheel. I could hear my children in the background, getting their after school snacks and yelling and screaming about their days and the fact that it's Friday.

I didn't want to "do it" with my wife on the phone, and she is telling me to stay with her; I can hear choppy breathing as her anxiety levels shoot through the roof.

"Don't hang up the phone, Jim, stay with me!"

The house phone started ringing in the background, and Chris could see that it was my sister Monique, and she says, "It's your sister—hold on—stay there—you have to stay there!"

Monique had decided to surprise the family with a visit because she wanted to go to the craft fair with my daughters, and she's half a mile behind me on I-95.

So, there's my wife, standing in the middle of our bustling kitchen, with her cell phone and her suicidal husband in one hand and in the other hand, the house phone with the suicidal husband's sister. She was trying to keep it together so that our children didn't go into a complete panic and were not scarred for the rest of their lives.

This moment in time was a microcosm of our life; Chris had been able to provide a happy and well-balanced life for our children despite my "dis-ease." Yes, my children will have residual effects of growing up with a parent that suffers from severe depression. However, those effects would be far worse if they did not have their mother.

Since my sister is familiar with the protocol of suicidality and my wife knows that I won't kill myself with her on the phone, they decide together that Chris should "talk me off the road" immediately and that my sister would meet me at the exit where I leave the highway.

My wife half yells into the phone as she scrambles into the next room and shuts the door.

"Just stay with me and get off the highway...can you do that?...Jim?...Can you get off the highway now or stop driving right now?!"

I was approaching exit 59, Goose Hill Lane, and I was trying to decide if I wanted to stop, if I should stop or if I should just get it over with...

I thought, *You've waited so long, you've talked about this in your head for 30 years, you're finally here, don't stop, KILL the pain.*

Chris was talking into my ear, "Jim, I NEED YOU TO STOP; I LOVE YOU; YOUR FAMILY NEEDS YOU, YOU ARE LOVED!"

Those words cut through all the racing thoughts, all of the mud that had become my brain.

I went from 110 MPH in the left lane to a dead stop (no pun intended) at the traffic light on Goose Hill Lane in about 200 yards. Chris stays on the phone with me and literally talks me through the left turn to Goose Hill Lane and into the commuter park and ride lot. The lot was empty, and I was so exhausted, I pull in and sit, slumped and sobbing behind the wheel.

Chris said, "Where are the keys to the car? I want you to take them out of the ignition, now!"

My sister pulled in next to me within a minute and guides me into her car. I collapsed into the passenger seat of her '98 Volkswagen Beetle, and I just felt lost. I felt like I had lost complete control of all that I was, as I've just given it up to the Universe. I was afraid, and I was full of hate for myself. I never wanted to let the world know how much I hated myself and how scared I was of living for another day, and now...well, now, it's all over. Regardless of what happened next, it would never be the same again. I would never be viewed as the one that had his shit together.

I had left the world, but I was still alive—I had left my world, the world that I created in my mind.

CHAPTER 2

THE HAND OF THE UNIVERSE

Do you believe in the hand of God, or angels, or the Universe, or some dynamic Universal Force?

I had not been a religious person up to this point. Having been raised as a Roman Catholic who was forced to attend church every Sunday as a kid, I loathed structured religion. I fucking hated going to church, I hated God for putting me here, hated anything about connection to some other-worldly being. Further, because of my depressive state, I didn't believe that there was a God. I certainly do now.

A word about "God." I certainly believe in some Universal Force that creates connection and causes miracles to occur, which cannot be explained and defy any logic. I call it "Universe"—you can call it what you want. For purposes of this story, let's agree to call it God. However, I am reticent to use the term because it conjures the guy in the sky that people pray to and is attached to so much ideology and a fear-based life of belief, judgment, and other shit that I just cannot support. That's my disclaimer about organized religion.

My sister lives in Princeton, New Jersey, and she is an experienced and professionally trained advisor for students at Princeton University. She knows how to handle the emergent nature of suicide, and in that split second, my wife made the decision that my sister's help would be really effective.

This is where God entered the room!

What my wife didn't count on was that my sister was on Rt. 95 at the exact same exit that I had just passed, only a short distance behind me; in fact, I probably drove past her at 100

MPH. Did I mention that my sister lives in Princeton, New Jersey? And she hadn't been to my house for months, and we had no idea that she would be visiting that day?

Sick and Tired

My sister drove out of the park and ride lot and onto the highway heading south toward Yale New Haven Hospital. I heard her talking on the phone to Chris and telling her that she was taking me to Yale Psychiatric Emergency and that I was out of immediate danger.

On the 15-minute drive down to Yale, I could hear her asking me questions, "Jim, how long have you been thinking about killing yourself? Have you been drinking today or taking any drugs? Have you been sleeping?"

Slowly, I explained that I often have thought of suicide over the last 30 years. The first time that I thought about it as a way to end my suffering and to get out of this world, a self-created world of unhappiness and anxiety, I was 12 years old and in the sixth grade. That day, I laid on the deck of a decrepit old wooden boat that sat on concrete blocks in my backyard, and I stared at the sky and thought, *This life sucks; I do not want to stay here...*

At 40, I had finished waiting for things to change, for the one event that would bring me the happiness that I had been seeking—*it's not going to happen, not now, not ever.*

Billy Joel's song "River of Dreams" was playing over and over again in my head. I was tired; I was absolutely frickin' exhausted and had decided that I just couldn't fucking take it any longer.

"I had a conversation with mom yesterday," I told my sister. "Mom explained her lifelong struggle with depression and anxiety. She told me that she had been to a doctor who diagnosed her with depression, and she was going to start taking some medication that would help her mood levels."

My mom told me that it was something that she was suffering from for most of her life, but that she never really paid much attention to whether life should or could be "happy." That was for other people.

"Her rambling on the phone with me, you know, the way that she goes on and on about herself in the most inane manner—I'm not really listening to her, and I'm thinking— you have got to be fucking kidding me?! You want me to listen while you tell me that you didn't know that life could be happy? All those years that I was miserable as a child, alone in my fear and confusion, all of those years that she could have helped me in some small way. Mom could have acknowledged her feelings of despair and isolation. I was alone in my thoughts; she never reached out to me. As I listened to her gibberish, I grew angrier and angrier. I wanted to scream at the top of my lungs. I just couldn't believe what I was hearing. I mean, for fuck's sake, I was never seen.

"Now, I'm pissed off. I'm pissed that she never shared any of this with me, that she had four children, and that three of them exhibited signs of mental distress at one time or another, and she never said a damn thing. That infuriates me. As a child, I tried to sort through feelings of extreme anxiety and depression on my own because I was alone. I was physically and emotionally abandoned beyond what any person, especially a child, should have to manage."

The thought of knowing that this could be genetic was just the icing on the cake. Could that be the most prominent legacy that my parents have bestowed on me? Looking back at our childhood structure and events, to understand why we are the way we are, is an important reckoning. It helps us see why we see things in certain ways, how we are built to manage or not manage specific events, and that understanding helps mold and shape our evolution for the future. It is not a point of blame; it is a nutritive exercise in learning. Looking back that day, all I could see was a life road littered with potholes, rusty guardrails, and abandoned hub caps.

The Longest Day Continues

After we arrived at Yale, my sister escorted me into the emergency room. I had a tough time seeing what is going on around me, but I could see the clocks on the walls and the people lying on the floor in the psych ward. They take my belt and my shoelaces at check-in and lead me to a room at the end of the hall, where I sit, holding myself for hours. It might have been only minutes; I just didn't care about time anymore. That was somebody else's problem. I had given up.

The next thing I knew, I was lying in my bed at home, feeling very tired and very groggy. My wife, faced with placing me in the Yale psych ward for a stay of an indeterminate amount of time, just couldn't leave me there. She was strongly advised by my personal doctor and the professionals at Yale that I was a danger to myself and others and that she should not take me anywhere. They told her that she wasn't equipped to manage the situation and that I might do something to hurt myself and potentially somebody else, and that would be something that she would have to live with for the rest of her life.

Chris is a woman with a tremendous amount of wisdom and intuition. Intellectually, she knows that the doctors were right, but in her heart, she felt that it wouldn't serve my needs. The ethos of the Yale psych facility is extremely institutional—just too extreme for Chris to get her heart around. So, she took me home, armed with some potent sedatives and a prescription for an antidepressant that would require weeks to take hold.

Chris is confident that she and my sister can get me to sleep and monitor me 24/7 until they find a facility that would be more appropriate. That night, thanks to the sedatives, I slept like I haven't slept in my entire life. The racing of my mind had eased a bit, and I was able to sleep without interruption until mid-morning, only awakened once for a medication reload. Unfortunately, my thwarted attempt on the highway has not deterred me from the desire to end my life, and my imagination is preparing a myriad of ways to accomplish this goal. As a former college athlete, I was trained to be very goal-oriented, and once I have a goal in mind, I typically fulfill it—good or bad.

I spent the weekend mostly horizontal, drugged with sleeping pills and antidepressants, and an antipsychotic. The antidepressants take weeks to kick in, but the sleeping aids work instantaneously.

We have a picture window in our bedroom that faces south and overlooks a picket fence and concrete path that winds its way around our swimming pool. I stood at that window, trying to establish the right angle of trajectory and running speed that I would need to a) break through the window and b) impale myself on the picket fence below. Of course, I didn't want to live through such a failed attempt, so I was taking my time with the process of establishing the correct path out the window. A few times throughout the day, I stood here, my train of thought broken by my wife or my sister, who walked in and led me back to the confines of my bed. It didn't help that I was so doped up. A few times, when I thought I was staring out the window and getting ready to leap, I was actually in bed. Much of what I was "seeing" was a hallucination.

That afternoon, Chris thinks it might be good for me to get some fresh air, and she takes me to CVS in town to pick up my new meds. As we drove down the bucolic main artery in town, Rt. 79, heading south toward the Long Island Sound, I was trying to engage my arms and mind simultaneously so that I can open the door and jump out onto the blacktop with the hope of cracking my skull open and killing myself. It was an incredibly stressful ride. I wanted my family to be free of my fucked-up mind and my self-created worthlessness. I hated myself for not being dead, for still being the miserable prick that I have felt like for the past 30 years.

Chris and my sister spent most of the weekend trying to get me into what they think will be an appropriate treatment facility, but it seems that everything is full. Apparently, there are a lot of crazies out there.

Life, As I Knew It, Was Over

After some serious intention, Chris received a call from Silver Hill Hospital in New Canaan, CT. Silver Hill is a world-class facility that has been around for a long time and has treated some of the most famous celebrities in the world. That doesn't automatically mean that it is a top-notch place, but it does provide perceived credibility. It was the first facility that Yale and my doctor recommended as an alternative to Yale Psych.

In her first conversation with Silver Hill, Chris was told that they do not have room in the acute care unit and they referred us to another facility. In a second discussion, Chris was told that a room has opened up and they can take me on Monday morning. A prayer answered! You see, the hand of "God" had now reached down to us for the third or fourth time in two days.

One of my best friends pulled up to the house in his BMW 750 sedan on Monday morning. He had volunteered to drive Chris and me down the hospital because he wants to help in any way possible. Chris had learned very quickly over the last few days that help comes when you need it and it is best to accept it when it is offered. This was not how we lived up until then. We were very self-sufficient and completely self-reliant.

I climbed into the back seat, and Chris buckled me in and tells my buddy to "lock the doors and windows" so that I can't jump out. I saw the look of horror on his face as he stared at his formerly optimistic friend, trying to comprehend that that was even a remote possibility.

My friend, Bill, is a strong guy, but he is also pretty closed off and distant at times. For him to be faced with such an emotional trauma must be extremely difficult to bear, especially since he knows me as a pretty funny and "fun" person to hang out with—great at a party, fun on the golf course, and always trying to make people laugh.

It was almost exactly two years to the day that our friend Dave had jumped off the mountain at Sleeping Giant State Park. He had stopped his depression medication and just went into a complete stupor that ended with him taking his life while on the phone with his sister. I remember talking to Bill and his brother at the time, and we all agreed that we wouldn't let something like that happen again—we would always try to reach out so that people would know that there were friends that cared.

Unfortunately, you cannot help someone that doesn't want your help, and this is especially true if that person believes that you, his friend, will be much better off if you are not subjected to him again.

We stopped at the Fairfield rest area on the way down the Merritt Parkway because Chris needs to use the restroom. Bill opens the back door and asks me, "What does it feel like? Where are you?"

Trying to be honest and coherent, I said to him, "My mind is telling me that it is time to die, that to continue living in this bullshit is not worth it anymore, that I am tired of the lack of fulfillment that I feel. Bill, there has to be something else, it just doesn't make sense to me anymore."

I explained to Bill that I can't accept a life of numbness any longer, that I wanted to die, that I did not see any other option, that I didn't want to be in therapy or on medication for the rest of my life, that I didn't want to be labeled as the psycho friend, and that I didn't want people to know that I am weak.

His next question is too much for me to handle emotionally, but it is one that I will ask myself many times in the coming years.

"What about your kids? What about your wife? They love you, how can you just decide that it is time to go? We don't get to make that decision!"

Again, I took measure of my friend, of myself, and I break down crying while he holds me.

We snaked our way through some back roads in Norwalk and into New Canaan and pull into Silver Hill Hospital. It was founded in 1931 in a hillside farmhouse. Now, it's spread over 40 acres, comprising 14 buildings, a gem hidden in the Connecticut hills.

However, the building that I was being led into is not the cozy cottage near the gate that looks like a bed and breakfast. It was a secure facility up on the hill. I knew as I am led to my room that life, whatever it was to be, would never be the same again.

CHAPTER 3
RELINQUISH CONTROL

I sat on the edge of a twin bed, very much like the one that was in my college dorm room. Metal frame with a small wooden headboard, a white pillow that looked pretty damn inviting, and a clean set of sheets and blanket, complete with impressive hospital corners. As I sat there taking it all in, I was trying to piece together the events of the past few days. Some memories were there; some were just hazy streams of people moving in and out of my world, and the smells that they brought with them.

There was a small wardrobe closet with hooks and shelves and a bathroom with a shower stall. There was a three-foot space between the bed and the wooden desk at the foot of the bed that sat beside a double window overlooking a nice scene of grass and trees. I imagined myself sitting on the edge of the bed at a Marriott Hotel that I had recently stayed in on a business trip to D.C. The scenery out the window was very much the same. Unfortunately, I wasn't readying myself for a walk down to the fitness room or dinner. Instead I was preparing to start drooling down my shirt and sleeping for a month.

I heard a slight commotion coming from somewhere down the hall; apparently, someone didn't want to leave her room for the "group" session. I did not know what a group session was, and I was pretty sure I didn't want to do anything that involved that person.

The screams of anger and pain were shrill as she yelled, "NOT today; I'm too fucking tired, please, not today!"

All I could think of doing was what I had wanted to do for a long time: crying. I dropped my head into my hands. Weeping into my hands felt good; it felt like a release of all that had been weighing on me. It felt like letting go of a life that I could no longer live.

That feeling lasted about a minute.

Then I started feeling like a pussy that had given up on life—a weak and beaten little wuss. Shame coated me like wet plaster being poured from above. I knew that my room was the next to be visited by the staff nurse that was rounding everyone up for whatever the fuck a group session was. I didn't want to go either. I just wanted to be alone. I wanted to curl up into a little ball on the floor and just fucking quit the world. I could not believe that I was there. I could not believe that I was alive.

Why am I still alive? To what purpose can I possibly continue to be here? Have I not had enough failure, enough self-loathing, enough pain, enough demotivation, enough dishonesty, just ENOUGH!? I mean what the fuuuuuuck?!?!

The desk was a pine veneer, looked pretty solid, and like something that I might be able to pick up and throw through the window. I thought about Chief in *One Flew Over The Cuckoo's Nest* when he throws that huge sink out the window and takes off into the abyss of the world. Then the thought hit me, *Where the hell are you going? You can't go home—there is no home, you made sure of that—you erased home the moment you decided that you didn't want to live anymore.*

You said to your family, "This life that we've all created, that I have been a driving force to, well, it's been a lie, and I have perpetrated a complete ruse on you all. Your husband, your father, your "go-to" leader—I'm just a phony, and you will all be better off without me in your world."

Giving Up to Be Safe!

I had no clothes except for the three t-shirts, seven pairs of underwear, two pairs of socks, and two pairs of pants that were neatly folded in the wardrobe. I didn't even have a pair of shoes; they took those when I walked through the front door— the laces posed a threat as a potential ligature around your neck, so they left me with my flip flops. What else was there? Oh yeah, there was a toothbrush, toothpaste, a bar of soap, and a hotel-sized shampoo bottle on the corner shelf in the shower stall.

The screaming got a little louder.

"I'll come down what I'm good and fucking ready to come down, today I need to sleep—just leave me the fuck alone."

The desk was empty except for the blue registration folder that I was given when I checked in. It had the beautiful seal of the facility, the simplest yet most succinct logo that I have ever seen—just three lines that illustrate rolling hills, with the tag line: "Restoring Mental Health since 1931."

I was sure that I was about to force them to change the tagline because it isn't going to be true in my case. I'd been carrying around the insane thoughts and scars that go along with constant mental anguish. *Restore?... I think not.*

There was a stack of high school textbooks on the floor next to my new roommate's bed. Physics was on top, and there were a couple of notebooks and workbooks on the pile. I was told on the way in that since they only had one bed available in the unit, I would be sharing a room with a teenage boy who has been here for some time and was very troubled.

"Well, that makes two of us."

I was so tired. I didn't care who was in the room with me, I just knew I wanted to sleep. I just wanted to end my pain. I just wanted to get out. I was there with the goal of being safe, but the loss of control over my world was causing more stress. I could not get the thoughts of wanting to hurt myself out of my head—they just wouldn't stop.

I was struck by this young kid who was barely 17. He was so stressed and anxious that he couldn't deal with life, he was contemplating suicide, he was miserable, and couldn't sleep... he was me. That was me at 17! I was reviewing myself in this mirror image that reflected me from over 20 years ago and said to myself, *God, if I had just done it then, I wouldn't be putting my family through this pain.*

I heard what seemed like a very distant knock, my mind not willing to accept the present reality. The doctor was back in my room, sitting on the bed opposite mine.

"Tell me, Jim, can you share with me why you are here?"

"Well, doctor, all I can tell you is that my wife promised that I would enjoy a nice car ride in the country; next thing I know, I'm given a pair of white pajamas and a straight jacket, you got the wrong guy, I'm happy."

Of course, this is not what I said.

As with most uncomfortable situations, I wanted to use humor to ease my anxiety, and I was reminded of a joke that I heard many years ago. A joke that I had told many times over those years, mostly when I had a few drinks to make me happy.

A guy goes to an insane asylum and starts looking through the windows in the doors at the patients. At the first window, he sees a guy standing on his bed with his arms out, and he's yelling,

"I'm Superman, and I'm flying through the air, faster than a speeding bullet; I'm flying out the window to freedom."

At the second window, he sees an enormously obese guy with boxing gloves on his hands, and he's hopping around saying, "I'm the world champ; I'm Ali, I'm Frasier, nobody can beat me, one more victory, and I'm getting out of here."

Then, at the third window, he sees a guy with a walnut on the end of his penis, and he's thrusting his hips in and out, and he says, "I'm fucking nuts, and I'm never getting out of here!"

Out in the hallway, a phone rang, and I heard somebody say, "Hello? Steve? Hold on, I'll see if I can find him."

There were two payphones in the hall, to be shared by all of the patients, and phone use times were pretty limited. Whoever it was that answered the phone dropped the gray receiver. I heard it dangling below the phone and swinging back and forth, the spiral metal cord making a grinding sound as it scraped the steel base of the phone box. It reminded me of what it was probably like in a prison corridor when an inmate gets a call, and somebody needed to find him in his cell or something.

I looked up at the doctor, this time I answered out loud, "I haven't slept for more than two hours at a time in the last 15 or 16 days, and I'm just exhausted. I own a business, and the financial pressure of the world that I have created is just too much for me to want to handle. I just want to die—that seems to be the only relief for me—to kill myself."

He made some notes on his pad, then looked up and said, "You're going to be OK; we will take care of you, but the process is a difficult process, and you have to be willing to let go and be of the process. I can see by the notes that you are an athlete, a marathon runner, a lacrosse coach, a tennis player—well, that's great. You know the physical work and commitment it takes to run a marathon? That's the kind of work ethic you will need to get through this—to be healthy. There will be discouraging moments, times when you feel like you can't run another step—those are the times to take a break and just know that you can and will take another step—just let the process unfold for you."

Nurse Patty came into my room and gave me some medication.

"These will help you calm down, you will need to take these every 12 hours, and we are having a group session in an hour; group sessions are mandatory."

"Isn't everything mandatory, Patty? I mean, I am locked in here—aren't we all insane? Are you saying that we get choices? Giving choices is not a good idea; it's my bad choices that have led me to be sitting on the edge of this fucking cot and taking medication meant for people with split fucking personalities or to put a rhino to sleep for a few days. I'm not, you know, Sybil!"

Patty smiled as she jotted a note on her clipboard and left me sitting on the edge of my bed like a child waiting for his mom to pick him up from the nurse's office at the elementary school. You know, like when I got sick in Mrs. Glaser's fourth grade class at Plaza Elementary School and they gave me some loaner clothes and one of those lumpy screw-top ice bags. They called my mom, but since she worked in Brooklyn, it would take hours before she could get me, so I'd be staring at my fever-ridden reflection in the shiny linoleum floor.

I realized that while there appeared to be choices, the team was very adept at making sure that there was minimal risk in the choice that was made. For example, do you want to go to group therapy at 11:00 or 11:30—you see, that's a choice, but it's only the time that you will be attending, not the actual attending.

A professional-looking man, wearing a white coat, walked to my door, which was at the furthest end of a very antiseptic and institutional hall; he knocked three times and asked, "Hey Jim, can I come in?"

"Yes."

"I'm Stephen, I work the day shift here on the floor and wanted to introduce myself and—"

"Take me down to group?"

"Yup—to group."

"What if I don't want to go to group, sounds like at least one other person doesn't want to go today either."

"While I'm not going to drag you down the hall, it is something that we strongly encourage because one, it's your first day, and we want you to meet everyone who is here and, two, we don't want you sitting down here in your room all by yourself."

I heard a shout from somewhere outside of my room, "Don't believe a fucking word he says; he will drag your ass down the hall!"

I was waiting for Stephen to make that "cuckoo" circle near his temple that people make when they think somebody is acting pretty frickin' crazy. Unfortunately, he didn't give me the satisfaction because it wouldn't be proper loony bin etiquette.

That's when it hit me. After all of the events of the last few days, after wanting to kill myself, after scouring the bathroom for pills and poison, after staring out the picture window in my bedroom thinking that I could jump through it and impale myself on the picket fence around my pool, after driving down here in the backseat of my friend's car, locked in like a two-year-old, after all that, it wasn't until this young guy walked into my room with his name tag around his neck on a string and a clipboard, that I fully comprehended that I had completely given up.

I had quit on my life—I had thrown up my hands to the gods and just said, "Take me out, remove me from said life; I am all done."

I am a 40-year-old husband and father of three. I own a business, I have earned a significant amount of money, I am a former NCAA Division I All-American athlete, I have a big house with a built-in pool and a white picket fence (literally), I have a mortgage, a stock portfolio, a money manager, I have a labradoodle, I am married to a beautiful woman, I have three gorgeous and intelligent children, I took my family to Jamaica and rented a house with an entire full staff for our last vacation—I have it all! I am the epitome of the so-called American Dream. Yet, here I sit on the edge of my bed like an 11-year-old who is home from school with the flu. Here I am, looking up at this young Black guy, and I am completely at his mercy. I have nothing but linen pants, a t-shirt, and flip-flops that I am wearing. I am nothing—I am lost, I have given up, I have succumbed to the insanity that has plagued my mind for so many years. FUCK!

Again, I didn't say any of this.

Instead, I said, "Sure, group session sounds like fun."

Stephen went over a checklist of the personal items that they have locked away for me; toiletry kit, one leather belt, one pair of New Balance sneakers and shoelaces, and one gold necklace.

Tears began to fall from each eye and slowly cooled the hot skin on my cheeks as they forged a path down my jawline. Stephen sensed my frailty and put a hand on my shoulder.

"Follow me to the common room, and I'll introduce you to our group moderator for today's session, and you can meet some of the other patients."

I could hear my flip-flops on the tile floor and could sense that my legs were moving beneath me as the patient rooms floated by me on either side. My friend's question popped into my head, "Jimmy, what is happening to you? What does it feel like inside?"

I have often thought about this question for myself. Depression is a tough thing to explain to people that do not experience it. Recently, my daughter illustrated the feeling of being depressed in the most poignant visual that I have heard yet; it is like living underwater. That is precisely what it feels like for me—you're in the world, but surrounded by water, which is preventing you from hearing clearly, from seeing without cloudiness, and from moving without energy—just like you experience when you're at the bottom of a 10-foot pool. The deeper you swim, the more difficult everything becomes. It's harder to hold your breath, your vision is blurred because of less light, the pressure and force of the water makes it more stressful for you to move your arms and legs. All of your actions become further impaired as you dive deeper into your travel into your depression, and the more difficult all of your actions become as well. The only difference is that your mental acuity is also affected, and you feel as though there is water inside your head and pushing on the outside. It's utterly terrifying.

For three days I had been slipping in and out of lucidity, and when I had tried to focus on one continuous thought, my mind just shut itself off. The thought of the question my friend asked brought the memory of that moment into view; I looked at my friend's eyes and saw myself looking back; I saw sympathy, empathy, sorrow, and most of all—I saw fear.

Many moments in life are not to be forgotten, that we remember as if they happened this morning or yesterday afternoon. That candid moment that I shared with my friend at that rest stop on the side of a highway that I have driven hundreds of times will never leave my memory. It is one of those healing moments that we can weave with other healing moments and create a quilt of happiness and strength. Those are the moments that I reach for in times of contemplation and deep thought. Sometimes it works quickly, sometimes it takes a long time, and I must go around the block a few times before I can ease into that perfect parking spot, the memory that will cause me to sit up and say, "Yes, that's why I love life!"

Later on in my life, those moments are the sweetness of being a survivor of mental illness.

I heard my feet shuffling down the hall again and could see a large nurse's station that looked as if it were carved into the glass—kind of like a huge fish bowl filled with people, computers, filing cabinets, medical charts, and phones. Beyond the nurse's station, there were two steel and glass doors that led into what looked like a small cafeteria. I heard voices coming from my left and turned to see a few people walking toward us at a bit of an angle. I realized that the hallway that I have just come down is one of two identical and converging wings that meet at the crossroads of the nurse's station here in what is called by the hospital, the ACU—the Acute Care Unit.

When I arrived the day before, I didn't see any of what I was looking at this day. The details were pretty muddy. The ACU was on 24/7 lockdown, so anybody coming in or going out had to have a pass or be escorted by a staff member. There was a set of double doors that led into the main portion of the unit that I was standing in at this point, while I waited for Stephen to grab a bunch of clipboards from the nursing station. He was prepping for the blood pressure and heart rate monitoring that occurred several times a day. As you entered through that set of double doors, you could get through the first but couldn't continue through the second set of doors until the first set closed—whoosh—behind you. It was like a vapor lock unit on a spaceship, keeping the universe out or, more aptly keeping the "clientele" from escaping.

As I was waiting for Stephen to continue escorting me into the common room, I thought about walking into the unit yesterday. Upon arriving in the unit for the first time, walking through the vapor lock sections of the doorway security was daunting, especially when you don't know when you will be leaving. That fear of the unknown jolted me into the gravity of the situation that I had created for myself. I realized at that moment that Chris saved my life and that my sister and her "god-like" appearance on the highway were signs from the Universe that I was to live. I realized that while I had created this emergent hospitalization, I had actually saved myself and had gotten myself to a place that would keep me—and my family—safe.

Now, I was there, on the "other side" of the doors, and there was no option but to hand over any and all claims that I had on how things were going to go. I noticed that everyone's movements were carefully watched from the nurse's station at the head of the unit. Two long hallways extended out in parallel lines from the nurse's station, and each had about 20 rooms, ten or so on each side of the hall, and all of the doors were open. All of the rooms that I walked by on my way in were empty, although I could tell that people were living there because most of the beds were unmade and there were clothes on the floor. I could hear the group of patients getting ready for the group therapy session in the common room, where both hallways ended and conjoined through a large double door. Another observation was that this place was like a sanctuary. It was very clean and had a peaceful energy, despite the obvious trauma that was taking place within each of the people within those walls.

Walking into the unit was like entering a scene from the film, *One Flew Over the Cuckoo's Nest*, complete with a medication window, electroshock therapy room, one television in the common room, and people in various stages of sanity and pain. In addition, everyone was dressed in all kinds of clothing from pajamas to jeans and t-shirts.

When I arrived the day before, my wife was with me as we walked down the hall to my room, along with two others, a social worker that was there for my wife and a social worker, Peter, who was there for me—he walked me through the intake process into the facility. I looked into a room as I was walking past and could see a human form huddled in a blanket on a chair, feet up on the seat, kind of in a fetal position but leaning forward with his head in his hands. He was just rocking back and forth as if to soothe himself—he looked like I felt.

Peter categorized and inventoried all of my belongings; shoelaces were removed from my sneakers, my belt was taken and placed in a box, which would be taken to a locked facility within the unit. Chris packed my toiletry kit, which I hadn't used since my last business trip, so it had all of the stuff I would have brought with me. Peter explained, "I am removing any sharp tools, toe clipper, razor, a pair of scissors, and the dental floss, sorry buddy, but I need to remove anything that would allow you to cut, strangle or harm yourself or somebody else—it's for your safety."

Everything was safely packed away in a very methodical and thorough way. I signed an acknowledgement that I had witnessed this process. Next, my luggage was being examined for any food that I might have snuck in; sugar and caffeine were a problem for mood swings. When they were trying to regulate medication levels and emotional balance, that was a problem.

My mind ran back to *Cuckoo's Nest;* I replayed the scene when McMurphy is complaining to Nurse Ratched about the treatment they are getting, and he says he's going to lead a mutiny. She clues him in to the fact that most of the patients are there voluntarily. The irony of that scene and the incredulous look on his face hit me like a sledgehammer. I now understood that my wife would be leaving me there, that I would not see my kids, that everything that I had in this world would be outside those double-locked security doors.

I could hear Chris talking with the doctor and could hear her running the events of the last three days; she said,

"I had no idea how distressed he was; I just didn't know; Jim did a really good job of hiding his sadness from me."

That fact is, I had done a very good job of hiding my sadness for many years. Yes, my wife had known of my unhappiness, but she had not known, could never know, that I had seen myself as a huge problem in her and my children's lives, that I just wanted to fucking die. That was not something that I had shared with anyone.

It was time for goodbye, and Chris and I embraced and cried deeply. She told me that I would be OK, that she loved me and that the work must then begin. Her strength of mind and character were far beyond anything that I could have asked for. Just as she could not understand depression and unhappiness, I could not understand her passion for life, her pure happiness, and joy, her positive attitude—it scared the shit out of me. As I melted into her arms and listened to her words, tremendous fear overcame me, and I just began to weep and tremble. She left me in my room, and I heard her steps moving away from me down the hall toward the locked doors, and then, I heard her say goodbye to the doctors, and she was off. Woosh, the doors vapor locked, and I was on the inside—alone.

At this point I lived in a small room with two beds, two desks, and a large window—exactly like my college dorm room. I had traded my beautifully decorated 4,000-square-foot house for a 200-square-foot concrete box that I shared with another person who wanted to off himself. Aaaah, the shit that we create for ourselves is just frickin' wonderful.

CHAPTER 4

THE COMMON ROOM

I walked into the common room and saw three or four couches in a big L formation around a small television. There were 30 or 40 VHS tapes on the bookshelf with all genres of older movies, along with 100 or so paperback books. It wouldn't be a general-purpose room without the requisite five or six cafeteria-style tables and a couple of dozen plastic chairs. There was a door that led to a beautiful deck, but the door was locked. The deck, while completely open to the sunlight and trees that run up the hillside behind the building, was completely wrapped in cabling and wire mesh so that it would be impossible to "bust out." There were 20 or so people in the room; an equal number of men and women, all heights, sizes, ages, and colors. They all were facing the TV, but it was completely black, and I thought, "Holy shit, these people are so fucking crazy that they are watching a blank TV screen"—and I imagined they were watching some '60s show, like *Bonanza.* Then, I realized that I was crazy too.

A woman on the periphery of the group was staring out the window, and she held her hands together in a ball and pointed them straight away from her body. It was as if she was holding back some force that was trying to invade her space.

A man walked in with a folksy, yet authoritative look to him. He was wearing the lanyard and badge that identified him as a member of the staff. He took a chair to the front of the room and sat right in front of the TV. He called us to order and brought us into a semi-circle on the couches.

"Good morning everyone; I am Tom, today's group session leader."

Tom was a very Irish-looking guy, the kind of guy you would sit next to at your local pub. I learned much later on in my multiple sessions with Tom that he spent far too many days doing just that, drinking himself into oblivion. His white hair was combed back over his head and his beard was white with flecks of gray and black. I could tell right away that this guy was very intelligent and he was doing what he was born to do—helping people with addictions and other psychological behaviors that were destructive to themselves and those around them.

That's why all that we do is done for a reason. Had Tom and his family not gone through the suffering of alcoholism, we would not benefit from his experience and passion for teaching others. We went around the room and gave our name, age, a little background information, and why we thought we were here.

I spoke slowly and quietly, barely a whisper...

"Uh, well, I'm Jim. I am 40 years old, I am married and have three children, and I am here because I tried to kill myself."

The words left my mouth before I had a chance to prevent them from being said. I could not believe I said that out loud. It had been hard to be so brutally honest, both with myself and anybody else.

Without warning and within a split second of my closing my mouth, the woman next to me, an early-30s-looking, heavy-set, white woman with dark stringy hair, leaned forward on her cushion and yelled at me, "Another fucking failure—another fucking failure—if you really wanted to die and you weren't such a fuck up, like me, you'd be dead—that must feel really shitty!"

Shock is not the right word, and anger didn't come close to the surface—it was more fear laced with shame and embarrassment. Feelings that would haunt me for many months to come. *Is this therapeutic? These people are fucking insane!*

Tom doesn't skip a beat. "So, Jim, tell us what you're hoping to gain from being here."

"Well, I am hoping that I can understand why I have been so sad and why I have wanted to die."

45

On the periphery, there was a regal-looking 72-year-old woman named Doris. She leaned forward on her chair, which was directly behind the couch. She was in the room, but not in the group—well, at least not physically. She was short and plump and very well dressed. I could tell that her clothing was made for her, and she had a Louis Vuitton bag that looked like it was flown in from Paris.

"My sister is coming to get me today," she exclaimed with a great big smile.

I felt happy for her as she said this. I saw the comment as a bright spot on a very tough day.

Trish, the fucking psycho who had already laced into me, said, "Doris, you have said that every fucking day that I've been here for the last three weeks—your sister, if she exists, is not coming to get you—give it up."

Trish turned to me again, "You know, big boy, if you had killed yourself, then you wouldn't be taking time from our little group here!"

Tom had had enough of Trish's outbursts and asked her to join him in the hall outside the common room.

"Fuck you, Tom."

"OK, Trish, let's talk in the hall."

"No, I'm good right here—I'm going to sit here on my fleshy white ass until I've decided that I'm ready to get up and leave."

"My sister is coming," said Doris.

The room was filled with tension, an intense mix of uneasiness and angst. We all felt the frustration and fear that Trish felt, yet, she was the only one who said how she felt through her rants.

David, a 40-something Fortune 100 CFO, rubbed his thick 40-day growth of a beard.

"I feel like every session breaks down as a result of Trish wanting to be the center of attention, and the rest of us are left with the thought that we are spending time learning nothing."

Tom responded, "This is what life is about, it's about working with others to achieve a level of balance and harmony, so, you are all learning something, but, I would rather have the conversation center on what steps you can take to make better choices—but, first, I need to see Trish in the hall."

I was thinking, *Tom, please leave Trish alone; she's going to take her wooden yogurt spoon and gouge out my eyes—please just let her sit here.*

Trish had decided that she was the 800-pound gorilla and that she was going to sit wherever she wanted to. Tom looked to his left, nodded a little, and raised his hand in a gesture to the nurse's station. In walked two guys that I hadn't seen yet, one was about six feet tall, and the other was five feet 10 inches and both looked like they were confident in their ability to handle any situation. They were not muscular, like bouncers or the classic insane asylum orderly you might see in a movie; they just looked and moved in a straightforward and confident manner.

Trish clamped her hands around the chair's silver metal legs, stiffened her body, and thrust her legs straight out in front of her. I chuckled at the memory of my second daughter doing the same thing when she didn't want to cooperate and sit in her car seat on long road trips. Trish immediately turned her head and looked at the source of the chuckle, and I felt as if someone just poured hot candle wax on my eyeballs. I felt terrified. I was there to try and get my world under control, to try and get some comfort. I'd been there for an hour and what seems like the craziest fucker in the room wanted to rip out my heart and eat it with her morning oatmeal. This would certainly solve the problem of wanting to die—Sybil here could just put me out of my misery. Steve and Eric gently took hold of Trish's arms, extricated her from the chair, and gently led her back to her room.

CHAPTER 5

ONE OF LIFE'S STORIES

Later on in the session, which lasted about 90 minutes or so, I was asked about trauma as a child.

You mean like being left alone by parents that didn't know what they didn't know, or sexual abuse and molestation, or a narcissistic father that psychologically abused all of us, or a severely depressed mother that was the victim of all victims, watching people verbally abuse my sister, calling her retarded—is that what you mean?

Of course, I said none of that; in fact, many of the memories of some of my abuse wouldn't come back into my recognition until I'd put in a few years of therapeutic work.

Now I could feel the anger boiling up inside me. I could feel my loneliness lashing out. I could feel myself getting to a new layer of the onion peeling away from moment to moment.

"How about something that you would feel comfortable telling the group?" Tom asked.

I began telling this story.

As I began my junior year of high school in 1981, my life was that of a typical Long Island jock. In no particular order, that life consisted of school, girlfriend, lots of friends, TV, training for my chosen sport of lacrosse, and a yellow 1973 Oldsmobile Cutlass Supreme. I bought my first car from its original owner for $1,000; the guy was a co-worker of my dad's in New Jersey. The '73 Cutlass had two doors that were so long and heavy; the hinges would sag under the pressure every time I opened the door. In the winter months, I had to lift the door when closing it to get the proper alignment so the lock mechanism would catch and the door would stay closed. More than once, that frickin' door swung open on sharp curves because it didn't *catch properly. This could be pretty scary since nobody wore seatbelts in 1981. I had more than one friend see his life flash before his eyes when the door flew open, and he watched the asphalt flying by beneath him at 40 or 50 MPH. I would always, without skipping a beat, say, "Next time, lift the door to close it tight."*

I will never forget the first time I got behind the wheel of that car—my magic carpet to independence. Inserting the key on the steering column produced a feeling of pure elation, and when I started the engine, the feeling of power that ensued was proof that there was a God. The faux leather grip, with plastic lacing wrapped around the wheel, crinkled under my clutching fingers and palms as I squeezed tighter and tighter. To ease my excitement and eagerness to "punch it" I reached down with my left hand and felt for the metal toggle switch to adjust the electric bench seat. Yes, "electric," I was living large. A couple of years later, that knob was broken off by my sister who was home from Europe. Although, I am sure she'll deny it. That was the same sister that just helped to save my life, so, all is forgiven. All that was left of the control knob was a little nub of a metal edge and to adjust the seat, you needed a screwdriver or pointed knife. When I finally upgraded my car in 1986, my mom inherited the '73 Olds Cutlass and I showed her how to move the seat and told her never to move it again once she found the right spot for herself.

As I was getting into my story, mayhem ensued inside the room. Trish ran back into the room, momentarily dodging her keepers, "I want somebody to succeed in killing themselves, I want them to come in here and tell me they succeeded..."

"Uuuhhh Trish, that's pretty much impossible, no matter how crazy you think we are, we know that somebody that kills themselves is not coming in here!" someone replied.

Doris: "My sister said that she would be here by 1:00, so I hope the meeting doesn't run over today."

David: "I think that I'm going home on Friday, hopefully for good this time."

Susan: "I'm a cutter."

Denise: "I'm so tired, what movie are we watching tonight?"

I adjusted the 10-inch rear view mirror, turned the stereo on, complete with push button station changers. This wasn't the digital crap that teens get to use today, you had to have really good dexterity to change the stations—had to put all your weight behind the push so that the little orange line would move from one station stop to the next. I immediately adjusted the presets to my ideal five stations by stopping on each one and pulling the button out to release the earlier saved stop and pushed each one in—one by one—knowing that these would deliver the ideal music of rock, alternative rock, and pop available in the New York City market (92.7 WLIR, 95.5 WPLJ, 102.7 WNEW, 103.5 WAPP, 92.7 WLIR). Then I did the same thing on the AM stations—not. Rule #1—No fucking AM radio in my independence train. "You want AM radio—hit the fucking bricks." I had nightmares growing up listening to 1010 WINS in my Dad's car, "...you give us 22 minutes, we'll give you the world!" while he chain smoked his Marlboros like the end of the world was imminent.

The song on 102.7 was Lunatic Fringe by Red Rider. I cranked it up.

Susan: "Yeah, when I get anxious or sad, I cut myself, see?"

She extended her arms so that we could all see the red and blue slices that ran the length of her arms from her wrists to her mid-bicep. I had never seen the result of a cutter's self-inflicted wounds, moreover, to that point, I had never even heard of cutting. These cuts were almost identical, about two inches long and spaced about two inches apart.

She continued, "My mom remarried about two years ago, my dad hates the guy, but he's loaded, we live in a huge mansion in Greenwich, nine bedrooms, an elevator, wine cellar, sauna, pool—but the guy is a dick, he's been hitting my mom when he drinks and I'm afraid he's going to kill me."

The engine of the '73 Cutlass was a 350 V8, it was clean, it sounded incredible, and it was very fast. I stepped on the gas and revved it a few times, the front end dropped down and to the right with each stomp on the accelerator. I grabbed the shift column knob and eased it toward me and down into Drive. I looked at my Dad in the rearview mirror and pounded the gas, leaving a 20-foot skid with the rear wheels. Fuckin-A that was fun. I didn't find out until later that it took my Dad 10 minutes to pick all of the dirt and gravel out of his hair and off his clothes. He was pissed, but he knew that I had experienced the all important, "first car, first ride" ritual to the fullest, but he couldn't help himself and he didn't talk to me for a week. It was one of the few times when his emotional blackmail terrorism tactics didn't mean a damn thing to me.

Life was better with a car, each ride was as exhilarating as the first. I was older than most of my friends since my birthday is in December. I was one of the first kids with a license and a car, so I was picking people up all the time and I loved it.

My friend Satch-mo (aptly named after one of the Bowery Boys) and I spent hours in that car, meandering our way through the "white bread" streets of our hometown, Baldwin, NY and through the emotional train wrecks that were our mid-to-late teens. Radio Rule #2: if a Police song was on, you had to listen to it, you couldn't change the station until the song played all the way through. Radio Rule #3, no crap, and no fucking Country. There weren't too many other rules that I can recall; we pretty much did whatever the hell we wanted to do. Both of us were from broken homes and our moms worked a lot. I think that our moms were just happy to have us show up at home alive at the end of each day. Well, I know my mom was happy, Satch's mom —maybe not so much. He was like a brother to me and I loved him like a brother.

In early December of 1981, the Olds was having transmission trouble, slipping out of gear or not slipping into gear right away. I called my dad one day and explained the issue. He promptly told me it was the transmission and that I should have a can of tranny fluid in the trunk at all times. He told me to park the car overnight in a dry spot—in the morning—back the car up and check the ground for wet fluid—if there's fluid on the ground in the morning, she's leaking tranny fluid. I did as instructed, because at 16, your Dad still has some of the answers and when it came to cars, my dad really knew his shit. As December wore on, the problem got worse—a combination of the leak worsening and the weather getting colder. The colder the weather, the thicker the fluid would get in the transmission case, that would exacerbate the problem. All I know is that when I added fluid and put it into gear, it would take a minute and then slip into drive. It got so bad that once I got the car into drive I wouldn't take it out for any reason unless I had to shut it off. I would park the car, nose into a wall so it wouldn't roll, with the emergency brake on or Satch would put his foot on the brake while I ran into the store or Burger King for a chicken sandwich.

On New Year's Eve 1981, the "last tranny straw" occurred. I planned a NYE dinner with my girlfriend. We went to dinner at the Milleridge Inn in Jericho. It was a popular holiday spot, a big theme type restaurant that was fancy and definitely a hot spot for upper middle class Long Islanders. The Milleridge had a faux miller's water wheel and it also had a full page ad in the yellow pages, which was the reason I picked it.

I remember that we were the youngest people there by at least 30 years. We planned an early dinner—early seating, and back to her house to hang out and watch the ball drop. I always felt like a 17-year-old in a 40-year-old's life. I always wanted to grow up more quickly than I was—I never enjoyed the moment, always striving to fulfill my next grown-up fantasy. Like, eating at the Milleridge Inn would impress my girlfriend, so she would think that I was better than I was. That was a pathetic emotional trend that I continued for another 20 years.

Everybody in the room, as in life, was living in their own heads and the disruptions continued throughout "my time." I heard Susan, "Yeah, so, because of the stress of this guy and my mom, I started cutting pretty aggressively and then two weeks ago I drank a bunch of chemicals from the maid's closet and woke up in Stamford Hospital. I knew the place immediately because that's where I was when I was bulimic."

After dinner, my girlfriend and I walked through the fully decorated Christmas village between the restaurant and the three-football-field-sized parking lot. The twinkling lights and the festive atmosphere, coupled with the thought that I was able to make this night happen because of my car, made me feel a sense of euphoria and power over my world that I had never experienced before. Confidence was dripping off me like water drops from a shower head —I was the Master of My Universe. I had the world by the balls. As I looked beyond the lights, I saw the moon glistening off the huge yellow hood of my '73 Olds, and then I glimpsed its round headlights staring at me like an ominous glare.

Then it hit me, the fucking tranny! I heard my dad's voice in my head, "you better get a bottle of fluid, it gets worse in the cold..." Shit. My head was reeling as I immediately left that moment that I was in, my palms started to sweat despite the below zero temperature. I knew...I just fucking knew that this night was too good to be true, that I was too big a fucking loser to pull off a grown up date and a normal relationship—shit, shit, and shit.

Each step we took toward the car was agonizingly long, and the cold air was whipping around my head like the hands of an evil demon there to fuck with my world. I held the door open for my date. She got in and "eeked" when her butt hit the frozen plastic bench seat.

I lifted the door a bit and slammed it shut. The last thing I needed was her falling out of the car and tumbling down the Southern State Parkway. Her parents already hated me because I wasn't Jewish —trying to explain that I didn't lift the door handle to seal the door and their youngest child bounced along the highway like a rubber ball was not going to ingratiate me as a member of the family.

As I walked around the front of the car, I could feel my heart pound in my chest—I was in a full-blown anxiety attack. At that point in my life, this wasn't an unusual event—it pretty much happened every day—so I was well-practiced at hiding the symptoms. You know, sweaty palms, headache, diarrhea, gas pains, leg tingles—I was having a full-blown fucking stroke. At the age of 17, I was going to drop dead of a frickin' stroke in the icy-covered parking lot of the famed Milleridge Fucking Inn!

I inserted the key, praying, and hoping and asking every God known to man to let this night, not be the night that the transmission just quit on me. The car leapt to life and I let it warm up, the whole time just hoping that things will work out and I'll survive this fucking ordeal. Looking back on that event now, and understanding my dramatic mood swings, I am sure that the energy that I was giving off was palpable and filled with very intense levels of angst. It probably created a strange aura of fear.

I grabbed the brown knob on the gear shift, pulled it toward me and dropped it into drive. Nothing! Not even the usual whine of the transmission trying to help me out—not a fucking thing—damn. I quickly dumped it back to neutral for a minute or two hoping that it would warm the fluid enough so it would engage. In my head, I promised God that if I could get some help here, I'd never ask for another thing again—ever. I also suggested that since my girlfriend was Jewish there was some closer connection to Jesus than most people. After waiting an interminable amount of time, I put it back into drive—then my dad's words screamed into my head..." Eventually it will get so bad that it'll just cease to work..." Fuckers! My girlfriend was very cool about it, but I was a bundle of nerves. Somehow, the fact that the transmission on my 10-year-old car needed to be repaired was a complete reflection on me and my inadequacies that were laid bare for the world to see and scoff at.

I opened the glove box to hit the trunk-release button to grab the spare fluid I have in the wheel well. Nothing...the mechanism that opens the trunk was frozen. I got out, opened the trunk manually, grabbed a quart of Aamco transmission fluid, popped the hood and prayed again.

I walked around to the front of the car, the yellow hood glistening with frost under the bright December 31st moon. I move my fingers in the slots of the grill to find the hood release, knocking icicles off as I slide my hand back and forth. My fingers are numb and getting colder by the second. With an oomph and a shove, the 60-pound hood goes up with a loud "kafwang." Pulling out the transmission dipstick, I can see that it is bone-dry, not a good sign. I turn the fluid bottle upside down and slowly drain the new fluid down the cold and dirty pipe leading to the only thing standing between my sanity and a friggin' rubber room.

Moments like this underscore the mania that my mind can go through, from very high highs to very low lows. There is no middle ground.

After I drained the bottle, I put the stick back in and closed the hood, the whole time muttering various prayers—mostly now appealing to the fact that I have to get this girl home safely and on time.

I said to God, "You can do anything you want to me after I get her to her parents."

My thought was that if I didn't deserve the positive outcome of a prayer; I figured I could sell God on another more doable thought, helping this girl who really didn't have to suffer because her boyfriend is a shithead.

I throw the empty bottle back in the trunk, slam it shut and get back in the driver's seat, let the car continue to warm up and downshift to drive—nothing. "Holy shit! Who am I going to call at 10:00 PM on New Year's Frickin' Eve? '82 is going to be one shitty year!"

Then after about one or two excruciating minutes, the transmission gently slips into drive. Prayers answered! Hallelujah and all that bullshit.

I drove about 90 miles per hour down the Northern State Parkway, exit on to the Meadowbrook Parkway heading south and get off at Merrick Road West, and 10 minutes later, we are back in front of my girlfriend's house. I explain that I cannot take the car out of drive for fear that I will never get it into drive again. Believe me, her parents would not want me and my crappy car stranded at their house. Her father would rather have me dead than give me a ride home. She was a very nice person, I often refused to accept the fact that she was from the gene pool of such a miserable fucking prick .

I drove directly to the Pawnbroker, a local pub where I spent a considerable amount of time. The bar was small, however it had a video game, a jukebox, and about 100 misfits like me and my buddy Satch. I park the car across the street, pointing south on Grand Avenue. I figure that if I can't get it started, Satch can drive and I can push the car a couple blocks to the nearest service station. Back then, gas stations provided service and most of them were owned by guys that were mechanics.

After a few hours of drinking pints of Bass Ale and doing shots of tequila and Alabama Slammers, we spill onto Grand Avenue, and it was now 1982. There's my sleek yellow Olds Cutlass Supreme, the moonlight continuing to shine off the hood and windshield; what a great car! The earlier evening stress had been doused by a couple gallons of ale and other forms of alcohol.

"God, I love having a car."

We walk across the empty main north/south artery running through our town, and get in. I am trying to explain my earlier tranny snafu to Joey while he sparks up a Bob Marley joint that he scored earlier in the bathroom. I insert the key as I do my best to hold my toke in my lungs for as long as possible.

The alcohol stupor isn't enough to deaden the pain of my world—a couple of hits of herb is just what the doctor ordered. Of course, I'm the doctor or Joey is the doctor, it doesn't matter who the frickin' doc is, the learned medical advice is always the same: drink, smoke some pot, eat Burger King on the way home and call me in the morning.

I turn the key and now, the fucker won't start. We're prepared; I pop the hood, reach under my seat and hand Satch a can of starter spray. He climbs up inside the hood and unscrews the wing nut on the huge air cleaner cover, opens the carburetor flaps and shoots fluid directly into the four barrel carb, four seconds later, the Olds is humming and Satch puts the air cleaner cover back on, drops the hood and gets back into the car. All in a night's work! Kids today don't know how lucky they are that they get to miss the mechanical shortcomings of the cars that were built in the '60s and '70s. My kids will never climb under the hood of some old clunker to fix it on the fly. Computers are running all of our vehicles today, so, even if I wanted to work on my car, I'd need a degree in nuclear mechanics.

My story gets interrupted by Dave, "Yesterday, I left a bagel with some cream cheese on the table and one of you ate it. Where's my bagel? It's not that I want it back right now, it's just that I don't understand why people are so damn inconsiderate! My problem with the world is the lack of decency and support, I just don't get it."

I drop her into drive—it immediately kicks in and we're off, we head south on Grand Avenue passing LH Martin's, the entrance to our high school, Grand Avenue Cinemas, Carvel, Baldwin Music Store, the frame shop where my sister works, Fong's Nursery, where we buy our Christmas tree every year, Peaches Pub and Baldwin Beverage Center. It's only about two miles and we turn left into Burger King and hit the drive-thru for a Whopper, chicken sandwich and two cheeseburgers. We always get two extra cheeseburgers because when I'm stoned, I need to eat. Seriously, the feeling of knowing that there is more food after you've eaten what you think is all the food you have, is just amazing.

I take Satch home and head home myself, pulling into the driveway on New York Avenue around 4:30 am and hit the hay really hard, not waking up on New Year's day until about 2:00 pm. I spend the first day of the new year watching football and thinking about the year ahead. On January 2nd, I break down and bring my car to Aamco Transmissions on Sunrise Highway in Rockville Centre. The guy tells me it's going to be a few days. Little did either of us know that those days would change my life forever.

CHAPTER 6

HUGE TRAUMA

Trish was back in the room and she looked like somebody hit her with an electric cattle prod, she was completely calm and very agreeable.

Trish said, "I'm sorry that I yelled at you and I'm glad that you didn't kill yourself, I just get so angry with myself for having not found a way to eliminate my own pain. I've been moving in and out of these facilities for years and nobody can find the right medication balance for my bipolar disorder. I am a trained emergency room nurse, I wasn't even diagnosed until I was 25. Up until then, things were pretty good, although my mania would shut me down from time to time." She stifled a cry as she spat out, "Now, I don't think I'll ever be able to live on my own again."

Over the next few days, I shared more and more of my story.

January 6, 1982 was not an unusual day to start with, it ends with me in the hospital trying to hold on to life. Oy, the irony. It's ironic because I've spent the better part of the last six years thinking about dying, planning my suicide or subconsciously trying to kill myself by drinking enough alcohol to drive my car off the road into a pole, or better yet, off the highway, down an embankment and into a large fucking tree. Now, I could die and I don't really want to, I feel like a misguided and weak failure. I feel that my cowardice and fear knows no boundaries.

Back to January 6, 1982. With my car still in the shop, I bundled up for the walk to my job at Rockbottom, an early CVS-like pharmacy discount store in the Sunrise Highway Shopping Plaza just west of Grand Avenue. I started with a long black wool scarf that my great-grandmother knitted for me a few years earlier, just before she died. Then I put on a pair of cowhide gloves and topped myself off with a winter coat that I got for Christmas a week earlier. It was a goose down coat, blue and white, with zip off sleeves so it could be worn as a vest. I pulled the scarf up over my nose and head out into the freezing morning air for the half-mile walk to the store.

I don't remember a damn thing about the day itself, just your typical high school kid at a typical high school kid job, unpacking inventory and neatly stocking shelves with toothpaste, mouthwash, dental floss, and rubbing alcohol. Goddamn, the amount of rubbing alcohol being consumed in Baldwin at that time in history was staggering. What they were doing with all the fucking rubbing alcohol was beyond my knowledge or imagination. Working at Rockbottom was a lot of fun, and there was a great crew of people. Eric, Paul, Annetta, Joyce, Jill, Donna, Joe, and the list goes on. People that loved to laugh. We worked hard to keep the store clean and organized. I think it was store #57 or #51 and I think it was one of the better stores in Mr. Otto's chain. The owner's name was Richard Otto and he would come in once in a while for a surprise store inspection and to see if his managers were doing their jobs representing his brand. I don't know what happened to Mr. Otto but I'm sure he made a shit load of money when Duane Reed bought the chain in 1998 to buy up distribution and eliminate competition. It was always fun when a hot chick walked into the store. The unwritten rule was that if you were the "spotter" of said hottie, you immediately had to personally notify every guy working in the store, outfit color and aisle. Everybody would move like flies to a picnic. It was hilarious to watch guys camouflage themselves behind shelves and boxes so that they wouldn't be noticed. Hey, we were high school adolescents just doing what thousands of years of evolution would have us do.

The main floor wasn't that big, probably 7,500 square feet, but it was well stocked with a front-to-back 12 aisle layout with the front-end having four or five registers that were elevated about two-feet above the floor level. At six-foot tall, I could see everything in the store from the register vantage point, but I hated ringing on the register. Way too much pressure. First, you had to manage all the pricing inputs and department identifications, no pricing scanners back then. At the end of the shift, you had to "prove" your register which meant that you had to reconcile every penny that came and went. Invariably, my drawer was always off, a couple bucks here and there. I never stole a thing, but, at the end of any shift that I worked the register, I always dipped into my own pocket to balance the register. It was easier to do that then have to work backwards and actually go through the entire register roll print out to verify all transactions. In order to truly prove it out correctly, you had to identify the specific transaction that may have led to being underfunded. Unfortunately, I was never over, I was always under, which I don't understand. I mean, I was a good math student, however, details and I do not get along.

The other huge selling products were Fleet Enemas, holy shit, at 50 cents a box, they were more popular than chewing gum. Baldwin must have had the demographic with the cleanest intestinal tracts in Nassau County in 1982.

Anyway, toothpaste, paper goods, makeup, and of course, cotton balls. One day, a woman walks into the store and up my aisle directly to me.

She asks, "Do you have cotton balls?"

With a perfectly straight face and without skipping a beat, I respond, "No, do you have wool tits?"

After she walks away and is gone for about 30 seconds, I can hear Paul the manager's feet coming up the aisle next to mine. Paul was the regional manager and a great guy to work for. Paul has the woman with him, a woman, by the way, who wouldn't know a funny line if it bit her on the ass. He demands that I apologize, which I do and then, he gives her a free box of cotton balls as compensation for my sophomoric behavior. If that had happened today, the company would be sued, I'd be fired and probably brought up on harassment charges.

The one thing that I'm sure of about that day was that it was payday, which was a good thing since my car was going to cost $300 to repair, which was almost 1/3 of what I had paid for the entire vehicle. One of the good things about Rockbottom was that they allowed us to cash our checks in the store on payday, which I did at 7:30 just before the 8:00 PM closing. I pocketed my $168 and bundled up for the walk home.

It was a cold 10-degree and very still night. I walked across the parking lot heading due east past Red Lobster and up to Grand Avenue. The thing that was unusual about my trip home was that I was walking. Normally, I would have run if I wasn't driving, but for some reason I was enjoying the walk. I turned left onto Grand Avenue heading north past the post office and the Koch building. Koch was a real estate and insurance brokerage office on the corner of Sunrise Highway and Grand Avenue. It was a beautiful building that combined with the building across the street, framed that section of Grand Avenue nicely. On the second floor, I noticed the sign for Mr. Hodge's law firm. His son Chris was "the" star athlete of my high school in the early '80s—that kid had it all. Good looks, intelligence and athletic ability. He starred in football, wrestling, and baseball and went on to attend the US Naval Academy. I ran into him a few years later at the Naval Academy when I was attending Navy Prep, and we talked about his stardom in high school with his roommate. His roommate couldn't believe that Chris was a standout athlete. I remember thinking that Chris was a big fish in a small pond in Baldwin and now at the Academy, his athletic prowess had dissipated and he just blended into the fabric of the Navy. The last time I had seen him up close, prior to that encounter, I was a sophomore in high school and was only about 5' 10". This time around, I was 6' 1" and a very accomplished All-American lacrosse player, and I didn't feel intimidated at all. It's amazing how your perspective can change as you grow older and more confident. The mystique of the BMOC Hodges was over at that point. He was now just another Naval Academy student and a small fish in a bigger pond.

The light changed and I walked across Sunrise Highway thinking about a sister of a good friend, Laura H., who had been killed several years earlier one intersection to the west. During bad snowstorms the Nassau County road plow team would form these huge mountains of snow at each intersection, right in the middle of the fucking road. When you were traveling east or west on the highway and wanted to make a left, you had to negotiate your field of vision around these huge manmade mountains, to see the oncoming traffic. If you weren't careful and experienced, it would be easy to assume that you could make the turn without a problem. When Laura and her friend were traveling east on the highway in front of Raay Nor's Cabin Restaurant, preparing to make the left onto Chestnut Street, Laura's friend, who had been the driver and was neither too careful nor experienced, thought she had the time to make the turn, and she wheeled into her turn and appeared from behind the snow mound, the guy driving westbound didn't even have time to slow down. He hit them broadside and killed them both, instantly. I was in seventh grade when that happened, and it was the first funeral I attended that wasn't for an old person. To this day, it breaks my heart to think of the way that Laura's family was tragically changed in the time it takes to blink an eye. For years, they couldn't bring themselves to change anything in her pink room. I do not clearly remember who the other girl was, but Laura was beautiful, intelligent, nice, athletic and a promising high school kid getting ready for college. What a loss, and why?

Walking under the Long Island Rail Road train trestle, the rolling steel wheels of a commuter train rumbled above my head. I was always fascinated by the LIRR trains.

I turned left onto Brooklyn Avenue, walking past Wick's Florist and OTB. The Off-Track-Bar, OTB to the regulars, was about 20 feet across Brooklyn Avenue from the main commuter stairwell that led to and from the LIRR station. At 6:00 pm during most weeknights, the OTB was filled with suits numbing themselves after a long day in Manhattan.

As I walked down the hill, a newer model yellow Ford Mustang drove by me on the right and turned onto Spruce Street. The sighting of a new car in my neighborhood of working-class people was unusual, especially the new Mustang. It was a somewhat boxy-looking car with a straight back window that kind of disappeared perpendicularly into the trunk. What was even more unusual than seeing this fairly cool new car was that the driver was a Black guy. You see, in 1982, Baldwin was as "lily-white" as any upper-crust Connecticut town is today. Seeing a Black guy at night, on the street, caused me tremendous anxiety for many years to come.

At the corner of Brooklyn Avenue and Spruce Street was a street light on a telephone pole that was on the corner of a parking lot for Balboa Tile. Years earlier, I had etched my initials into the fresh concrete of a new curb that was installed in front of that building. Also on that pole was a red light next to where the street light arm attached to the utility pole itself. That little light indicated a location for a fire emergency call box.

Several years ago, I opened that box to see what was in there, and pulled the grease-covered white trigger that tripped the alarm. Then I ran like I was on fire! We were threatened with severe punishment and jail if we messed around with the fire alarm boxes. Many of the men in my neighborhood were big-time volunteer firemen, which was a prestigious rite of passage for the blue-collar folks that I lived among. I, of course, was punished severely and lectured by my neighbor, Mr. Fortuna. Ironically, his house was 30 yards from where that call box was and where I met the occupants of the Mustang.

Across Spruce Street from Balboa Tile was a huge white concrete wall that stood between the street and the inside of the old Cott's soda distribution center. Mr. Balboa, the guy that owned the tile shop, was a big Italian who drove the biggest and newest blue four-door Lincoln Continental I had ever seen. He seemed like a nice guy in retrospect, but at the time, we were all convinced he was mobbed up and would fit us with cement boots, throw us in the back of his huge Lincoln and drop us in the Great South Bay, if he ever caught us on his property.

So, we generally stayed clear of the building, which was why I was so proud of having carved my initials in his new concrete curb when they put it in. That raised my credibility in the neighborhood quite a bit, and I was quite the juvenile delinquent; you know, for a fairly quiet and not very tough kid.

I cut an angle across the Balboa Tile parking lot, cutting off the corner, which was a steep downgrade for a generally flat geographic area. About halfway across the lot, which was only 30 feet wide, I see these four Black guys walking toward me and away from the now parked, late model yellow Mustang.

The tallest guy was 6' 2", a very big dude, looked to be in his early 20s. As I was walking past them, he says, "how's it goin'?" then punches me in the side of the face with a left hook, which seemed to move in slow motion across his body.

I immediately started to run forward, but their zone defense outflanked me. I made it about 20 yards to the other side of the street, directly against the white concrete wall of the Cott's building. I knew that wall very well and you will learn more about that later on in the book. I was stopped from running by a swinging baseball bat to the face. It hit me square in the nose and the blood seemed to explode in every direction and the pain was intense. In short, it fucking hurt!

I turned the other way and saw another bat coming at my head and I instinctively put up my left hand to block it, and the bat, more like a thick broom handle or stick ball bat, made contact with the outer side of my hand. It was better than getting hit in the face but I could hear the bones shatter. Time had slowed to a crawl and I was fully prepared to die.

The entire attack could not have lasted more than three or four minutes, but it seemed like an hour. Every movement, breath, grunt, spasm, smell, bone crunch, all of it, was extremely detailed and pronounced. It was like I was watching myself being beaten by four people on slo-mo on my VCR. This slow-motion view of it all in my mind confirmed for me that I was dying.

Not only that, but the thought of, "Is this really happening, or am I dreaming?" ran through my head several times.

Having realized that I couldn't get away and I couldn't fight four guys, I bent into a crouch with my hands over my face for protection. I told myself that if I fell to the ground, they'd kill me, so I concentrated on keeping my feet under me, bent at the waist in a ball, while they swung bats into my back like a lumberjack swings an ax to split logs.

Then, it got worse. Much worse. I felt something very sharp cutting into the top of my head. Four blows to the back of the head, each creating a gash three inches in length, the thick blood was dripping down over my hands, over my ears, into my eyes and mouth. As I am writing this, I can still smell and taste its salty and pungent metallic essence. Blood is thick and when it hits cold air, it gets a lot thicker, and the clumps of blood were falling from my hair onto the ground at my sneakers.

I guess they got tired because they stood me up, flat against the wall, and that is when I saw the blood-covered pistol, the black gun-metal brightened from the reflection of the street lamp on the corner.

Two of them held my arms out while one of the four swung the bat in my ribs and stomach; once, twice, three times, then the littlest kid (I learned later he was 14!) says, "shoot this white motherfucker!"

Those words echo in my nightmares to this day.

The fourth guy, the big one who swung the first punch, raised the gun and put it against my forehead.

He said, "Gimme your money," and they let go of my arms so that I could comply.

They got my week's pay, $168, my license, and some pictures that were in my wallet. Scared is not the right word for that type of moment. The surreal nature of such an event leaves it with no description that can adequately describe its emotional magnitude and the imprint that it etches on you at a cellular level.

Life passing before my eyes? Well, I did think about my family, how dysfunctional it was, and I did firmly identify the irony of being killed against this wall, the spot that meant so much to my growth as a well-trained and highly skilled athlete. It was hard to comprehend the callous nature of these people. The way that this guy held the gun against my head without so much as a minor tremble was awe-inspiring.

Later on in my life, I became the attacker and experienced the power of controlling the destiny of another's life. That was a moment, as depraved as it was, that brought me back to the deep black eyes of this guy's internal abyss. I am sure that he has lived to regret attacking me, and I am sure that if he is not conscious of that regret, that at some point in time, perhaps when he has left his physical body and in his life review, he will experience the pain that he inflicted on me on that cold Wednesday night in January.

Literally 30 yards to my left, just at the end of the wall, was the front door of the Fortuna's house. Mrs. Fortuna didn't miss a thing that happened in the neighborhood. Unfortunately, the Cott's wall extended far enough to the sidewall that it blocked any sightline that she might have had to where my life was being extinguished, and *oddly enough, she was in her kitchen, which was at the back of their house, and she was on the phone with my mother!*

How crazy is that? What does that mean? Were the pieces put together by a twisted God or was this the work of Satan or was it just four guys from Roosevelt out for a drug-induced joy ride in their grandmother's car, which they had stolen a couple hours earlier? These are all questions that I would ask myself over and over again for the next 20+ years.

The beating stopped, but only so they could blow my fucking brains out.

The big guy says, "Run, you white piece of shit so I can shoot you like a fucking dog."

My brain tells my feet to get the hell out of there. I already have an escape route in my head, which included cutting left at the end of the wall and up the little alley between Cott's and the Fortuna's eight-foot wooden stockade fence. I could hop that fence about 20 feet in and into their backyard and potentially see the license plate number on the Mustang.

Unfortunately, the guy with the Louisville Slugger had other ideas, and as soon as I turn to run up Spruce street toward that alley, thud, he connects with my forehead; I reel from that blow and am back against the wall and I can feel my legs getting wobbly beneath me.

In the movies when people are fighting, the sound folies put in really neat smacks and thwacks and all kinds of noises that keep one engaged with the excitement. In reality, when a bat comes in contact with a human head, it sounds like a brick when it hits the pavement after being dropped about 10 feet. A real thud, a dead sound, nothing exciting or engaging. It is a sickening noise, to this day, when I hear that sound or a similar one, my stomach turns upside down.

"Nah, the other way you stupid fuck."

I start to run down the sidewalk returning in the direction that I came from toward Brooklyn Avenue. I take a hard left, running three or four yards, then a hard right, another four or five yards, then repeat the same move as I run a serpentine pattern down the street.

I heard the gunfire and braced for the impact. I suppose that if I was going to be hit, I would have felt the shot before I heard the sound, but at the time, that did not process.

They seemed stoned, and I was lucky, because the shot went by me and into the stone above the retaining wall right in front of me. I got to the corner of the Cott's building and turned that corner like I had never turned that corner in my life. I felt a sheer wave of panic and fear, because I was now on a very wide and unprotected area of the street. They could easily have jumped in the car, made a U-turn and doubled back to run me down, either in a literal sense, by hitting me with the Mustang or just by pulling alongside me and shooting me like the dog that they thought I was.

What is it that causes that kind of anger and hatred? Why do races have such issues with each other? I have read Baldwin, King, Buscaglia, Dyer, and many others. They have all talked about the human condition, James Baldwin getting very close with his understanding of the condition that exists in the Black community because of their roots dating back to when people were taken off the beaches in Africa, hauled across the ocean, and sold like animals. The collective pain of this wound has oozed and festered for hundreds of years. I lived it too. I grew up on the other side of the coin, learning that "Blacks" and "spics" and "ricans" were the problem. They were the reason that there were unsafe neighborhoods and social programs that diluted the rest of society's benefit from taxes. They were the source of graffiti, robbery, assault, rape, murder, drugs, and hatred. It wasn't the white folks that I lived among. It was us against them, they were the problem and now, I had the proof of this. I had a less than five-minute encounter with four guys from Roosevelt who tried to kill me.

I now wanted to get even. I wanted justice. Justice in the punitive sense, not legal justice, but street justice, in the sense that I wanted to inflict pain on a Black man for every blow that I endured. True, I did not understand their pain, I did not live in their world, just as they did not live in mine. I was never pulled over by a cop while driving, just because my skin was dark and my hair was curly. I was never refused a job or looked down upon by my teachers. I was never followed through a store while I was there to buy a pack of gum. I was never led to believe that my life should be confined to a specific town line, to stay in a place like Hempstead, Roosevelt, Wyandanch, Compton, Detroit, or Harlem. The thought of crossing the Hempstead town line into Garden City on my way to work or the store, never created anxiety because I was afraid that I didn't belong. I didn't watch the race riots of the '60s and early '70s with fear that I would be persecuted.

The reality is that I have absolutely no understanding or possible inkling of what these guys were living or feeling. The anger and hate that I felt as I ran up that street, blood oozing out of my head and the swelling slowly forcing my eyes to close up, was real and powerful. Where does it go? Can something positive come from this? I hated my mom for trying to teach that racism and bigotry that I heard from my father and my NYPD neighbors, was not accurate. In that moment, I hated her for trying to teach me that it was a negative way to live and that she wanted me to live a more "Christ-like" life.

At that moment, as I ran up Brooklyn Avenue wondering whether I would see another day, I was really pissed about my mom's tolerant teachings. I learned later that she endured a very difficult life and her belief in forgiveness was well-worn and real.

I ran about 100 yards up Brooklyn Avenue, just past the end of the Cott's parking lot, and took a sharp right into the driveway of a house that backed up to the Lubitz's house, which was across the street from my house. I bolted up the blacktop drive and hopped a cyclone fence into their yard, ran another 50 or 60 feet to a wooden stockade fence, and jumped as high as I could so I could grab the top of the fence. Fortunately, this side of the fence had the crossboards that held the fence together which gave me a foothold and I jammed my right foot into the board and in one motion, swung my legs up and pushed with my arms to vault the fence. I landed on the grass, about 50 feet from the back of the Lubitz' colonial, on all fours, and for the first time, I felt the pain coursing through my back and my head. I could feel the blood dripping down my face and off of my chin.

The adrenaline was wearing off as I got closer to the safety of home and increased the distance between me and my attackers. I pushed myself forward in an aggressive motion, realizing the strength that I had developed over the last year while training to play lacrosse. I could feel the action and reaction of my calf and quad muscles as I sprinted toward the wooden fence in the front yard that was put up to contain their Afghan hounds.

The fence was five feet high, with wooden spindles that were about four inches apart and ran the length of the yard. While still in a gallop, I put each hand on a spindle about a foot apart and leaned forward and jumped. My pants leg got caught, and my head immediately headed straight toward the concrete sidewalk, and the blood splattered on the walk.

That was the first time that I saw the amount of blood that was seeping from my skull. I put my hands out to brace for the fall, and the impact caused my head to jerk forward; a red puddle splattered onto the sidewalk about three inches from my head. I didn't stop, my heart was racing, and my breath was shallow, and I had another 50 yards to go to get to my side door. I looked down the street toward Spruce Street as I crossed New York Avenue, looking for signs of the yellow Mustang. They were long gone, but my paranoia was keen. I ran down the north sidewalk and cut across my front lawn, feeling woozy and sick to my stomach. The damage from the head wound was now in full swing, the concussion causing an upset *stomach and the contusions causing blurred vision and a headache that didn't go away for almost a year.*

I wrapped my left hand around the doorknob and turned it— as I did, my legs collapsed beneath me; my brain knew that I had made it and told my body to let go. I fell inward, and onto the brown linoleum flooring of the small landing that was a step down from the kitchen floor, the yellow wall in front of me was covered with blood from my head and my hands.

I heard my mom yell, "What happened, what happened? Evelyn, call 911, Jimmy just collapsed in the kitchen, and he's covered with blood!" My mom was actually on the phone with Mrs. Fortuna—the woman whose house was about 50 feet from where I was being beaten half to death.

Time started to move much more quickly, after having dragged on for what seemed like an hour or two since I left Rockbottom. Everything was now a blur of motion and time, my mother was in full-blown disaster recovery and management mode, a role that she was well practiced at having dealt with my sister Lisa's many medical emergencies. My mom was happiest when she had something to do that kept her from facing the harsh reality of her life and her deep sadness and depression. And, she was good at pushing her stuff aside and jumping in to help others.

In the moments after she hung up the phone, the sirens were blaring at the Hose Company 3 firehouse around the corner on Baldwin Avenue and my mom called Jackie Lowery, my godmother, who was a nurse and lived three houses down.

All she said was, "Jackie I have a serious emergency, Jimmy has a head wound and I need help."

Mrs. Lowery was in the kitchen with a dishcloth against my head within 40 seconds. That was the kind of world it was on Long Island in 1982, people willing to help people when they needed it, no questions asked.

News traveled fast across the Baldwin Fire Department radios, and an ambulance, fire truck, and four or five police cars were in front of my house within minutes. I was seated at the head of our small table, on a metal kitchen chair that had a red plastic-covered seat cushion. I was hunched over my legs in a fetal position, just as I was 15 minutes earlier protecting my face and midsection from the attacking blows that were coming down on me. I was watching the room peripherally as I stared down at the linoleum floor with blood pooling around my feet.

My mom was a bit of a mess, this was well beyond her typical disaster, and there were six or seven rescue guys in the kitchen along

67

with one detective and two uniformed cops from the Nassau County Police Department.

Word had quickly spread that a young kid had been brutally attacked by a "gang" and that it was a white kid in Baldwin and a group of Black kids from out of town. It was bad enough that any attack had occurred, but having it be racially biased, gave the cops and firemen even more fodder for their already racially charged beliefs. Baldwin was only a few towns east of Brooklyn and Queens, it was a suburban town that many second and third generation Italian, Irish, and German Americans moved to, to build better lives for their own and subsequent generations. There were folks that grew up during the '40s and '50s and '60s through the racial plight that was a never-ending hangover of the slavery of the nineteenth century.

I grew up at the knees of some of the most bigoted and racist people in America. Yes, I am sure that there was much deeper hatred toward blacks in the southern states and of Puerto Ricans in Florida, but to have it in your face as a child every day was confusing at best; at worst, it helped foster an "us versus them" mentality. It also stoked fear.

Remember, many of my neighbors were New York City cops, they saw the worst of the worst crime in places like Brownsville, Bedford Stuyvesant, Harlem, and Queens. The fear that was created from those experiences was pervasive and permeated everything that they thought about anyone of color.

I had a friend whose father would shake hands with us with his left hand and as a "joke" would say, "lefties for niggers."

I remember, at the time, feeling like what he was saying wasn't a good thing, but at the same time, I got the joke and it was a sadly displayed racial insult being taught to the 11-year-old friends of his son. Then, he would crack his Budweiser and turn on whatever sporting event was coming on. It was all a very normal part of the routine. He has now passed into another life and I think about those handshakes and that statement often and I shake my head at the ignorance and the sadness. I do not judge, and I know that his anger was squarely being projected from his feelings of himself.

I remember seeing the half-covered legs of some of the firemen that were in my kitchen. They had their canvas and neoprene boots on with the big black loops that protruded on either side of their knees. Those boots seemed an odd site when there wasn't a fire, and there certainly wasn't a flood of any kind. I pictured my mom having to clean up the bloodstains and the fireman boot tracks tracked around the house after they walked through the puddles of blood on the kitchen floor. She was quite excessive about having clean linoleum.

At some point, Detective Cooney walked into the kitchen. I cannot remember the exact moment, but I do remember he had a small pad and pen for taking notes. He introduced himself and apologized to my mom for having questions, explaining that it is best to start immediately while the victim has the crime fresh in his mind. Detective Cooney was related to Gerry Cooney, who was a famous boxer nicknamed "The Great White Hope." The irony of that name is not lost on me. Gerry Cooney lost a title bout to Larry Holmes, the same year I lost my bout with four Black guys from Roosevelt. Detective Cooney was no stranger to race-related incidents and did not pull any punches about his feelings regarding the guys that attacked me.

He was very professional, and at the time, I thought that being a detective might be a possible career because of my exposure to Detective Cooney. He started asking me what happened and I slowly recounted much of what I have just written, but I was still in shock that what I was telling him actually happened.

At some point, I was expecting to wake up and roll over to go to the bathroom and wake up from this nightmare. The thing that jogged my head back to reality was the white flashlight and smelling salts that an EMT was using. His name was Doyle or Duncan and he was a nephew of the Fortunas by marriage, and he was the first guy to arrive. He was using the flashlight to continually check my pupils while they were strapping me to a bodyboard and gurney for my ride to the hospital. I had passed out for a moment. That night, I learned that the reaction to smelling salts that I had seen in the movies is very accurate. The chemical smell is intense and tells your head to wake up STAT.

Two of the EMTs eased me onto the gurney on wheels and strapped me down across the chest and waist. They put an IV into my arm, secured my head, right around the forehead, and fastened those straps to the gurney. I remember being in a semi-inclined position, not being able to move at all, and feeling very vulnerable. After having just run for my life, my brain was telling me that flight was the safest possible reaction now. I felt akin to a trapped prey as they lowered the gurney to carry me out the side door, the door that I just collapsed through, into my kitchen. It was not a comfortable sensation, having to give myself over to others and giving myself over to anyone had become something in my life that I was not accustomed to, and at this particular moment I was reacting in a very visceral way.

All I could think of was that I had to get out of there, that danger was looming large, that I was in imminent danger of being killed, that I couldn't trust anyone, that I wasn't safe. There were two guys on either end of the gurney as they passed me through the door and slowly lowered me to the driveway to wheel me down the path to the ambulance, which was waiting with the doors open, bright red and white lights swirling around on top. I also caught a glimpse of about 50 people standing down there in the street, all of my friends from the neighborhood and all of my neighbors.

As a kid, we chased ambulances and fire trucks all the time, so that we could get a "good seat" when they carried some poor son of a bitch out of their house because of a heart attack or a trip and fall in the bathtub. This time, I was the poor son of a bitch, not some old-timer who slipped on a bar of soap. The fear and desire to run overpowered me, and my usually reserved and shy self was pushed aside, I exploded verbally.

I couldn't move, so I rebelled in the only way I could; I started yelling.

I yelled directly at my mother, "you want me to trust the world, to accept people, well the niggers that you want me to tolerate just tried to kill me. People fucking suck! The miserable sons of bitches are there getting their jollies by beating your son's head in. Do you feel better now?"

Then I turned to all of my neighbors and overdramatically exclaimed, "It's not safe. They're taking over! Protect your kids!"

It was not one of my better moments and I was shocked at how quickly I developed the hatred inside of me to want to kill, to kill somebody with dark skin. My poor mother had to endure this tirade while watching her son lay on a gurney, not knowing if I was bleeding internally, if I had broken bones, if my head wound would result in brain damage, and if I would survive the blood loss. On top of that, she was living through this without the support of a husband or mate to share in the pain and confusion. I didn't comprehend that experience for her until recently. I am sure that it created a tremendous amount of stress and emotional trauma and anxiety for a woman who already lived a lifetime of stress and anxiety.

Looking back, I would like to have maintained some grace under pressure, and right now, I wish that my mom was of a conscious mind so that I could share with her how I understand a little and I can finally empathize with her loneliness and depression.

The door to the ambulance closed tightly and my mom and the EMT were all huddled next to each other. Detective Cooney was in a car directly behind us and would continue his questioning at South Nassau Communities Hospital in Oceanside.

The ride to the hospital was quick and it was really loud. It was loud without having three frickin' cracks in my skull, but having a *headache of such intense proportions only amplified the siren sounds that were blaring around me. I asked them to shut it off, but they said they couldn't take the risk of slowing down and talked to me about football.*

I knew they were only trying to keep me somewhat focused and coherent, and I felt pretty good knowing what was happening around me. However, my mind was having trouble executing strings of thought and specific words, and my head hurt —a lot!

As the adrenaline slowed inside, the pain started to appear throughout areas of my body where I'd been hit. My back was swollen and covered with welts and lacerations. My left hand, which had blocked the oncoming baseball bat, was as big as my head and throbbing like a stubbed toe. It was painful to breathe and the EMT thought I had some broken ribs, which turned out not to be true, but it sure felt like it.

It seemed as though every inch of my body was reacting to the beating that I'd received on my head, shoulders, and back. In addition to the physical effects of the diminishing levels of adrenaline, my emotions were also changing. Bottom line, I had survived and now my body was allowing me to experience the emotion that follows something like this, and that would be complete and utter fear.

As I stared into the group's eyes back in the all-purpose room in New Canaan, I said, "I did not realize until today, sitting in this room in a mental hospital, that I had lived much of my life in fear, a feeling that was as comfortable and known to me as anything else that I have felt. It is that fear-based life that causes anger, anxiety, self-loathing, and wanting to cause self-pain. As I sit here today replaying this story to people that I have never met, I am sharing a story that I do not discuss, and it feels good to let it go, to release a piece of anxiety that has plagued me."

Tom: "Wow, thanks for sharing that."

And with that one story and Tom's acknowledgment, I had engaged in my first group therapy session.

Trish: "Is it my turn yet? Because I do not want to talk today."

David: "I'll go, Tom."

Tom: "I'd like to hear Doris a bit. Doris, why are you here?"

Doris leaned forward, "I'm tired. My medication isn't working anymore and they're trying to figure out how to stabilize me."

Tom: "Why do you take medication?"

Doris: "I'm bipolar."

Me: "What is bipolar?"

Tom continues with Doris, "Doris, do you sleep well?"

Doris: "My sister is coming to get me today."

It is amazing how quickly people can move in and out of their psychosis. There are some questions that are just too painful to face and require separation from reality. I am struck by the intelligence of every person in the room.

Ninety minutes after it had begun, we recited a prayer.

"God grant me the serenity to accept the things I cannot change, the courage to change the things I can, and the wisdom to know the difference."

Holy shit!

Those words were on a small plaque that hung in my kitchen for my entire childhood. I had no idea of the relevance of the Serenity Prayer and that my mom had lived those words the best that she could.

I left the room and went down the hall to the payphone bank to call home. I was tired, I was defeated, I was scared, and I was still holding on to the hope that my life wasn't completely over.

Chris answered the phone, "Hello?"

"It's me."

She said, "How are you?"

I said, "You need to get me out of here, these people are fucking crazy!"

Chris replied, "You're fucking crazy and you are where you belong right now. We all love you and you are safe, and so are we."

Me: "Ok, thanks."

I stood there in the hallway, with the phone receiver in my hand and I wept uncontrollably for a while as I tried to make sense of still being alive, accepting that life was changed, and feeling sorry for having put my family through the pain that I had been living in my head for so long.

Sharing that story of the violent assault that I endured was very cathartic. It was the start of the process of healing, although, at the time, I did not comprehend that the process had begun. The road to health and peace is a journey that requires discipline and focus.

Following the assault, I had sustained some broken bones in my left hand and three gashes in my skull that required 75 stitches. I had a concussion and my nose had been broken. These injuries all healed relatively quickly and I was back on the lacrosse field in late March. I played that season despite having had a concussion. I suffered from severe headaches that I did not share with anyone. I was a Junior and was trying to be recruited to play in college and I knew that if I didn't play, I would not have that opportunity. As my kids say today, I am intelligent, but not very wise.

CHAPTER 7

THE PRACTICE OF HEALTH BEGINS

That night I was given a few drugs; Seroquel, Effexor, and Ambien. Yet again, it was just like *One Flew Over the Cuckoo's Nest*, complete with the half door opening to the pharmacy closet and those little Dixie cups with the pills in them. I took my Dixie cup with a few pills on the bottom, put it to my lips and the pills ambled into my mouth. Then the nurse handed me a cup of water and I swallowed what would be the beginning of my accepting medication into my life to help me manage my chemically driven imbalance.

I slept for 14 hours straight!

It had been more than a month since I slept for more than two or three hours at a time and a week since I had slept at all. I had never felt more rested in my entire life.

Each one of the following days brought some sense of relief to a mind that had been plagued by anxious thoughts for over 20 years. Each hour was like a rebirth and many months after I left the hospital, I described my time there as if I had unzipped a thick neoprene suit that had enveloped my being and I then stepped out of it. Every day, a new suit would be unzipped and I would step out of it, getting closer and closer to the real me. Little did I know at the time that it would take a full four or five years of hard work and examination of self before I would be comfortable and in love with "me." It had been that long since I was me and there were many layers that I had created to protect myself, hidden and buried within the masks of what I thought that people wanted to see from me.

Each moment in the day was filled with as much interaction as was possible for each of the residents in the acute care unit. At different points of the day, that interaction varied for each person, just as all of our personalities varied. The one common theme for each person was that there was trauma at some point in their life, there was a genetic predisposition for some level of addiction, there was self-loathing, and a strong lack of self-esteem, and there was pain and fear. I have learned since then that all people suffer from the same feelings of fear and pain from their experiences here in this world. The stories are all very different, but the resulting feelings are all the same. In the hospital, you could have substituted any one of our stories for others and the resulting feelings, outcomes and destructive behaviors were all exactly the same! This is not true with strong chemical imbalances; that is an entirely different situation altogether. I am simply talking about all of the other experiences that I was encountering throughout my time there. It completely opened my eyes to the pain of the human experience that we all suffer from.

I have seen a car bumper sticker that I didn't fully understand before, *"Don't believe everything you think."*

A few days into my hospitalization, group therapy was an arts and crafts period. *What the fuck? Arts and Crafts? You have to be kidding me!"*

I'll say it again—*Arts and fucking Crafts.*

The tables in the common room had been pushed together and placed end to end to create a larger than average picnic table area 15 by 15 square and a chair for everyone around the outside of the square. On the table were 10–12 plastic boxes filled with all kinds of stuff that would have made a kindergarten class jump for joy: markers, glue sticks, glitter tubes, beads, shells, scissors, colored paper strips, tongue depressors, popsicle sticks, pipe cleaners, hemp string, styrofoam pieces, and the list goes on.

I sat there taking in the scene, thinking, *If I see one piece of shell macaroni I'm walking right the fuck out of here and finding something sharp so that I can gouge my eyes out. There is no fucking way I'm sitting in a looney bin making macaroni necklaces.*

We made picture frames out of popsicle sticks and tongue depressors and shells and beads and glitter. We drew pictures of whatever came to mind. We made paper cut-out people and strings of crazy designs. Then 90 minutes later, the group session leader Lisa, said, "OK guys, you have done some great work and it's time to clean up."

I heard myself saying, "What? I'm not done with this necklace, can't we just have another 15 minutes?"

The group arts and crafts time went by so quickly. I couldn't believe that I could focus on something for more than five minutes. I am an avid New York Times crossword puzzle enthusiast. I love the Sunday times for lots of reasons, but if they got rid of the crossword puzzle in the magazine section, I would cancel my subscription. However, over the past few months, I had not been able to spend more than 10 minutes looking at the puzzle. My thought process and ability to concentrate had been reduced to small spurts. It felt like there were conversations taking place in my mind that would pull me away from what I was trying to focus on. It was happening more and more throughout the day and I was becoming less and less productive with each passing day. During that group session, I was able to concentrate for 90 minutes—holy smokes, I was excited!

I am sure that if anybody had looked in on that scene, they would have thought that this was a bunch of crazy or developmentally disabled people. That thought drove a little sadness in me and I realized that the desocialization of this kind of fun had been driven out of us by a society that puts no value on continuing these simple little events from our childhood. Arts and crafts are fun, social, and creative. What else do you need from your world?

That afternoon, I was given a black and white composition notebook which would become the first real journal of my life. Between the arts and crafts and now this old school composition notebook with its marbled cover, the memories of my childhood flooded back into my head. The instructions from the teacher that day were simple, "Just write down what comes to mind, there are no right or wrong entries, just start to acknowledge things as they come up in your mind. Please try to do this every day."

I started to write that day, and man, I couldn't stop. I called Chris that evening and asked her to please bring me some composition notebooks. I upgraded my journaling process by including my wife in this practice. I would write during the day and when she came to visit me, which was almost every day, I would hand her a full journal and she would give me a new book to write in.

I started the process of talk therapy with my soulmate and shared thoughts with her that I hadn't shared in our 20 years together. I filled eight or nine notebooks in a few days. I could not stop the flow of feelings and revelations that were pouring forth. It was very liberating. It was also scary because I could feel memories come to the fore that I had chosen to bury deep within my psyche. The honesty was critical to developing love for myself. It was allowing me to let things go in a way that I hadn't been able to do in my entire life. Sharing all of this with my wife was a leap of faith because I felt that I had ended any and all trust she may have had left in me, and anything that I shared was now suspect, at best, and for good reason. However, I felt that I could no longer hide from the things that I had been doing and the ways that I had been slowly destroying myself and my relationship with Chris. My behavior was self-destruction on steroids.

I heard my name being called from down the hall, "Jim, you have a phone call."

I slowly stood and put my feet into my Tommy Bahama flip flops and shuffled down the hall toward the phone bank. It was 10:00 in the morning on my third or fourth day of being locked away in the cocoon of health and safety. I picked up the phone, "Hello?"

My sister was on the other end, "Hi Jim, it's Vicki."

"Hi."

"I heard about what happened and I am calling to let you know that I am thinking about you. Do you need anything? How is Chris? Can I do anything?"

My sister Vicki is an amazing person. She has endured much trauma in her own life and is also in the mental health business and has been doing what I call "God's work" for many years. My sister is highly educated, having worked to put herself through college and earning her Master's Degree in Special Education. She is retired now, but spent her career investigating the treatment of residents of group homes to protect the mentally ill and those who cannot take care of themselves. She was driven in this work like the hand of God had led her down this path because of the way that she saw my sister Lisa treated when we were growing up. Vicki was also the person that raised me. She took care of me through elementary and junior high school because my mom worked so much and was also detached because of her own struggles with depression. Vicki was always there to make sure that I was taken care of. We had lost touch in the years prior to my breakdown because she was doing her own work and she had successfully detached herself from her past so that she could protect herself from the memories of her own emotional trauma.

The phone call from my sister was both comforting and upsetting at the same time. It felt great that she was reaching out to me and I could sense the love that she had for me and her concern to make sure that I was in good hands. On the other hand, it made me realize that there was a whole world outside of the walls of this facility, a world that I had not survived in and one that I would have to return to at some point.

At that moment, I wanted to die again. I couldn't shake the feeling that suicide would have been the right thing to do. *Fuck it, it should have been over before that phone call.* I said to myself, *I don't want to do this. I don't want to be medicated. I don't want to be in therapy. I don't want to hurt my family anymore. I don't want Chris to be subjected to me anymore. She is still young, she can easily find someone that will take care of her and love her the way that she deserves and I don't want to face my inadequacies any longer.* These are things that I would repeat to myself for the next several months.

Out loud, I said, "Thanks for calling, I am ok and they are taking care of me. I don't need anything. I have to go now."

"OK," Vicki said, "well, call me the minute you get home."

I knew that that was a phone call that I would not make. I knew that I was never going to call anybody—ever.

Six years after that phone call, I got a chance to sit down with my sister and her husband at a diner on Long Island. I said to her husband, "I want to thank you for staying with my sister, she deserves to be loved and taken care of in her life. She deserves happiness after a tough life and I thank you for working through your relationship with her."

To my sister, I said, "I want to thank you for raising me, for being there for me when I was a child. Your relationship was very important to me and saved my life. I am so happy to be here and I love you very much."

So, six years later, I made that "phone call" and was able to speak the healing words that we both needed and it felt better than great. It was one of those moments when every cell in your body vibrates with joy and healing. That's when you know that it's right and in rhythm with who you really are. It doesn't have to happen on any schedule or time frame. It happens as it should and when the Universe delivers it.

As James Taylor explains in his song, "Secret O' Life," time isn't real, it's just a societal construct and it really depends on how you look at it.

On the fourth day in the hospital, I started to feel somewhat human and my thoughts were relaxing a bit after getting some much-needed sleep and being in a calm and healing environment. My medication regimen was starting to kick in a bit and it was creating some physical changes that were not welcome, but I was patient with "letting go" and being "of the process." I experienced some pretty intense body sweats, involuntary hand movements like shaking and trembling, and my eyes were twitchy. I must have looked like shit, and I was starting to come out of my fog. The feeling that I was safe and that I didn't actually need to do anything provided an incredible release and allowed me just to shut down my brain.

At 10:00 in the morning, I noticed that the doors to an outdoor patio were opened up for the first time since I arrived. Everyone lined up like cows waiting at the barn door to be milked. I had not seen this doorway since I arrived, and I asked Trish what was going on.

Sue turned to me and said, "Knucklehead, every day at 10:00 and 2:00, we go outside for a smoke—where have you been?"

I said, "I thought I was here but I guess not."

I walked through the double glass doors onto a deck that could have been used for corporate events at a Marriott Hotel, and I felt like Dorothy Gale looking in Munchkinland for the first time as the color kicked in. The sun was shining brightly through the leaves of birch, elm, spruce, oak, and maple trees. The bright blue sky was dotted with the whitest stratus clouds and they hung there like the fluffiest cotton balls I have ever seen. The sky was electric, and I could feel the blue as it poured over me and surrounded my being, like being held in the arms of mother nature herself.

The deck was pretty big. It was L-shaped and hung off the back of the common room and was about 50 feet by 15 feet. There were tables and chairs in the center area and bench seats flanked both walls. Then I noticed the entire area was closed in by a fence that rose up from the floor to a height of 20 feet. It was scalable, but the drop to the ground was at least 30 to 40 feet and was definitely not doable by anybody in this group.

In all her tact and gentility, Trish said, "Holy shit, your eyes are the same color as the sky."

"Uh, thanks..."

In my mind, all I wanted was for nobody to see me, especially Trish. I just wanted to fly under the radar and be left alone.

"No, really, I thought your eyes were gray like a river of mud, when you got here, wow, it would have been such a waste to kill those eyes!"

"Thanks, it feels good to still be here."

At that moment, I decided that it really *was* good to be here. To be alive, to have made it to....well, to be here; wherever that was and wherever I was heading to.

I laughed as I thought about Spanky on the Little Rascals, when Alfalfa asked, "Hey Spanky, where you goin'?" and Spanky replied, "I don't know but I'm on my way."

Then, I smelled the cigarette smoke that was billowing up from the mouths of the group. I looked around the deck and everybody was smoking. Well, there were three of us that were not, but, the other 21 were each sitting or standing or leaning and smoking a butt that had been doled out by Joe, the social worker that was carrying everybody's cigarettes in plastic bags with their names on them. It was snack time for adults.

The smell brought me back to sitting next to my father at the movies as a kid. We always sat in the back of the theater, the smoking section, and he would smoke five or six butts during a two-hour movie. I would leave the movies feeling nauseous and smelling like a fucking ashtray.

I carried myself over to a wooden bench, sat down, put my head in my hands, and started to cry.

Trish came over, sat down next to me, and said, "Hey, you ok?"

I didn't say a word.

Trish said, "Yeah...I know."

She did know, in fact, everybody on that porch "knew." We all knew that whatever happened to us in our lives was just too much for our minds and bodies to continue to bear. There was no judgment from those people, just empathy. At times, the feelings of personal frustration about our own situations bubbled up and exploded in the form of anger, but it wasn't based on the judgment of others, only the judgment of self.

That anger, stemming from frustration and self-loathing, was always right there under the surface, ready to be launched in the form of attack or destructive behavior and continued self-mutilation.

Being in that environment, with others that were "feeling" my pain, was exactly what I needed to survive that which I had created for myself. After 20 years of abusing my family, my friends, and myself, I was finally in a place where I could release it all and just let go.

I cried some more. In fact, throughout my stay at Silver Hill, and for months after, I cried quite a bit as I mourned the pain that I had lived and the moving on to a better life. It is like mourning the death of an important person in your life and it doesn't matter if that person was a positive or negative experience. The finality of death brings waves of mourning and that is what it felt like.

The next morning, I was moved down the hall to a room with a single bed. Steve, a middle-aged guy that had been there for 45 days was released, and because I was so much older than my high school aged roommate, they felt it more appropriate to put me in my own space. The solitude, especially at night, was very much in order. However, I did what my habit had always been when the anxiety kicked in, I retreated to that space as much as I possibly could during the first couple of days after the move.

I grabbed a book off the shelf over the 20-inch TV and immersed myself in the fictional work Michael Crichton had created in *Prey*. The story had no nutritional value for my mind, but I was enthralled with this newfound ability to concentrate because I could now focus on something for longer periods of time. It also provided me enough escape for a few hours that I relished opening it and used it as a crutch to be alone and quiet.

As I lay on the bed in complete and utter aloneness at the end of the long shiny hall of hospital rooms, I was interrupted by a knock on the door. Again, the door was open, because that was the rule during the day; you couldn't close your door and shut yourself off from the world.

Nurse Barb asked, "Jim, what's going on?"

"Just reading."

"I'd like you to read in the common room."

"It's too distracting down there with the TV going and everybody around."

"Here's the thing, isolation is part of your reaction to your depression. It's one of your symptoms, and I'd like to start changing that habit a bit."

I felt a little edgier as the ego-anger bubbled up like a teenager being told to clean your room, "You mean, I'm not capable of making my own frickin decisions?"

"First, you are capable. Second, have your decisions led you down a good path in the past?"

Fucking touché! I stood up, took a deep breath, and walked with her down to the common room. I sat there continuing to read and found that the presence of everyone in the community room was actually very calming and pleasant. Damn, isolation doesn't work and only continues to further my disease.

Then, one of the social workers came in and said, "Everybody, this is Stephanie, she is joining us for a bit, please introduce yourselves at some point today."

Stephanie was a 24-year old blonde woman, with the kind of physical appearance that you only see in the movies. Her face was striking, like a face that I had seen on the cover of Cosmo a few weeks ago as it stared up at me from our kitchen table. As it turned out, Stephanie was a soap opera actress from New York City and was taking some time to rehab herself while her on-screen character was struggling to regain consciousness from a long-term coma. That is how the world operates. Things just keep going on as mental disease is masked in some way.

I looked at Stephanie and was amazed that someone so beautiful, so young, and so successful could possibly have a problem in the world. Ironic, right? I caught myself in mid-thought, again reminding myself that Stephanie was me and I was her. That was the first time I realized that judgment of others had taken hold and it was masking the things that I felt for myself. And that is what judgment is; it is a direct reflection of what you see or don't see in yourself, not the person you are judging. You are actually saying all of those things to yourself, and it will not help you to be in that space of "negative speak."

The next day, in our group session, Stephanie fully introduced herself and talked about her life. The life that she had tried to extinguish a few days earlier, by swallowing a bunch of pills and drinking a fifth of bourbon. She had small scars on her wrists. Both wrists. Each wrist had marks that were about an inch long and ran across the light blue veins and arteries that ran from her hand into her forearm. They were very faint from a couple of plastic surgery skin grafts, but, as someone who had spent years dreaming of suicide, they were the unmistakable marks of complete unhappiness, that drove someone to want to die.

Stephanie shared, "My father raped me when I was nine years old and my mom was sleeping in the bed. She had to know, I mean, I was next to her and could hear her breathing as I stared up at the ceiling while my father pounded his hips into me. I hate that motherfucker! When I was 11, I met a kid that lived around the corner from us. He was in high school. I think he was 17. I went to his house every day to hang out with him and he would get me to give him blow jobs, and eventually when I was 13, we started having sex. I was pregnant a year later, and I had an abortion. I was always an "A" student in school, it seemed like the right thing to do, and whenever I had the chance, I would fuck anything that moved. Girls, boys, men, whoever, and whenever. It felt like that was my purpose in life and I hated myself for it. I started drinking heavily in college and haven't stopped since. It's been five years of going from studying regular academic stuff and acting. Every day I followed my routine of studying with a bottle of vodka and coke. It was just never enough of a numbing, and I continued to take as many mood-altering substances that I could and of course, continued to fuck anybody that would use me for the reason I was put here.

"God has cursed me with beauty that runs about a quarter-inch deep into my body. People see me and think I'm beautiful. I know that, but I feel so fucking ugly that I cannot stand it any longer. I earned over $250,000 last year, and this year I'm going to make almost double that. I'm 24, and my father called me last weekend because he wants to come to New York for a visit. I hung up the phone, smashed it on the ground as if that would somehow protect me. I realized at that moment that the only way that I could get away was to finally get away from this existence, to close the book on this soul's choice for this life. This is not life, this is a death sentence and I cannot take it anymore. I tried to kill myself four times, and each time, I have failed."

Trish didn't say a word this time.

Stephanie continued through her sobbing, "I don't know where I go from here. I just know that I am broke, I am broken, and have finally hit bottom, at least I think I have anyway."

All of us, every single person in that room, even Doris, who was sitting in her usual seat outside the circle, was crying. That included the session moderator, who, for today, was a Hawaiian-born and trained Buddhist healer named Kalika.

I took in what Stephanie had said. I mean, I tried to get my head around it as best I could. That's the thing that I have always tried to do, get my head around stuff. It was time to stop with the head and start with the heart. The heart is the real you; the head is driven by our imagined and real experiences. Some years later, I was introduced to Byron Katie (Byron is her pen name and everybody calls her Katie), who has written several books that have changed my life immensely.[1]

Stephanie had spent 30 minutes telling us all about ourselves. She told us about our fears, our self-loathing, our hate, our anger, our misperceptions of self, our abuse, our destructive behavior, our suicidal ideation and actions, our destroyed family relationships, and the one particularly scary thing, all of our "I DON'T KNOW WHERE I GO FROM HERE" fears.

My time in the hospital was a much-needed safety zone for my family and me. I wrote extensively, talked to therapists a lot, cried multiple times a day and night, slept soundly, read, got my medication cocktail in rhythm with my needs, and learned that it would be possible to move on in life. This wasn't who I was, it was just part of my journey, and then, Chris came to pick me up.

Leaving a facility where you are locked in for a period of time is very scary. I cannot imagine what people who live through long prison sentences feel as they catch their first breath of freedom's air. They must be scared shitless. I know that I was.

I went through the exit process, getting all of my belongings back, having a post-hospital continued care plan that included required weekly therapy in both an individual and group setting, signing off on all kinds of hold-harmless

---

[1] Around the topic of following your head instead of your heart, Katie has written an incredible book called *What Would You Be Without Your Story* that is so simple in concept, yet so difficult in practice.

documents for the insurance risk factors of the facility, signing off on the bills. *OH SHIT! The bills!* And lastly, saying goodbye to all of the patients and the staff. I saw us all as a family of complete fuck-ups that had deep-seated respect and understanding of our collective journeys to follow this shared evolution of spirit. That included the staff. While they were not mentally ill in the way that the rest of us were, they were very much of the world that we had all created, and in my opinion, much of that world was skewed toward the unreal machinations of the fucked up mind.

Chris was there to pick me up. This time, she arrived alone, in the silver BMW that weeks earlier, I had wanted to take my life in. It was a hot pre-summer day, and she put the top down. Sitting in the passenger seat, I leaned my head back on the leather seat and breathed in the fresh air as I stared up, looking at the green trees that lined the rural winding road that leads to and from the incredible gift that is Silver Hill Hospital.

I cried as we listened to *Train*, a band that wrote some songs that helped Chris get through her journey and process.

We both knew that the hospital stay, the suicide attempt, and the pain and anguish that I brought to my entire family was just the beginning of a road that would be carved out as we moved forward. There were no Operator's Manual or "Depression for Idiots" books to read to grasp where we were.

As Stephanie had said, "I don't know where I go from here."

The thing about going through a journey of self-evolution is that you go through that journey while the rest of the world continues down its own path. Chris sensed that this would be a huge part of the continued healing that we all embarked on.

She said, "We need to talk about how you want to proceed with the world. As I see it, you, we, have a few choices. One, we can tell people that you were sick in the hospital with some dread disease and now you're back. Two, we can tell people that you were away on business. Three, we can tell people the truth and let them deal with their own issues and judgments about it. Since we are going to be hit with a lot of judgment, misunderstanding, and ignorance, I want to make sure that we both agree on how we should proceed."

I looked at Chris, her beautiful flowing brown hair blowing in the breeze as we got on to the Merritt Parkway in New Canaan, and I was shocked by her stunning face. She was glowing in a way that I hadn't seen for many years. The unzipping of the suit of dysfunction had brought me back to see her again.

I said, "I think that we should be honest. I am ready to be honest about who I am."

We chose honesty and that was the start of my life of honesty—although it would be another full year of self-examination before I was prepared to be fully honest with my soulmate about the depth of my self-hatred and destruction. Some of that continued "dishonesty" was conscious and much of it was not. I had repressed some serious trauma that I had experienced as a six-year-old boy and I was not ready to go there yet.

For the conscious choice of continuing to hide some of my behavior to my wife, it's a time and choice that I wish I had back, but, it just wasn't time and everything in life happens in perfection, just as it should. But, neither of us understood what was to come and the magic that life is.

CHAPTER 8

DIAGNOSIS OF DEPRESSION

I left the hospital with my new "life suit" and felt like I had been through a war with myself. The good guy won.

Unfortunately, as I said earlier, when you go through dramatic change in your life, it is your change, and the world continues to go on as it had before. I had a tough road ahead of me to try and heal some of the broken pieces that were the relationships that I had with family and friends. Pieces that I left along that road. In some cases, those pieces were small fragments. In others, there were whole buildings that would take years to clear away for the possibility of paving a new road. I felt strong, but I was also frightened of being in the world again. It is a daunting task to go back to a world that has been successful at crushing you at a cellular level.

The doctors at Silver Hill diagnosed me with general anxiety disorder and major depressive disorder (clinical depression) with bipolar tendencies.

OK, so I had my labels. We love to label everything in our lives—if there isn't a definition, we have to create one. In a lot of situations, I reject the need we have to label everything. In my case, beginning to understand what was occurring in my body, which was dramatically affecting my mind, was a huge wake-up call because it would lead me to understand how I could manage my depression.

What is depression?

Here is some information from the University of Michigan Center for Depression[2]:

What is depression?

- *Depression is not the same as a short-term feeling of sadness or emptiness. It's more than a temporary case of "the blues".*
- *Depression is a brain disorder, caused by abnormalities in the levels of neurochemicals in the brain.*
- *Clinical depression, also called major depressive disorder (MDD), is a serious, long-term illness that can affect a person's daily functioning and relationships.*
- *There is no single cause known for depression; a number of factors may be at work, alone or together, including a family history of the disease, a recent trauma or loss, or encountering an uncommon level of stress.*

What are some of the symptoms of depression?

- *Recurring feelings of sadness or hopelessness*
- *Loss of interest in hobbies or favorite activities, including sex*
- *Pessimism*
- *Fatigue or decreased energy*
- *Changes in sleep such as early morning wakefulness, excessive sleeping, or insomnia*
- *Changes in appetite (either an increase or a decrease)*
- *Persistent aches, pains, or digestive problems*
- *Thoughts of suicide*

As you can see, depression has some pretty varied causes and as many variations of symptoms. It has become a bit of a "catch-all" to many healthcare providers, who can send people down the wrong path for their individual situation if they are not experts in the diagnosis and treatment. Just as everyone is not the same, the depressive episodes that people experience can be very different.

As a result, the causes of those episodes, the resulting behavior, the addictions, and the understanding of it are critical to the individual patient. I decided that I needed to learn as much as I could about my depression if I was going to take back my life and live it to the fullest.

---

[2] (https://members.depressioncenter.org/docc/)

My depression resulted in the following symptoms: chronic sadness and emptiness, lack of sleep at times, too much sleep at times, suicidal thoughts, severe anxiety, self-loathing, chronic lethargy, over-eating, alcohol abuse, dangerous and illicit behavior, isolation, fear of failure, manic mood swings from highs of laughter and fun to lows of complete suicidal focus, anger, and back pain.

It is important to understand that when I write something like the word anger, I don't mean it in the sense that most people might experience or define anger. I mean, it's almost impossible to drive on a major US highway and not experience anger—right? I'm talking about unhealthy levels of anger that result in wanting to cause physical harm to someone or myself. Anger that isn't appropriate for a given situation causes blackouts in memory of what I did or said. There was no barometer for my angry outbursts. I was either seemingly calm or off the charts pissed off resulting in lunatic rantings of foul and threatening language and behavior.

Depression can result from as many varying factors as there are symptoms and behaviors. My depression was the culmination of the perfect genetic storm that started when my parents met in the '50s and decided to mate and have children.

My parents, James and Bertha, were about as mismatched as any two people could be and are living proof that there is a lid for every pot. However, as I have read and learned about life's relationships and why we have them, it makes perfect sense that these two souls decided to connect.

In his book, *Keeping the Love you Find*[3], Harville Hendrix, Ph.D., explains the importance of healing self as the reason why we meet certain people in our lives. As I have looked at my relationships in my life, Harville's philosophy rings true. Essentially, we meet people in our lives that will mirror people from our childhood that bring up "stuff" that we need to work through and heal. If we choose not to heal and then divorce the mate that we have chosen, we will go out in the world and meet yet another person that will bring up the same stuff, and we will eventually have to work through it. If not, we will ignore the healing required to fully engage in the reason you and your mate have met in the first place.

Unfortunately, my parents never got that far. They separated when I was about a year old, and my father moved to

[3] Hendrix, Harville. *Keeping the Love You Find*. Atria Books: 1993.

New Jersey, where he lived alone until his death several years ago at 79. My mom passed away a few years back after having moved back to her hometown in California's San Joaquin Valley. She remarried and experienced the love that she rarely got to receive before she was reunited with an old elementary schoolmate back in her hometown.

Perhaps some background is in order.

My mom was born in the 1930s in some of the best farm country in the US—the San Joaquin Valley. She lived in Livingston, Merced, further north in Sebastopol, and a few other places that her mom dragged her to as she was growing up. It was not an easy post-depression era life. Her story is riddled with physical abuse, sexual abuse, alcoholics coming and going, a dangerously promiscuous mom, and a 13-year-old sister who had died by suicide after being raped by one of her mom's drunken lovers.

As my mom grew older, she longed to get the hell out of that existence and dreamed of big city life with dreams of landing a man that could provide for her and the family that she hoped to have.

James Francis Rinere, II, my dad, was born in Brooklyn, New York, also in the 1930s. He was the son of one of the meanest people that I have ever met—my namesake, James Francis Rinere. It is a name that I have not been comfortable with for many years. My father was subjected to severe physical abuse from an alcoholic father and his childhood was not unlike my mom's, unhappy at best, miserable with suicidal thoughts at its worst. They both struggled with obesity issues as children, although my father in his very early years did play baseball and football. Football was his sport of choice because of his size. However, because of their obesity, they both suffered from bully attacks when they were younger. It was much worse for my mother because my father, being physically stronger than most kids his age, was willing to fight it out if he needed to. He was a real Brooklyn greaser, complete with the Harley Davidson and leather jacket. My mom did not fare as well, and she suffered many a stoning from her classmates in elementary school.

Yes, stoning.

I remember the first time that she told me the story of being stoned. I was a junior in high school, and she said that I was so lucky to be physically fit.

I asked, "Why?"

She said, "Because kids can be so cruel. When I was in elementary school, I was stoned by the other kids."

I said, "You mean, you got stoned with the other kids? I didn't know that you smoked pot back then!"

She said, with a straight face and a white as ghost expression, "No, because I was so fat, they put me up against a barn and threw rocks at me until I started to bleed."

I looked at my mom through the tears that had formed in my eyes, and I saw that child that could not take care of herself. At that moment, I experienced a rage toward my father for having left my mom so many years earlier. It was an anger that I didn't release until a few years ago.

My parents met in the 1950s in California while my dad was on leave with the Army, after having come back from the Korean War. He was a wounded war veteran after taking grenade shrapnel to the leg that left him with a huge scar running up the side of his knee and thigh.

My mom wanted to get out of the farm country, and my dad wanted to show somebody how worldly he was. It was a match made in "ego-heaven" for each of them. The kicker here was that they both suffered from severe bouts of depression, my mom was diagnosed in the '70s and my dad wasn't officially diagnosed until much later because he detested doctors and anything having to do with him taking care of himself. They both had the genetic predisposition to depression, alcoholism, and suicidal tendencies. It makes perfect sense that I, their youngest child, would enter the world with a predisposition to addictive behavior and depression. My sisters have had their own struggles with mental health as well. We have all had our issues with depression, eating disorders, and suicidal ideation at one time or another. It would be somewhat improbable to grow up with that gene pool and not have some of those problems.

While my parents were tortured souls early in their lives, their individual issues manifested themselves in very different ways.

My mom became an extremely passive victim, but she was the kindest person that I ever met. My mom believed with all her heart that God put us here to serve others, and she did that pretty much every day of her life. This "serving of others" began with her first child, Lisa, my oldest sister, who was born with Down syndrome in the late '50s.

The doctor walked into my mom's hospital room after my sister's birth and told her, "There is a facility in upstate New York where you should send the child, forget about it, and try to have another immediately."

My mom, despite not knowing the first thing about a disability like Down syndrome, would not have her child sent away, in her words, "to die a loveless existence."

So began her life's work of caring for her first child, who was in and out of hospitals for much of the first ten years of her life, with open-heart surgery, lung development issues, and many other ailments. The medical issues were just the obvious things. The larger issue that we dealt with every day was the world's ignorance about "mongoloids" and "retards" as they were cruelly referred to.

I remember getting out of the car at the Pathmark Supermarket after having parked in a newly created handicapped parking space, our official New York state handicapped sticker prominently displayed in the front windshield of our '68 Oldsmobile Delta 88.

As we turned to walk toward the store, a man coming the other way said, "The only place she's handicapped is in her brain. She can fuckin' walk like the rest of us."

My mom didn't miss a step and said, "You are right, she is handicapped and that's why we get this great spot in the front of the parking lot. You should get to your car before I have my daughter talk your ear off."

I was deeply hurt by these small altercations and took them on as if people were saying things about me. It happened all the time, pretty much anytime we went anywhere in the world. It helped me to understand the deep ignorance of people around the unknown and their own fears. However, it didn't help me with my own issues of self-esteem, and I would often be so nervous to go anywhere that I developed stomach pains and diarrhea.

Later on in life, as I grew older, bigger, and stronger, I became much more aggressive toward people that would make comments or stare at my sister. One time, in the same Pathmark parking lot, it was just Lisa and me and I parked in the center of the lot because I didn't have the handicap card in my car.

A large 40-ish man got out of his car next to us and looked into my passenger window as I was getting out of the car.

He said to his passenger, "Charlie, look at the retard."

I said to my sister, "Hey Leese—stay in the car and I'll open the door for you."

I walked around to the other side of my car, straight toward the ignorant jerk that had decided to say the "R" word on the wrong day, to the wrong person.

I grabbed him by his too tight t-shirt and threw him against the back of his car while continuing to hold onto his shoulders so that I could drive his head into his trunk with as much force as I could. I was a freshman in college, a division one athlete, and had been lifting weights six days a week for a year. I weighed 200 pounds and was 6 foot 4 inches. The entire force of my being and all of the anger that I felt from years of these kinds of people saying stupid things came down on this guy.

He crumpled to the ground like a toppled snowman, his car keys flying one way and his body going the other.

I turned toward the passenger, Charlie, and he said, "Don't hurt me."

I said, "Yeah, just as I thought, a couple of pussies picking on somebody that cannot defend themselves. You say one more thing and I'll kick both your asses all over this parking lot—you ignorant pricks!"

My sister, waiting patiently for me to open the door, turned her head toward me as I opened her door and said, "Are you going to open the door or what?"

To Lisa, violence and anger didn't exist, and I was immediately sorry that I had put her in danger. We walked into the store, and I felt like I had gotten some retribution, but the anger that was so quick to bubble up was something that would plague me for many years to come.

My mom believed that my sister was the most special being she had ever known—and she was right.

My dad, on the other hand, did not espouse the philosophy of service to others. His issues manifested themselves in the diametrically opposed way of anger, bigotry, and racism. Not to mention all of the abuse that he inflicted on himself—alcohol, cigarettes, isolationism, and overeating.

As with all of us here on this wacky planet, my dad was quite the study in dichotomy. He was extremely intelligent, a member of Mensa, had a Broadway-quality voice, and could tell a joke like nobody's business. He was also an excellent cook and when he was in service to others, it was usually around creating a great meal.

His personality reminds me of a story that I heard a few years back:

A Native American chief and his son are sitting on a rock overlooking their village below.

The son says to his father, "Papa, why are some men good and some men bad?"

The chief, sitting there in his best headdress, turned to his son and said, "Our ancestors believe that inside of every man is a good wolf and a bad wolf, fighting for control. It's a constant battle between two very powerful forces within each of us."

The boy thought for a minute and said, "Papa, which wolf wins the battle?"

The boy's father says, "The wolf that you feed always wins."

My father fed his bad and angry wolf most of the time. He just didn't know what he didn't know, and his habit, which had been learned early on, was to believe that he was worthless and did not deserve happiness.

CHAPTER 9

THE JOURNEY OF DEPRESSION BEGINS HERE

Unlike my parents, I had been given this diagnosis of depression at an earlier age and I decided that I would need to learn as much as possible about the disease and my life of suffering with it. While I didn't know it at the time, it was an opportunity to break the cycle of disease that ran through generations on both sides of my family.

I started to write in my journal one day and prayed on when this all started for me. That led to a memory of the first conscious experience that I had with suicide.

I was 11 years old, a 6th grader—the young master of my world. On a typical day, my mom left for work early, usually catching the train to Brooklyn by 6:30 in the morning. That left me to my sister's care, and she made sure that I was fed and dressed, and off to school. Many days, although my sister was very responsible, I was left to get myself out the door and to school by the first bell.

My life went down a winding and treacherous path on a crisp fall day in October or early November. It was a day that included a boat, lots of leaves, sunshine, and tremendous solitude.

As I said, it was a crisp morning, not cold, more like "coldish", a day that was one of those autumn days that leave you thanking your God that you live in the Northeast and love the change of seasons. It was chilly when I woke up, with a brilliant sun shining and glistening on the frost as it was melting on the grass. I love those types of days, when it's warm enough for a pair of shorts but cold enough to wear a sweatshirt over a long sleeve shirt.

In the fall of 1975, I was an 11-year-old in the 6th grade; unfortunately, the sweatshirt with shorts look was not in my wardrobe. That would have been way too preppy for a kid growing up in the blue-collar neighborhood of New York Avenue in Baldwin. I probably wore a pair of Lee jeans, or Wranglers, or worse, a pair of corduroys, along with a nondescript t-shirt, a zipper hooded sweatshirt and a pair of Puma sneakers. I wasn't much of a fashion plate back then; I think it was just a positive thing that I actually had clothes to wear. I'm not really much of a fashion plate now, either, but I do have a much nicer selection of clothing than I did at the time. Although, the '70s fashions were painful for all, so that can probably be said of anyone who remembers 1975.

It was the kind of day that gives you a feeling of excitement; that some event is going to occur that involves growth and a promise of great change. I have experienced that feeling many times since and have learned to embrace the possibility of dramatic change or shift in my inner self. At the time, I didn't realize the significance of what was going to occur within me, and I also was not equipped to deal with it.

I grabbed my books and reached for the brass doorknob of the wooden side door to head out to school, it was about 7:45 am. I pulled the door open, pushed on the screen door, and stepped down from the gray threshold to the small brick stoop and one more step to the concrete driveway. The driveway of our house was pretty unique, in fact, much of the street was unique—there was little uniformity in a neighborhood of houses that were an eclectic jumble of capes, colonials, ranches, and some funky designs that I would classify as small and ugly craftsman bungalows.

Our house was one of the "triplets" that sat side by side by side in the middle of the north side of our street. These three homes were part of the real estate holdings of the Verity family. Mr. Verity, who I was deathly afraid of as a kid, was the meanest prick you would ever want to meet. My mom kissed his ass whenever she saw him, for fear that if he got pissed off, he would sell the houses and we'd be out in the street. The guy was like 90 years old for 20 years. My mom lived in fear that he was going to die, and the houses would be sold. We paid $200 a month in rent for most of the '70s and '80s.

After I stepped out the door and landed on the concrete driveway, I headed toward the street; the driveway sloped downward at about a 15% decline for 20 feet and ended at the blacktop where the street began. I took a right, walked across the front lawn and headed due west up the street toward Chestnut; the streets in my neighborhood were named after trees, Native American tribes and cities.

The neighborhood was a hodge-podge of spec homes that were built from the late '30s through the '50s, by people who were building one or two homes for investment purposes and selling them to the blue-collar folks that managed to scrape together their nickels and move from Queens and Brooklyn and were now inhabiting our 'hood.

The occupant of #626 was Mr. Sigilo. I'm not sure if that is the spelling or not, but I know it sounded like SIG-A-LOW. He was a dark featured man, very Italian looking, and he had a very gentle energy about him. He lived with his mother, and when I was young, I remember her sitting in a chair in the driveway while her son did his yard work, and one day, she just wasn't there any longer. Mr. Sigilo was very fastidious about his yard; he had five fig trees that ran along his driveway. Every winter, he would wrap those trees up with brown burlap from the base to the top. At the top, he would put a plastic bag around the branches, and then a garbage pail or something to cap off the highest branches. As a kid, I never knew what he was doing or what those trees were. It wasn't until later in my life that I learned that those were fig trees, and they were common for Italian immigrants all over the New York metro area and each winter, they needed to be wrapped up for warmth so that they didn't die of frostbite.

I remember walking past the house that morning, as I did most days when I walked past, I thought of Jennifer Quirk. Jennifer Quirk was the twin sister of a friend of mine from elementary school. Jennifer was accidentally run over and killed by Mr. Sigilo when we were in second grade. It was the first time that I was really touched by death. Whenever I walked past that house, right up until I moved away, I thought about that death and what it must have done to both families.

I continued up the street and took a right on Chestnut Street. When I got to Chestnut, I had an eerie feeling about the day. I felt that if I went to school that day, that something really bad was going to happen. What does an 11-year-old do when he decides that something bad is going to happen? Talk to his parents? Call a friend? Well, this 11-year-old really had nobody to turn to at that time of the day. My mom was in Brooklyn at work, my dad was—well I have no idea where my dad was—so, I decided to take matters into my hands; to fend for myself, to create an adventure.

I got to Baldwin Avenue about 30 seconds later and took a right, continuing around the corner on my way back to my house. However, I couldn't go back to the front of my house for fear that one of our nosy neighbors would see me and snitch. I traveled east on Baldwin Avenue for about five or six houses until I got to the lawn of Mrs. O'Leary, whose backyard abutted my backyard.

Mrs. O'Leary was a very elegant older woman who lived alone in a very well kept home on Baldwin Avenue. Mrs. O was the mom of the woman who married my mom's brother Douglas, her name was Kathleen. I decided to cut through the O'Leary yard and hop the fence into my yard. Going in the back way was definitely the way to go—a much more concealed approach.

I jumped the white wooden picket fence into my yard and landed directly behind the boat that was on blocks in my yard. The boat, The Wee Tree, was a 23-foot wooden Chris Craft that had been up on blocks in my yard for many years. It just sat there as a monument to all that was my father's dysfunction and failure as a parent, husband, neighbor and all-around member of society. I had seen pictures of all of us out in the mud, clamming and oystering, with the boat in the background, anchored in the bay. I guess my parents got tired of the charade.

Unfortunately, I was either too young to remember those few days as a family or I was blocking it out because of some emotional trauma, or a little bit of both.

So, there this boat sat, a reminder of the stagnation and breakdown of a family unit that barely got started before it was put on blocks to collect leaves and wood rot.

It was at that moment that I knew what I was going to do that day; I was going boating. I was going to relive one of those family days and I climbed up over the back wall of the boat, the transom, and pulled myself into the engine well. I paused there for a moment and pulled myself up over the transom to look for any neighbors that might have seen me ditch into the boat. The transom was filled with leaves, and I could smell the morning dew as it lay on their surface.

Have you ever laid in a pile of wet leaves? They have their own muskiness. When I smell them to this day, I am immediately back in the transom of that boat.

The sun was angling from the East, above my garage and the rooftop of the DelCastillo's house beyond that; I could tell that the wetness on the leaves would only last for a few more minutes. Once the sun hit the leaves full on, the wetness would dissipate into the warming fall sky. I lay in the transom for a few minutes, afraid to raise my head for fear of being seen by anyone.

The reality was that nobody really gave a shit what I was up to. At least, that is where my 12-year-old head was at on that particular day. As I smelled the leaves that surrounded me, I pulled on the mass of steering cables as they crisscrossed in a tangled web of interlocking pulleys and rusted steel lines going through the holes that gave them access from the wheel to the outboard motor.

The wooden sides of the transom well were still intact, not much wood rot at all, except the wood around the cable holes was all soft and much of it was chipped away. I tried to think about the days when we took this boat out as a family. I stood up and climbed over the rear gunnel to get into the boat, swinging my legs over then following with my body, I immediately lay down flat on the deck. Boat decks have a hollow sound because of the space between the deck and the bilge and the hollow sound on this boat was familiar to me. I played on this boat often and had gotten to know every creak and echo in the wood from bow to stern.

As I lay face up on the deck, I grabbed as many leaves as I could reach and pulled them around and on top of me. I imagined myself as a recon ranger in Vietnam, hiding from the VietCong. I had no idea what the VietCong was, but had seen enough news reports as a kid, to know that they were the enemy and if they found me, I'd be dead. I thought about the fact that if I was a 12-year-old in 1950, I would be hiding from the Germans, the VC had not become a threat yet—and hiding from the Germans seemed more acceptable to me because they were such a tangibly evil enemy. So, I decided that I'd reenact a WWII recon mission and I would try to infiltrate an enemy stronghold and was going to have to be clandestine through the entire day until nightfall when I would leave the French barn that I found refuge in after my jump from the spy plane that flew me into France unnoticed.

The thought of what lay ahead for the day was a bit nerve wracking. I didn't know what I would do for food, had no idea if the truancy patrol would find me, or what the hell I was going to do next.

At the time that I decided to skip school, which was about 20 minutes prior to my current thoughts, it seemed so exciting and adventurous. Now, I felt lonely and a little worried that I was going to get into major trouble for not going to school and being a bad kid. I was at the fork in the road; get up now and go to school down one fork or stick with the current plan and stay in the boat and be completely rebellious to my responsibilities as a student at Plaza School.

I chose the latter, that choice, unbeknownst to me, would be the beginning of thoughts that would plague me for the next 30 years.

I lay on the deck of The Wee Tree for several hours, staring up at the cloud formations through the myriad of branches of the cedar and oak trees that flanked the boat at the rear end of our property. The deck was covered with leaves, acorn shells, and sticks from the oak. I gathered some of the leaves up and started to cover myself from my feet up to my neck, and instantly felt the warmth that they held from the sun as the breeze of the fall day flowed around me. I grabbed a wad of leaves and put them over my face so that I was now completely covered from head to toe. The sweet smell of the leaves gave me a sense of the beauty of the nature around me and I was overcome with the feeling that I was very small and insignificant in this environment.

The world was such a big place, the tree whose leaves that I was covered with was like 100 years old, the sun had been going up and down for millions of years, the cedar tree, which I tried to chop down with a hatchet when I was eight, reached to the heavens with her long green covered branches.

I could hear the LIRR train going by as it left the Baldwin station bound for New York City. A plane flew overhead, out of JFK, heading to some exotic locale far from Long Island. I started to think about how long the world had been around, whether you believed in the Big Bang or Creation or some other source of Earth's beginning, the resulting feeling of being a minor blip on history's chain of events was overwhelming.

So many questions flooded my mind; I wondered why I was there, what was my purpose, why was I in this piece of shit boat, why did I have to go to school—it was so boring, why was I alone on this beautiful day, what was the point of church, how long does a tree last, why was this boat sitting in our yard like a symbol of the failure of my parent's life together, why did we rent our house, why was my hair brown, what was it like when the Native Americans lived here, what was the point of it all?

I hated myself for not going to school and defying my mom, I hated myself for being so fat, I hated myself for being so bored, I hated myself period! I had been hungry for what seemed like many hours and as my stomach growled with the pangs of the need for food, I was drawn to my mid-section. I rubbed my stomach under my leaf cover and was utterly humiliated with the feeling of my stomach fat beneath my hands.

I had gained 20 pounds during the summer between the end of fifth grade and the beginning of sixth grade as I gorged myself on everything I could get my hands on to feed my stress and anxiety, especially ice cream. I was partial to Dairy Barn vanilla with a couple of squirts of Bosco or Hershey's chocolate sauce. I loved it when the ice cream would get to a somewhat creamy/soupy consistency, and then I would swirl the chocolate sauce throughout and make cool spirograph-like designs, before inhaling what was left.

I was a very anxious kid with constant digestive issues; diarrhea, gas pains, vomiting—the full gamut. That particular year, '74–'75, I literally gained 20 pounds! Yes, I was growing taller, but most of the weight that I added that year fell on my face and my midsection. I had major body image issues, which only drove me to eat more.

My parents, being the disconnected folks that they were, did not acknowledge that I was developing a weight problem right before their eyes. I was just "big boned." I guess they were confused as to what to do because I was physically active up to that point and was still playing a number of sports. My abilities as an athlete masked the pain and anguish that I felt through most of my life. I experienced a trauma that occurred only 8 or 9 months before this day on the boat, that created scars on my psyche that I would repress until I was 42 years old. I will discuss this trauma, my first and most catastrophic, later. The mind can sew itself up tight to protect the being from deep-seeded physical and emotional trauma. I had no idea why I was eating—I only knew that I couldn't stop—and it was comforting with each gorging bite.

As I lay there staring up into the sky, with my hands on my stomach, I thought about the song that the kids in school had created on my behalf. It was written by a few of the girls, and it was something that cut me to the bone—a song that was so caustic that I had nightmares about it later on in life: *Green, Yellow, Red—Green, Yellow, Red.*

The colors were reference to the three shirts that I wore alternately through pretty much all of sixth grade. I only wore those three shirts because they were the only shirts I owned that I thought didn't make me look fat.

I can remember that the "Red" shirt was a Prout Memorial High School shirt from the school in Warwick, Rhode Island where my aunt worked, the "Yellow" was a Franco Harris Pittsburgh Steelers Jersey that I loved, and the "Green" has faded from my memory.

I was miserable as I thought about the kids singing that song behind my back; the anger welled up inside of me so severely that I developed an intense stomach ache. They weren't throwing stones at me, like my mom had endured, but the pain felt just as real. The thing about attacks, whether they are physical or verbal, is that they produce the same response in the brain. The resulting pain is just as real as physical cuts and bruising, and in some cases, more debilitating.

It's important to note that this was payback for my being a less than sensitive person at that age. I was so insecure about being in my own skin that I projected that feeling out to the world around me. I was given a good sense of humor, but at times, I used it at the expense of others. The reaction of others fed that personality trait, and my friends exacerbated my caustic behavior because they reacted positively to my jokes about others, thus projecting their lack of confidence and negative feelings about themselves.

It can be a vicious cycle when we humans get together and are closed off to the valuable differences that we all have and the concerns that we each harbor about our own lack of value to the world outside of us.

My stomach ached to the point of major activity in my lower intestines; I knew that diarrhea was coming next, as it usually did. That would be followed by intense flop sweats, potential feverish chills, and vomiting. It was this chronic internal stress that drove so much of my schedule through the course of my day. I knew when I had to be concerned about being within a two-minute walk or run to a clean bathroom.

When confronted with an adult that I felt was aggressive or an authority figure that seemed dangerous, my stomach would react like a drain that a plumber just poured full strength Draino into.

All I had to do was wait for the clog to clear and for the contents of my body to flow. Often, this resulted in my soiling myself because I couldn't get to a bathroom, or I miscalculated how long it would take for me to get to the safety of the toilet.

This caused further and more intense concern about when and where the next event would happen. I recall the first day of fifth grade. I was really excited about fifth grade, because fourth grade had been a pretty good year and the summer leading up to school was unusually fun. I walked to school on my own, thinking about the school year to come, my blue three-ring loose-leaf book under my arm. The loose-leaf book was one of those denim blues three-inch binders that can withstand the overuse by an 11-year-old kid who didn't care about what happened to that book. Not like the disposable binders that people, including me, are buying at Wal-Mart.

I can recall the tan pants that I wore, not khakis, more like a suede-ish felt, and the new sneakers that I was so proud to be wearing on the first day of school. That new-sneaker feeling is something that cannot be duplicated for a little kid. You feel faster, like you can jump forever, and when you walk it feels like you're on the moon. Everything is better in a new pair of sneakers.

I was doing well as I strode the eight or nine blocks to Plaza Elementary on DeMott Street. At the entrance to the school, there were four steel pipes that came up out of the blacktop, to protect from errant cars. As soon as I got to those pipes, I spied the fifth grade entrance to the school just past the "art room" that protruded from the main section of the red brick school.

In 1975, Plaza was a relatively big school with grades kindergarten through sixth. Each grade had its own entrance to the school which helped to separate the younger kids from the older and imminently more aggressive upper-grade kids.

As I looked when I walked between the pipes that provided a safety barrier from the cars whizzing by, the kids were about 50 yards ahead, all of my friends, and some kids I didn't know; everyone. I heard somebody yell my name and a bunch of kids turned to look at me—it was a great moment. This moment ended pretty quickly because something happened inside my mind, as I reminded myself that I was not the person they thought I was, that I was insecure and inadequate.

That thought drove my intestines into overdrive, and my bowels started to rumble very quickly. Bottom line; I needed to take a shit within the next 15 minutes, or it was going to be very messy.

I went to the door to try and get in—unfortunately, it was locked. I knocked because I saw the custodian sweeping the hall, and he came to the door and opened it a crack.

I can still smell his Marlboro laden coffee breath, and he said,

"Knock on this door again and I will take you straight to the Principal's office."

I said, "I need to use the bathroom..."

Before the last word left my mouth, the black door was closed in my face. I thought, *Shit, I "need" to shit.* So, what do I do?

As a very nervous fifth grader with little confidence in himself, I did the only thing I thought I could do. Have you ever had to go to the bathroom so bad that it literally starts to fall out of you?

If you just said, "Yeah, I do!" then you know what I was experiencing at 7:30 on that Tuesday morning in September.

My friends were all running around and playing pre-school games, wall ball, flipping and scaling baseball cards, tag, whatever. Nobody was really paying attention to me at that point, so I snuck around the large steel utility shed that stood outside of that entrance to the school and slowly slinked along the back wall to the door. I grabbed the large U-shaped handle to see if the shed was unlocked, and it opened. I slipped in unnoticed and held the rope on the inside to seal the door shut, just in case somebody saw me and decided to pull it open.

Then as I stood, my forehead sweating profusely, my bowels screaming, my legs wobbling from the immense shit that I had to get rid of—I stopped all tension and negative force and I just released my angst.

The shit fell out of my body into my Fruit of the Loom tighty whiteys. The relief that I felt in my stomach was overpowered by the intense fear that overcame me when I realized that I just shit in my pants on the first day of school in the custodian's utility shed. It served him right for not opening the door to a little boy that needed to relieve himself.

So, what do I do? Go home? No, I did what I would do again if I had to relive that situation. I dropped my pants as quickly as I could, carefully sliding each foot out of each leg, so as not to cause any leakage. I slowly slid my underwear down my legs and stepped out of them and flung them as far into the darkness of the shed as I could. They landed with a very unpleasant sound, against the wall and slid down to the floor.

I felt so much better, physically, but my mind was racing as to what to do next. I checked myself as best as I could in the dark, decided that putting my pants on would be uncomfortable but it had to be done. Once I got them up and connected the little metal clasps on each side, I slowly peered out the door to see who was out there—all of the kids were now lined up outside the door to be paraded in and up the stairs to our classes.

They could not see me because the line snaked from the door to a vantage point behind the shed. I slipped out the way that I slipped in and instead of walking directly home, I joined the line. I actually joined the line to go into school!

God, I would want my kids to leave school and call me immediately so that I could drop whatever it is that I was doing to get them, take them home and help them pick out some clean clothes, take a shower and then get them back to school asap.

First order of business in school was to get to the bathroom to clean myself as best as I could to get through the day. I did that and made it through the day, all the while, wondering if anybody else could smell the slight stench that was emanating off of me.

This happened to me once or twice a month, and my mother took me to the pediatrician to find out what kind of gastrointestinal issues I had. I don't remember the visit to the doctor, but it probably went something like this:

Doctor Rosenzweig: "Mrs. Rinere, what seems to be the problem with little Jimmy here?"

My mom: "Well Doctor Rosenzweig, he has terrible gas pains and has a hard time keeping his food in."

Doctor R: "You mean he vomits?"

My mom: "No, he has terrible gas pains that result in large explosions from his bowels, and he cannot control his BMs."

That is my least favorite acronym—the BM, or bowel movement, was one of my mom's favorite ways to find out how you were.

Me: "Mom, I don't feel well.

Mom: "Did you have a BM today."

Me: "Yes, mom, I took a shit."

Mom: "You know I don't like that language."

Me: "I don't like your acronyms!"

Doctor R.: "So, these gas pains create a situation where he cannot control himself?"

Mom: "Yes, and I cannot keep up with the laundry."

Me: "Hey—you know I'm sitting right here while you're discussing me crapping in my pants with a man wearing a rubber glove!?"

Doctor R.: "Well, let's just have a look at that bowel."

So, he proceeded to stick his protruding index finger into my nether region to check if I was impacted or irritated.

I didn't go to medical school and I'm no genius, but if a patient is in the room and his mom is telling you that he's shitting his pants all the time—I don't think that the problem is an impacted colon! Just saying.

As I laid on the boat thinking about the larger question of life and the why the fuck we are here, it dawned on me that this life pretty much sucked. I hated myself, I hated my stomach, I hated school, I was fucking lonely, I couldn't stop eating, I was shitting in my pants pretty regularly, my father lived in New Jersey, I had a sister that was constantly being ridiculed for being different, this boat was a pile of shit, my clothes didn't fit, and I just didn't understand why I was there.

CHAPTER 10

THE SUICIDE CYCLE BEGINS

On that day, on the sun-filled deck of an old abandoned boat covered with leaves, I thought about killing myself for the first time. Why not? I had heard about people that had done it, and it seemed to be a great solution to feeling really down.

Depression is real—as real as cancer, hepatitis, asthma, HIV, and any other dreaded disease that we experience in this existence. The problem with depression is that it is a disease that is not seen. In most cases, there are no physical characteristics to depression. If somebody you are close with is suffering from a bout of depression, you would probably see the physical changes that go along with poor sleeping habits, under/over-eating, or jittery behavior. But, if you weren't close with me, you would have no idea that I was suffering the deepest of "dis-ease." In addition, the ignorance that exists around mental illness is akin to the ignorance that my sister faced as she went through her life with Down syndrome.

People see depression and other mental illnesses as weakness, especially in men. So, most people are afraid to admit that they need help and do not seek treatment. They just drag themselves around from minute to minute and from day to day, trying their best to put on a happy face and get through the fucking day without killing themselves.

I experienced several severe bouts of depression through my teens, and at times I was very close to taking my life. One time, I pulled my car into the garage and closed the door while the engine was running. All I had to do was stay in there and go to sleep. I don't know what persuaded me to yank the heavy wooden door open after about 10 minutes. I was so pissed that I had chickened out and regretted it for years. I walked into my kitchen and ate a gallon of ice cream and a bowl of leftover meatballs, in that order. You can bet your ass that my colon was impacted after that binge!

Fast-forward 11 years, on the Long Island Rail Road train platform in Woodmere, New York. It was 5:20 in the morning; there was a chill in the air very similar to the one that I felt that day on the old boat. I was waiting for the 5:28 to Penn Station in Manhattan, with about a dozen or so other souls that would hump their asses into the city each day to chase the American Dream.

I stood at the northernmost tip of the station, where it intersected Woodmere Boulevard, about two blocks from where my beautiful wife lay sleeping and dreaming of being married to a man that could take care of her. My blue pinstriped Hart Shaffner and Marx suit with the 1.5" cuff and mild break over my wingtip Oxfords was pressed to perfection. My monogrammed shirt (with new gold cuff links showing slightly below the sleeve) was visible at the collar beneath my suit and my black double-breasted wool Bill Blass overcoat. My coat and my jacket concealed the silk red and blue paisley braces that held my pants up. I carried a black, two-handled, soft-covered leather briefcase. My hair was slicked back with gel, ala Bud Fox from the movie *Wall Street* and I had the New York Times folded under my arm.

I was a formidable sight as my 6' 4" body stood there waiting to get on the train that would snake through the NYC suburbs carrying the captains of industry into the business capital of the world.

Just as I had on that boat as a chubby sixth grader, I decided that I had had enough of this life. Once and for all, it was time to end it—to put me out of my misery. Yes, I loved my wife, but, in time, she would come to understand that she would be far better off if I were not in her life. Plus, she would collect some life insurance money so that she would be set financially.

I looked down at the tracks and thought about what I was going to do. I realized that at this point of the station, the train could probably stop in time to prevent any mortal damage, even in the dark. I walked south toward the Cedarhurst Station and the beginning of the platform. At this point, the train would be traveling about 35 MPH when it made the position at which I would jump. As I walked, I saw the headlights of the steel tube of a train moving toward me. They cut a swath of light through the early morning darkness like the hazy light of a lighthouse as it reflected off the ocean spray. I was only halfway down the platform as the train made the station and I could hear the brake pads pressing against the disc brakes—it was slowing down. Fuck!

I was 25 years old. I commuted on that train into New York, every day for two years. There wasn't a week that went by without thinking that I could and should jump in front of the fucking train. It was one of the worst periods of depression that I had experienced, and I could not get it to stop. So, I drank a lot and went out late at night with "clients" and spent many nights carousing around New York City doing all of the things that somebody with mental health issues should not be doing.

A couple of years later, my wife and I were relocated by her company, up to Westchester County, and settled in White Plains, New York. For a time, the excitement of the move and the change of scenery snapped me into a positive reality, but it wasn't long before the depression set in again, and my habitual self-abuse would continue. The bottom line is that I was dragging my soul through a career that just was not in rhythm with who I am. I didn't realize that at the time; all I knew was that I was miserable and blamed it on everything and everybody else.

On the fifth or sixth day in Silver Hill Hospital, I sat journaling about my first suicidal memory and trying to get a handle on my diagnosis. My wife, as I said earlier, suggested that honesty would be the way in which to handle the situation that we found ourselves in, and that is where the "Peace in Truth" philosophy started.

I started to work with a therapist that was suggested by the great team at Silver Hill, and that was combined with group sessions at the Yale Psych outpatient facility in New Haven.

We learned very quickly that the experience at Silver Hill was not the norm and that people that suffer from mental illness and their family members are pretty much on their own when it comes to figuring stuff out. There are not a lot of resources that can provide you with direction and support. This is changing slowly, but for the most part, people are left to their own resources and ability to drive the care that they need.

I had decided very early on in this process that I was going to devote my life to being at peace and that I was going to live, with unconditional love and loyalty to my wife, my children, and myself.

It's important to note here that the process of talk therapy had just begun. I hadn't completely opened up about the depths of pain that was being held inside of my repressed being, and I hadn't fully faced the fact that the relationship with my wife had been rocked to the core by my breakdown, which threatened the financial security that had been created by years of living a life that I couldn't continue. I knew that I loved my wife deeply, and I felt that we were meant to be together. However, over the coming months and years, I opened up a Pandora's box of shit that would have my relationship with Chris teetering on the edge of the abyss.

The first therapist that I was referred to by Silver Hill was a great guy. I really liked him, but it was obvious after a few months, that he could only take us about an inch down the 100-mile path that needed to be traversed to get to health. In fact, one day when Chris and I were in session with him, he said something that was one of the most honest admissions that I have ever heard a professional utter.

He said, "You two are maddening for me because I am not smart enough to help you. I cannot help you any further. I just don't have the expertise. You need someone that has a much deeper sense of intellectual ability."

It was blatantly obvious, kind of like the 800-pound gorilla on the couch, and it was a gift for both of us.

This mental health professional was asking for a life raft in a sea of tumult. You see, alone, I was looking for much deeper answers than the average person might have wanted. The average mental health therapist is overworked, underpaid, and is trying to provide each patient with the ability to function in the world. I wanted to go well beyond just functioning. I wanted to experience the fulfillment that only exists when you examine everything—all of it—and come away with the answers of why we are here, what life is about, and how I could live in joy.

However, when you put Chris and I in a room together, I guess "maddening" is a great description. We zig and zag like a boxer trying to work his way into the body of his opponent, and then we land body blows relentlessly.

You have to be relentless when you are seeking health and trying to advocate for yourself.

As with anything in life, therapy will take you to levels that you didn't think possible, but you must pay very close attention to making sure that when you plateau, you are aware of it. The plateaus are natural during the therapeutic process; it is impossible to continue to grow without some leveling off of the depths to which you will go. It feels great to work through a difficult process and give yourself some time to breathe at the top of the mountain you have just worked to climb, take in the beautiful vistas that you have created for yourself. Sit at the top of that mountain, give yourself a strong mental hug and recognize your hard work and your accomplishments. Catch your breath, and then, go to work on the next mountain.

It is far too easy to get to the top of one mountain peak and think that the journey is done. You need a support team that will continue to push you toward the next part of the process and so, it is critical for your therapist to recognize these peaks and plateaus and to work with you to know when to begin the next piece of the journey.

In many situations that I have learned of from talking with a lot of people, the process slows to a whining grind, without there being much movement toward any sort of resolution. The creative process can pretty much dry up and just showing up for appointments can become a chore. It is in those times that you must see what is happening and forge ahead. In my case, my therapist had tossed up his hands and it is usually the client that says, "No mas!"

It had been almost 18 months since I left the hospital and started to live a life moving toward happiness. I had taken a giant leap toward health, and over the previous 18 months that giant leap of growth had been reduced from the huge steps of daily work to smaller steps of growth, and eventually to shuffling toward a life of pain-free living. I was starting to stagnate and it was time for a change when my therapist made that decision for me.

If you ask for it, the answer will come. In my case, it was in the form of an introduction to a new therapist that was a simple referral from a friend.

Lisa said, "You know, I don't like to talk about it, but I have been working with someone for many years off and on and I think you might like her."

I said, "Thank you, I will call her."

That simple exchange with a long-time friend came at a time in my life when I was ready to hear it and my new therapist turned into the most prophetic angel that had ever been introduced into my world. Up to that point, the most prophetic angel had been my wife, now, we both allowed space for this miracle worker to enter our lives.

Together, we laid out a road map to health that has become the way of life for me and my family; most importantly, it has led to living an examined life and that path included intense hard work, pain leading to growth, and it required commitment.

My Initial Road Map to Health

1) Talk—Talk—Talk

Therapy can be such a negative term for some. I just call it talking, and it includes talking with a licensed therapist, friends, your partner, children—everyone. It is important that you work with a professional and someone that has experience in working with depression and anxiety.

2) Journal

Keeping a daily journal is critical to documenting the feelings that arise in you all the time. Recognizing these feelings is crucial to identify who you really are.

3) Exercise

Daily exercise is critical to keeping balance for mind and body.

4) Nutrition

Putting "bad" stuff in, you get "bad" stuff out. We self-medicate with food as much as we do with any other drug—alcohol, illegal drugs, addictions.

5) Meditation

Settling the mind for a few minutes a day does wonders to help you sort through the white noise of society that deadens the feelings your soul is experiencing and keeps you from yourself.

I include spirituality and a belief in a higher collective in the meditation work.

6) Honesty

You must live honestly. All that is said, all that is done —it all matters. Everything matters.

7) Medication

Balancing the chemical make-up of the body provides needed relief from what can be severe highs and lows. There is a steadying effect for the body that allows the work to be possible. If it is closely monitored by a professional and combined with the therapy work, I highly recommend it.

8) Read—Read—Read

I pursued a Ph.D. in "me", trying to read everything that I could get my hands on: self-help, spirituality, relationship, clinical, philosophical, existential, and as varied as the disease I was conquering.

9) Trust in Your Team

We are taught that to go outside and ask for help shows vulnerability and weakness. I ask, has that worked for you? If not, get a team of people to help you on your journey.

Trust in that team and include them in all of the things that go on in your life—doctors, therapists, spouses, partners, friends, etc...

These are your designated team members and must all work together on your behalf as well, which requires them to communicate.

As stated in the heading above, this was my "initial" road map to health. As with anything in life, as you know better, you do better and so this list has evolved over the past 15 years and I will update this for you in a later chapter.

The list of the books and authors that I have studied is vast. Over the past many years, I have read dozens of books and teachings by people such as: Wayne Dyer, Byron Katie, Leo Buscaglia, Harville Hendrix, Gary Zukav, Eckhardt Tolle,

Marshall Rosenberg, Harvey Diamond, Viktor Frankl, Thich Hnat Hanh, Pema Chodron, Buddha, Don Miguel Ruiz, Gael Chiarella , Albert Einstein, Julia Cameron, Lionel Ketchian, Tara Brach, Esther and Jerry Hicks, Abraham, Lao Tzu, and Neal Donald Walsch. Those are some of the more conventional teachers that I have hungrily followed.

Still, many others are a little more unconventional, and yet, their messages can be as prophetic: Bono, The Beatles, Bruce Springsteen, Indigo Girls, David Byrne, James Taylor, Billy Joel, Bob Marley, Black Eyed Peas, The Moody Blues, Paul Simon, Pink Floyd, Peter Gabriel, Tracy Chapman, Train, Green Day, Alphaville, Verve Pipe, Carly Simon, REM, Brandi Carlile, Neil Young.... and the list goes on.

Teachings are everywhere; you just need to slow yourself down to see them and apply them to your life.

Some of these teachers have completely changed my life, some have raised questions that I have pursued answers to, some have not provoked anything but served to keep me in the mindset of self-care.

I have also become a big fan of writing down some of the quotes of prophets that have walked the earth and left their mark of brilliance. I write them in my journal, on my computer, on slips of paper that I hang on mirrors in my house. Having access to these words of wisdom serves as a reminder to me of something that acts as a touchstone throughout my day to bring me back to the center of who I am.

Here is one of those quotes that I find helpful:

"The ideals which have lighted my way, and time after time have given me new courage to face life cheerfully, have been Kindness, Beauty, and Truth."
- Albert Einstein

CHAPTER 11

BUSINESSMAN & THE ILLUSION OF SUCCESS

When I see a successful person in the world, whether they are a world-class artist, a successful writer, an athlete, or a business owner that has built something that is thriving, I think about what we don't see, the stuff that people don't think or talk about often, and that is the hard work that leads to successful people being where they are today.

I have lived with my son, an artist, and watched him work for hours every day on his craft. I marveled at his commitment and the drive that pushes him to study the human form and draw thousands, and I mean thousands, of iterations of hands, feet, heads, eyes, and circles. People see his artwork and the first comment is usually, "Wow, you're so talented!" This is true. He is talented. However, if you ask him, he will tell you that anybody can draw, they just need to put the work in to learn the technique and nuance that is required to be truly exceptional. Yes, I agree that there is a little Universal Magic or God-given talent that can allow some people to elevate to different heights; there is no substitute for hard work.

As a successful athlete, I was familiar with the work that I had done to be good at my craft. The hours spent running and throwing the ball against a wall to practice my stick skills, lifting weights, running, and studying the game. All of it was what I did before anybody watched me play in college. When I left the hospital and Chris and I decided to learn and evolve, I committed myself to the work that would need to be done to live peacefully. I had no idea what that would require or how long it would take, but I knew that I did not want to live the life that I had lived and that the path forward would bring the change that I would need. When I was introduced to the person that I call my "Life Guru," I consciously decided to focus my energy on training my emotional and mental health as I had trained my physical body as an athlete. The concept was simple: train the mind, body, and heart for the most important success in life, to live in peace and grace. I worked at my recovery as an athlete would work to dominate in their sport.

The following chapters outline some of that process and some of the repressed things that we, my Life Guru and I, uncovered during that process. I think it's important to share that learning because it helps to show the work that occurred that was necessary for me to live the life that I am living today. I think that it is important to understand that this does not happen overnight and the things that I am going to discuss in the next few chapters occurred over a three-year period of hard fucking work. There were sessions with my Guru where I was on the floor on all fours, with my head on the ground, sobbing uncontrollably for an hour, and several sessions where I was so exhausted afterward that I couldn't drive myself home right away and I would sit in the car and collect myself. There were also many sessions where I would leave so energized that I could have run a marathon and I was so excited to call Chris and share the epiphany of that day's work.

I remind you, each person's journey is their own and your experience will be very different from anybody else's and will require patience and intestinal fortitude. The visual that I use for my learning process is that it started with a huge waterfall of change, and then there were some whitewater moments of flow, and then there were periods where it felt like a fucking dropper of water into an ocean. The learning ebbed and flowed and it was all cumulative, sometimes there were waves of energy that caused goose-bumps and at other times, the change was imperceptible. All I can say is that I only wanted to move forward and I was seeking a life of peace and love, and that drove me to work as I have never worked at anything in my entire life.

Here's a behind-the-curtain glimpse of learning to live an examined life.

Partners In Life

Physically, Chris is a beautiful woman, stunningly gorgeous, with a body to match. I fell in love with her in college, pretty much the first time that I saw her. I intuitively knew that she was an angel sent from God.

I was 20 years old, a typical college jock, captain of the lacrosse team and she was one of the hottest girls on the small and idyllic campus of Adelphi University in Garden City, NY.

On a warm Indian summer day in September of 1985, I stood with a group of buddies, talking about the Daily News Sports page, and she walked up the blacktop-paved path of the Quad, toward the main gathering spot of the University Center. The crowd of coeds parted; it was one of those moments in time that drips by slowly like hot wax drips down the side of a burning candle.

I was instantly drawn to her. Yes, she was beautiful, but there was some other force at work that to this day I cannot explain.

I was a big man on campus, and Chris selected well, from a pure innate human desire for protection, to be provided for, and the physical attributes that we as animals seek for our offspring. I was strong, good looking, smart, funny, and loved her. She thought that she had won the "husband material" lottery.

Chris was one of the more popular people on our small college campus. She was gorgeous, smart, funny, had a great sense of fashion, and was a phenomenal dancer. I had won the "eligible wife" lottery.

I pursued her for a few months before we started to really connect and on December 3, we started a once-in-a-lifetime romance. At times, which you will see, this romance seemed like a once-in-a-lifetime mistake. In the end though, as with many things, you have to get through some seriously challenging stuff in order to realize your dreams. That is the story to be told, that marriage or soul connection or whatever you deem an appropriate title for a relationship, requires a very long-term view and for better or for worse is either something you live or you don't. I believe with all that I am that being in a relationship is what was asked during our vows. "Do you take this woman to be your lawfully wedded wife, to have and to hold, for richer, for poorer, in sickness and in health, for better or for worse..." While, I don't espouse the structured religious aspect of the ceremony when you cut through the actual vows, regardless of your religious doctrine or if you are agnostic, it doesn't matter. If you choose to commit yourself to one person, the required work is baked into that commitment.

The foundation for our relationship was strong, starting with long conversations that would go on into the night. We built our soul connection laying about 14 inches from a stucco ceiling, on a wooden loft bed in my apartment, which was above a paint store on Hempstead Turnpike in West Hempstead, New York, about two miles from school. It was just us, two young adults, exploring our dreams together, while a Panasonic clock radio played soft rock from WEBE 107.9.

I learned quickly that Chris's physical beauty was only a small piece of her being. She was and still is the most loving and caring person I have ever known, with doses of wisdom that seem only to be available to a very select few people who walk this earth.

We were inseparable right from the start, which turned a lot of our friends off, but we let those relationships leave our lives as we had chosen to stick with each other. We have had so much fun together, and there is a strong love bond that exists between us.

Since Chris and I have basically grown up together, she has seen me from the beginning when I was much happier and easier going. That was the "me" that she fell in love with and the "other me" that she has always seen from time to time throughout our lives.

Over the years, my mood swings did not go unnoticed, as they might in a relationship where there isn't enough love or when people just aren't present enough to care.

Chris often inquired about my withdrawal from our life. During those conversations, I would come up with excuses, as if defending my reason for existing. But, the feeling of not wanting to let her down was always there, I loved her and I very much "wanted" to love her in a way that she could feel good about.

I have spoken with many people about the conversations between people in a relationship, the tête-à-tête of trying to negotiate the differences between what one person wants versus what the other wants. Our discussions were probably not dissimilar. However, the added complication of severe depression, something that was not understood, always made things that much more difficult.

When I started to feel like I was slipping into a funky feeling or heavy episode, I would want to have some time to myself. I would expertly pursue isolation like a drug user seeks out a quiet corner to inject. Chris could see these changes take place and would question me and where I was.

I was becoming very good at coming up with an excuse around money pressure, or work struggles—building a business or managing a department full of salespeople, my boss, the company, Wall Street's demands for return on investment; I had become a master of deception, often lying to her without a second thought.

It is important to understand, at this point, that neither of us knew that I was depressed or that there was a potential for treatment and that life could be so much better. I mean, I knew that I wasn't "right," but I thought that it would go away.

As far as deception, for example, I would come home from working a 12 or 13-hour day, very tired and in need of some solace. When questioned about my day, simple questions that any person in a loving relationship would ask with interest about the person that they are living with—not an inquisition—I met those questions with extreme defensiveness and anger that I was being attacked in some way.

These were efforts to mask my feelings of vulnerability and to hide the dishonesty of how I was living. The excessive drinking that was necessary to woo clients, the six or seven-hour golf junkets that would consume time away from my family, the overnight trips to cities where key decision-makers were, trips that I often took just to get away from my life and hide.

Let's face it, as the current business climate has proven, many meetings are just a waste of fucking time, money, and emotional energy.

In early March of 1992, my wife and I packed up a rented minivan with luggage, food, and all of our ski equipment and headed north from Woodmere, New York for our annual week-long skiing adventure. We were headed to Mounts Attitash, Wildcat, and Washington for some early spring isolation in New Hampshire's White Mountains.

This trip, like many others, was our chance to try and repair the chronic disintegration of a relationship that had been skirting the shoals since we said our "I dos" in 1988. Chris knew what she had vowed on that rainy November day; that marriage was a commitment that required love, patience, and faith. She had lived that faith every moment since we began our life as husband and wife. If not for her strongly grounded faith, the fact that her commitment was of the highest magnitude, we would not be taking this trip.

As we crossed the Throgs Neck Bridge headed for the New England Thruway, I was nervous about being "seen" and being found out as the fraud that I was. After all, spending an entire week with my wife would require conversation, affection, and sex. There would be no excuses for hiding, no work commitments, no long nights at the office, and no "man, I'm tired, need to get to bed early tonight" to avoid any potential intimacy, physical or otherwise.

I lived my daily life thinking that this would be the day that Chris would decide that enough was enough and pack her stuff and leave. I could sense that she was down to her last thread of commitment and that she knew that it wasn't going to get better, and potentially could get worse. Ultimately, this was not a good enough life for her—she wanted to live a soul connection, a genuine love story. It was how our relationship started, when I was open to being myself, and all of the vulnerabilities that go along with that presence in life.

As time went on, the demons that threatened my mind would not allow that kind of vulnerability for the long term and I was not capable of that, and I started to repel it as much as I could, without just throwing up my hands and screaming, *"I can't fucking do this anymore, I am broken, I am not worthy of you, you need to run away from me —far far away. RUN!"*

You are probably asking the question that Chris has asked me a thousand times, "Why not just walk away, why not let her go, why not just say, look, this isn't working, and I am tired of making you and me miserable?"

The simple answer is this: I loved Chris very much.

The more in-depth answer is that I knew somewhere deep down inside of my being her love and my love for her was the only way that I would survive.

You may think that is selfish, and I agree with you. However, I was living separate existences; one was the reality-based existence of love for somebody that I knew I was deserving of and who had me walking on air every time I saw her beautiful face, electric brown eyes, and radiant smile. The other was the illusion of self-hate and loathing that I produced due to depression, anxiety, and repression of trauma.

We checked into our slope-side condo after driving through a bad snowstorm for a couple of hours. It was a long and tiring trip. That was my first excuse to just drop into bed and isolate myself.

I remember saying, "That drive knocked me out, I'm going to get some sleep and be ready for a long day of skiing tomorrow."

Part of what I was saying was true. Driving in the snow, to this day, brings back some really bad memories of an ill-fated college binge-drinking trip that I had taken eight years earlier.

In 1984, my friend Satch and I took a road trip to see another high school buddy at SUNY Oneonta. Satch and I weren't due back for our spring semesters and lacrosse practice, me at Adelphi, Satch at St. John's, until the following Monday. We had three days to get up to Oneonta, drink our asses off and get back home in time to start classes and begin our respective lax seasons.

On Sunday morning, after hitting the party circuit pretty hard for three days of binge drinking and smoking huge Bob Marley joints, we got in the car and began our three-hour drive back to Long Island. It was 10:00 in the morning, and we were both stone-cold sober. We drove and listened to Madonna's first album on my International Scout's Clarion tape deck. "Burning Up For Your Love" was blasting pretty hard through the six speakers that I had installed throughout the cab of this jeep-like truck.

I drove up a hill in the town of Stanford, New York and at the crest of the hill, the road flattened out for about a half-mile. The wind had picked up a bit and this section of the, up to now, very dry highway was covered with about an inch of snow for 250 yards. I tried to slow down a little, but the fresh snow on the road had grabbed the knobby tires pretty hard and as I applied the brakes, we immediately went into a skid. From there, the car was on its own.

I tried to turn into the skid, as the motor vehicle book had suggested, but, at 60 miles per hour, it didn't matter. The only question was, when and where were we going to leave the road. Another wax-dripping moment as we hit the gulley alongside the highway about 50 yards later. The front left fender ran headlong into an old Oak tree and the inertia of a stationary object meeting a hurtling steel missile caused the energy to force the car into the air and back onto the road, upside down and rolling over and over. All I could hear was the deep pounding sound of my heart, metal on the blacktop, and the radio.

I was thrown into the backseat—what seat belt?

The car rolled over and over again. I think we made three full revolutions. It came to rest on the roof.

My first thought, literally, was that I was now dead and I had a sense of relief. Then I realized that I couldn't be dead if I was thinking. Then, I heard Satch scream, "My eye, I'm blind, there's glass in my eye, man it fucking hurts!"

I remembered that I wasn't alone and my instinct to help immediately kicked in. I pulled myself to the back of the car, dragging what I thought was a broken leg and I scurried to the back of the cab and kicked the back window open. I hobbled around to the passenger side of the car, shards of glass falling from my shirt and hair to the ground and I pulled the door open to pull Satch out to safety. I had images of a fiery explosion, as the wheels still spun furiously despite the car being on its roof.

The next song came on the stereo, "I Know It" by Madonna...

Satch and I walked away from the car, about 30 or 40 feet, assuming that this distance would keep us safe from the impending destruction of a gas tank that was full of fuel and poised to explode any second.

The ambulance arrived several minutes later, as did a NY State trooper and a tow truck. My car was totaled, my friend's eye was blinded with glass and my leg was pretty banged up—although not broken.

I was so pissed that I had been thrown into the back seat. If I hadn't, my head would have been crushed like an eggplant because the roof on my side of the car had collapsed and the steering wheel had been smashed into the road. That would have ended my habitual pain and hate for myself.

There are no accidents!

Since then, driving in any kind of snow is pretty nerve-wracking for me, so this trip to the White Mountains of New Hampshire was fraught with more than the usual anxiety I would have felt in going away with Chris and having nowhere to hide.

CHAPTER 12

LIFE'S PRESSURE BUILDS

The next morning, we woke up early and went to Mount Attitash to ski the freshly groomed hill. During the day of skiing, Chris had complained of being very tired and not in the "I didn't get a good night's sleep" tired, more of a "mentally I'm ready to go, but my body just won't respond" tired.

After six hours of going up and down the mountain, Chris couldn't take it anymore and we decided to head back for a nap before an early dinner. We stopped in at a local pharmacy to pick up some sundries for the rest of our week. We walked up to the register. I had bottled water, some aspirin, a couple of magazines and some chips. Chris dropped a box of EPT sticks on the counter.

I said, "What are those for?"

She said, "They are pregnancy tests."

""What?! Why?!"

There's only one reason why you buy pregnancy test kits—dumb ass!

That night, Chris peed on four sticks. Each time, the result was the same—yes to pregnancy, and yes to giving birth to a child in a relationship that was less than it should be with a man that was more than disconcerting.

Again—there are no accidents.

I spent the entire night, almost four hours, sitting in the hot tub that was off our deck, alone, my mind swirling with the responsibility of a child. Every fear that I ever had about my shortcomings of being a functional human being, let alone a father, just came at me the way nightmares can prey on a person who tries to sleep on a full stomach.

It was a long night. Outwardly to Chris, I was very excited to be having a baby. However, inside, my fear and sense of dread were intense. The thought of having a child with Chris was, at times, euphoric. As good as it felt at those times, the feeling of fear and anxiety was that much worse. I was terrified to duplicate my father's shortcomings as a parent and was afraid that I would fail and completely fuck my child up, which would cause her to hate me and every other man on the planet.

Of course, I never thought about the fear that Chris was experiencing and never had the personal mettle to ask the questions that she needed to talk to me about.

The number one question, "Are you afraid to have this child with me? Do you think that I can be the man that you need in your life"?"

I could never have asked those questions because I was too focused on my own shit and I was not stable enough emotionally to hear the honest answers without just beating myself into a suicidal frenzy.

It wasn't fair to my wife that I couldn't ask those questions, it wasn't fair that she couldn't talk with me about her fears, and it certainly wasn't fair to her that she was now locked into a marriage that she was close to ending.

Children change those easy decisions.

There are no accidents!

With depressive tendencies and anxiety-ridden personalities, it can sometimes be very good to have concrete goals and structured direction. My competitive masculine nature kicked in right away as I thought about having to provide for my wife and newborn child. It was good for me to have the thought that I must take care of us all—financially— that these people would rely on me to be strong, aggressive, smart, and driven. I repressed the fear and anxiety and hung my every thought on providing. Initially, it did help to know that I was going to be the breadwinner and that there were now three people relying on my ability to be successful.

That was the beginning of us creating the traditional roles of husband, father, and provider, and wife, mother, and homemaker. This was a decision that we made together and with planning and thought about how, why, what, and everything in between. This was not something that just happened—we went down that path together in a united way.

However, as a "man," I felt the masculine need to be the person that took on the outside world. I would pound my chest and head off into the jungle to find the food.

In many ways, despite the women's liberation movement, society has ingrained the male population with the role of provider, protector, and Master of the Universe.

I did not intend to lose myself as dramatically as I did.

Does anyone intend to lose their mind; to live in "dis-ease"?

It is so easy to get caught up in the mundane shit that we do in our lives; getting out of bed, taking a shower, putting on a suit, walking to the train station and riding the steel snake into Manhattan, then to the subway to get to the office, then at 6:00 pm, you turn around and do it all again.

Oh yeah, in between those two 90-minute trips on the sardine can of a train, you get the shit kicked out of you as you try to sell people stuff that they cannot put a value on, and you spend the day hanging out with other people who are going through the same bullshit.

Yeah, that's a fun environment to hang out in day in and day out; it creates an emotionally uplifting and spiritual ethos. Not!

For some, it's a great way of life, the money, the after-work cocktails, the client entertainment, the women, the ego-driven life of a Master of the Universe. I would argue that it's not a great way of life for anyone, that some, actually most, have chosen to not look inside to know what they don't know.

For others, it becomes a death sentence as they watch their lives melt into the cobblestone streets and run down the sewers of Manhattan. It's like watching all of the sludge that gets washed away when heavy rain hits Broadway on a Friday morning—all the shit and scum from the night before runs along the curbs, black and gray lines of dirt, piss, rat shit, soot, spit, and anything else that gets thrown into the street—it runs along the blackened curbs like the lives of the people walking by just slipping away from them to a drain that dumps them into the Hudson River.

When I started working in New York, it was intoxicating to be in a city that I had admired for so many years as a kid growing up on Long Island. New York was where you went to make money, be successful, and live the American Dream.

That was what I wanted; to live the American Dream, to make up for growing up without money and without a feeling of confidence. I always wanted to provide for my family in a way that my father never would or could.

I thought that money was going to bring me that feeling.

So, Chris and I thrust ourselves into the life that we had chosen together. I went after success in my career the way that I went after success on the lacrosse field; with intensity like there wouldn't be a tomorrow.

You either win or you die and if you're not going to win, you better kill somebody along the way.

I was good at selling and was really good at delivering results, taking my natural leadership skills to others to drive them to deliver returns for our company. I moved up in the ranks, stepping on people along the way—again, you either win or you kill somebody along the way.

My routine was simple: get out of bed at 5:00 AM, get dressed, and go, go, go.

From Monday to Friday, I worked as much as I needed to, which included being out with a client or a prospective client until 10:00 or 11:00 PM, or even later, if that was what was required. If I got home stinking drunk at 1:00 or 2:00 in the morning, I still got up for the train back into the city a few hours later. It wasn't easy, and it affected who I was—but, it didn't matter, that was what was required.

Well, I would rationalize that it was required.

I was a man; I was out there hunting in the woods to feed my family.

Bullshit!

I let myself go to places that I should never have gone to, mentally and physically.

The addition of mental illness, undiagnosed, driving much of my disconnected behavior, helped to increase the volume of the dysfunctionality. That is probably the most difficult thing for people with some mental illnesses, especially depression; they can be very functional in the world to an extent, and their illness is not seen—except perhaps in subtle ways by those that they live with. If they live with someone not attuned to mental illness and/or an enabler, it can be disastrous.

To put it simply, I suffered from deep depression for many years. I found the energy and drive that I needed to get through each day, believing that I must provide the money for my family. Living in what I call the "energy suck" of being something that you are not, causes you to hate yourself further. You cannot possibly understand what you are doing because you just don't see it consciously. You don't see that the more you do that is not you, the more you become in touch with who you are not and before long, "you" cease to exist. The person that you are living is out in the world, it is the "not you" and the more that person exists, the harder it is to function as yourself. If not working, I was chronically tired, chronically anxious, chronically disconnected, and I became angrier and angrier with myself each passing year. Of course, that anger, which was squarely centered on myself, would come forth into the world directed at all that I came in contact with. That's how deflection works.

To give you an idea of the disconnection, here is an illustration of events around a pivotal moment in our nation's history.

When the Gulf War started, when it was announced that our country was at war and the first President Bush had ordered the US military to attack the shit out of Iraq, I was standing at the dark mahogany bar at the Downtown Athletic Club, schmoozing with the Regional Director of Sales of my company.

I had a glass of scotch in my hand, Crown Royal on the rocks, with a wedge of lemon. Either that or Chivas, Glen Morangie, or...you get the picture.

I called my wife from the payphone at the corner of the bar; she was very alone and very scared at the prospect that we were bombing people on the other side of the world.

She needed to be held, to be comforted, and to be assured that she was safe, that she was loved. You know, the kind of normal behavior that a supporting partner would exhibit during this kind of experience.

"I know honey, I'm watching it on the television at the bar, yeah, I know, it's amazing."

"Scared?"

"No, I'm not scared, we should obliterate the desert and get all the fucking oil we can get our hands on—that's what I'd do..."

"Coming home?"

"This is really important, we're talking about relationship realignment, I think I'm going to pick up some great new opportunities for us..."

Sound familiar?

127

"Yes, I'm leaving soon and I will call you when I leave."

"Bartender, I'll have another one."

Eventually, I made my way home.

The damage of disconnection and aggression separated us, and Chris did her best to create some insulation for herself and our children.

And so it went.

My attitude took me away from my family, took me away from my wife—the only person on this earth who ever really knew me. As I slipped further and further into the rationalizations that I had to hunt and kill; I started to believe the thoughts that what I was doing was more important than anything else that I could be doing.

After all, at the ripe age of 31, in 1996, I was earning a mid-six-figure income. What wasn't working?

What could possibly be wrong in a life when you're making that kind of money?!

My wife thrust herself into her role as mother and homemaker as aggressively as I was working, creating a home that was far beyond any dream that I could have imagined. Chris managed the house finances, organized amazing vacations, planned family get-togethers, redesigned and decorated our home, created all of the holiday magic for our children, and pretty much did everything that didn't involve what I was doing at work.

She was a wife and mother extraordinaire.

She had to be for her own fulfillment, because I certainly wasn't helping her with her sense of being a woman, being a partner in life, being wanted for the person that she was when we met.

When you enter the hamster wheel, you need to keep running to keep things in motion. Unfortunately, what you don't realize when you're on the wheel is that you don't go anywhere. Sure, you start to fill your world with fancier stuff, nicer cars, bigger houses, more extravagant vacations, custom-designed furniture—whatever, but you don't go anywhere.

You are a slave to the wheel; subconsciously knowing that to stop the wheel would require you to face your partner, and worse, yourself!

I need to point out here that our life was not complete misery. We lived a great life, by the standards of the American Dream that we are all chasing.

However, we didn't know what we didn't know about emotional connection, living an examined life, and most of all, the ravages of a depression that would continue to tear me to shreds.

As life marched on, the emotional repression that I believe that I had mastered was slowly eating me from the inside out.

I was eating too much, drinking excessively whenever I could, not sleeping regularly, working way too much, avoiding intimacy with my wife, treating people like shit, going through tremendous mood swings, from high mania to low and angry sadness, going out at night as often as I could for business without communicating where I was going and who I was with to my partner, and just generally living an existence that was focused entirely on me. I was earning the money. I didn't think anyone should question what I needed to do to bring home the cash.

Questions from my wife about our relationship or our lack of intimacy were always met with the same responses.

"I'm exhausted, it's been a long week."

"Do we have to do this now?"

"It's always something."

Or the ever-popular, "I know, I know, I'm a fuck up— let's just cut to the end of the conversation when we agree that I am a fucking mess and not capable of happiness—I am sorry that you are stuck with such a miserable prick of misery."

Those are the kind of comments, especially the self-immolating defense of saying that I am a mess and you deserve better, designed by the ego to prevent any further connection and stop the dialogue immediately. It's like the robot from *Lost In Space*, arms flailing and screaming inside of your head, "Danger, Danger..."

Fortunately for me, my wife was not easily put off. She also had the benefit of knowing me when I was more vulnerable and more myself. So, she would keep on coming until she broke through the walls that I put up. Sometimes it would take an hour, sometimes days, but she never gave up. Oh, sometimes she would scream and yell and cry to get me to open up. It was the crying that always snapped me back into reality. In those raw emotional moments, I would see the pain that I was causing and would come around for a bit.

Those pieces of the conversation were real and very freeing for me.

Me: "God, I am so sorry, I don't want to push you away."

Chris: "I can't live this way anymore, I just don't deserve this, why are you so unhappy?"

Me: "I know that I love you, and I am sorry that I am causing you so much pain, I'm afraid that I don't deserve this and that it is all going to go away."

Chris: "I need to be loved and I need to be loved by you."

Me: "I don't know why I can't be normal—I feel broken —I feel like I'm never going to find happiness—I just don't know what it is."

You get the idea.

From this point, we would live in connection for some time—perhaps days, perhaps months.

The thing about depression that makes it such a moving target in trying to understand the disease is that the experience of it is different for everyone. The manifestation, the symptoms, the resulting behavior, and all of the complications associated with the disease of depression are unique to the individual. Yes, some generalized behaviors and symptoms are common indicators of depressive people, but the nuances can be hard to see without proper training and experience. This is especially true if you live day in and day out with people. It's like watching your partner lose weight over the course of a year. A 10-pound loss to you may not be seen at all. However, if you were walking down the street and ran into someone who you hadn't seen for a year, then you would see that weight loss immediately.

With depression, you can see that someone is struggling or unhappy, but you wouldn't see the daily gyrations that they are going through to hide the pain or the behavior resulting from their overall sadness. I have talked with alcoholics that were very good at hiding their liquor and sneaking drinks throughout the day. Sufferers of depression do the same thing. We hide our sadness from the outside world and the clandestine nature of that isolation becomes part of the addiction.

The wall, a creation of my mind that I built over time, was designed to protect me from any intrusion that caused emotional discomfort. I have recreated this wall in a physical setting in therapy sessions to see what it looks like for myself so that I can work on how to break it down. More importantly, to know and feel when I am starting to put it up in a given situation.

Here's what one of those sessions looked like: I sat in a nicely decorated room with several chairs, stuffed animals, a CD collection, rocks and seashells from the beach, decorative statues on the mantel over the fireplace, throw pillows, books, and other things that you would find in a room that was well decorated and lived in. I was asked by the therapist to spend as much time as I needed to re-create the emotional feeling that I experience at the moment that I am confronted with the need for a deeper connection with my wife.

In those moments, physically I go through some changes as well; slight stomach discomfort, increased heartbeat, reddened face and ears, cold feet, slight headache, itchiness on my skin, and other reactions from feeling anxious. I stood up, took three wooden chairs, and laid two down on their sides next to each other to create a solid base for the wall. The third chair was laid on top, sideways, and then I proceeded to fill in the empty spaces with as many things from the room as I possibly could. In the end, the wall stood four feet off the ground and was piled thickly with all of the items in the room that I deemed unbreakable. The result?

I lay on the carpeted floor next to my wall and visualized my wife on the other side of it. To get to her, I would have to climb over, snake my way through the crevasses of furniture and tchotchkes, and/or tear it down and throw the stuff all over the place. Just as she would have to do to get to me!

That physical manifestation of the creation of my mind was a profound experience for me. It woke me up to the separation that I had created from my wife and others in my life. Having that understanding and accepting it as part of my fear was the start of keeping the wall from going up. As I was confronted with those emotional inflection points, I could choose not to take all of the furniture in the room and pile it up to prevent anyone from closing in on me.

A critical part of this therapeutic experience was that my wife was open and willing to experience it. It was important for her to see the wall's physical reality and begin her understanding of the fearful being that existed deep within my outer body.

This is the essence of a relationship that has its foundation in the long nights that we shared in college, laying on that twin loft bed, inches from the stucco ceiling, listening to soft rock, and talking for hours. Night after night, despite what was going on around us—our love for each other was inevitable.

CHAPTER 13

MEN & A REPRESSED ANGER

What does living in this world require of us? I'm talking about the men, the people that are 50% responsible for bringing life into the world. There are people reading this book right now that are saying, "This guy is a pussy—he's a wimp." To them I say, "It is much more courageous and much 'gutsier' to admit fault and vulnerability and still succeed and prosper in life." From an early age, boys in our society are taught to toughen up—keep a stiff upper lip—there's no crying in baseball!

That's bullshit!

The "real" man is compassionate, empathic, physically strong and yet vulnerable, open, honest, caring, and present in life.

It is extremely difficult to make your way up through childhood and not buy into the social structure that makes little boys want to be tough, rough, strong, and dominating. As a successful former athlete, I know what it means to dominate physically and succeed in that world. I also know what that brought out in me on an emotional level. Mostly, emptiness and a feeling of aloneness.

My girlfriend, at that time, and now my wife, unconsciously and/or consciously chose me for all of the traits that came along with my being a dominant and strong man: physical prowess, good looks, aggressive, and protecting. I was a great example of someone that would be a strong provider and protector. However, she also experienced my sensitive emotional side and didn't count on my unemotional ego taking over my world as it was further bombarded in the business world with the male-dominated ethos's social structure.

Where does all of this anger come from and why does it continue to proliferate and permeate our society? As a youth athletic coach, I have seen the impact that fathers have on their little boys and the adult way in which little boys are treated. I have also treated little boys like adults, so please don't misunderstand my feelings here. I am not saying that I only saw this behavior, I was a party to it—of course I was, it was all I knew. Young athletes, little boys of 10, 11, 12 and 13 years old, are just that, little boys. They are afraid, uncertain, nervous, sensitive, and very impressionable. As they experience the athletic world, they receive accolades and ego-boosts through being the fastest, the strongest, the most aggressive, and the leader.

At that point, the young male athlete clearly understands how they are supposed to be and what will bring happiness to their male role models. With each other, they also start to form their own roles and try to dominate whenever possible; that is what brings popularity, attention from the opposite sex, and other ego-driven "feel good" experiences. At this point in their lives, if they were only interacting with each other, those behaviors would smooth themselves out through time and they would come to an understanding that that does not bring happiness and fulfillment. However, because their behaviors are being so strongly supported and praised by their male role models, that opportunity to "smooth out" is overridden by the overwhelming desire to please their fathers, coaches, uncles, etc.

As I moved more deeply into the therapeutic process, I gained a better understanding of what was driving my disease. This chapter will take you a little further into some of the shit that happens that helps to form who we "think" we are. I knew at an early age that I wasn't comfortable around my father and his brother, my uncle. They were strong male influences on me, and they were both angry and aggressive people whose anger could and would pop up without any restraint, at an instant. They had never learned any level of control mechanism around their feelings of anger and aggression. Their moods were either "not angry" or "I'm so angry that I'm going to kill you and your whole family." I spent a lot of time trying to understand where I came from and that brought me face to face with trying to reconcile with my father's life and influence on me.

My dad loved to fish. He loved the water and boats and the solitude of being out there in the sunshine with nothing but the birds and the boat slapping against the vast Atlantic Ocean. He had an innate love of the ocean and had learned the necessary patience and hit and miss that are fishing. He had knowledge of fish and how to catch them that many had only dreamed of gaining. This side to his complicated personality was at such odds with the rest of him that it would lull me into a false sense of comfort. The ocean-loving man that resided within my father was the real him, it was the person that I enjoyed being with. In fact, it was really the only person that existed within him that I enjoyed being with. As time went on, the trauma of spending time with the others that lived within him created so much fear that it drowned out the small murmurs of peace that he tried to utter from his fisherman.

My dad grew up in Brooklyn, New York. He was a greaser. He was one of those kids with the leather jacket, slicked-back hair, and the Harley Davidson motorcycle. He loved to work on cars and could strip a carburetor—clean it, lube it, replace, and gap the points and have it all back together before lunchtime. After lunch, he would strip the timing chain, recalibrate it and still have time to take his bike for a ride down to Sheepshead Bay for some night time striper fishing.

He would tell me that his ancestors in Italy learned to fish so they could eat and that the genetic understanding of "fish or die" had been passed down to him. I don't know if that's true or not, from what I understand from my mother, my dad's ancestors were masons and olive farmers that didn't live within a hundred miles of the sea. Does it really matter? In a sense, yes, it matters because the foundation of any relationship needs to be based on honesty, which ours was not. With that said, the guy loved the ocean and found solitude and a purpose in that endeavor that he didn't have in any other place in his life.

When I was eleven years old, we didn't own a boat and so, we spent much of our fishing time either on jetty rocks down at Jones Beach or on party boats out of Freeport or Sandy Hook, New Jersey. At the time, my dad lived in New Jersey and so, when I visited, we would head down routes 1/9 toward the Amboys and find some rocks to stand on to throw our lines into the water.

One day, my dad had found a place where we could rent a 19-foot skiff with an outboard motor. The place, a small marina somewhere under one of the route 1/9 bridges was called Frank's Marina. It was the kind of place that existed up and down the Jersey shore; tons of crushed oyster shells covered the parking lots and walkways, seagulls hung around waiting for fisherman to toss the entrails of their catch into the water, there was a coffee and bait shop that smelled like squid and doughnuts. There was a sole proprietor, who loved the water and seemed to be the son of Italian American parents, like my father. Frank was a very large man. In fact, Frank was just plain fat. His head looked like the biggest, roundest, fattest cantaloupe you've ever seen, resting on top of a neck that had rolls of skin that looked like three or four layers of tube socks wrapped around the top of his spine.

As my dad would say, "That fat fucker is one fat son of a bitch."

The irony of this statement was that my dad was fat and had been since he was a kid. He wasn't as fat as Frank, but his view of Frank was like Emperor Palpatine calling Darth Vader "one evil bastard."

I climbed onto the wooden boat with the three bench seats. It was high tide, so the boat was at the same level as the oyster-covered parking lot. My dad passed the rods and tackle box to me and went back to the car to grab the Styrofoam cooler that he had packed with sandwiches, soda, beer, and frozen squid. I sat there watching Frank in the next boat, the sweat was pouring off his forehead and the blue denim shirt that he wore was pasted against his back like someone had just doused him with a Gatorade jug after a big game. He had the cover off the 25-horse engine, the Evinrude logo was upside down, as it sat on top of the sun-streaked oyster shells. I watched him pulling the wires off the spark plugs and reaching into a ratchet set for the spark plug attachment. My dad returned, limping a little bit as he always did when he carried any kind of weight. He had been hit by shrapnel in the Korean War and had a nasty scar that ran the length of his leg. His knee was never the same again, especially since he really didn't exercise at all, so he lacked the necessary muscle strength to compensate for the lack of support in his knee.

Dad called out to Frank, "Hey there Frankie, beautiful day to drown some worms!"

"Yeah, looks pretty flat out there. Hey, we had some rain last night, so, some of these old engines are a little wet—if you have any problems, just let me know when you get back."

"What could be wrong on a day like this? Nothing, that's what."

The cooler, the rods and reels, tackle box, cushions and my dad and I are all in position and ready to head out in the Sandy Hook Bay, with its great views overlooking the Verrazano Bridge. The sun was high in the sky already and it was a beautifully warm day, as the skiff slapped along the water, the Evinrude outboard pushing us along toward our first drift point. The saltwater coming over the paint chipped bow was creating a mist that felt refreshing on my cheeks and forehead. I turned my nylon baseball cap around so it wouldn't fly off in the wind.

My dad cut the engine and we opened a can of corn giblets to start chumming the water for Flounder. Corn giblets were my dad's secret lure for the doormat shaped flounder that lay on the bottom of the bay. I would toss them in a few handfuls at a time, every few minutes. Whenever we caught fish, we always found corn in their stomachs, which I thought was cool. We sat and moved our sinkers up and down on the firm bottom, causing the bait to dance its alluring dance for the fish, so they would think it was alive and their next meal. After a half hour of drifting with the tide and bouncing around a bit from other boat traffic, my dad said, "lines up." We were heading back toward our original spot where we would continue our drift and take advantage of the corn giblet chum slick that we started.

I remember his hand gripping the black rubber cap to the pull cord and I remember the sound of the cord as it tightened and turned the fly wheel that would start the engine —"thwarr"—then it would recoil, and he would pull it again— "thwarr"—then recoil. After five pulls, he checked the choke switch which was a little metal tab that protruded just below the engine cover. "Choke's not on." He reached down to the throttle again, twisted the rubber throttle handle ever so slightly, so as to give the engine just a little gas and *thwarr*— recoil, *thwarr*—recoil, *thwarr*—recoil—"motherfucker"—*thwarr* —recoil—"shit"—*thwarr*—recoil—"you fat fucker"—*thwarr*— recoil—"Goddamnit."

The engine cover was now off the outboard and he was checking the wires, the fuel filter, the fuel line, the fuel tank, the connection from the fuel tank to the engine—he had that engine apart and back together in 10 minutes. He worked like a surgeon, like somebody who had been working on engines as if they were his symphonic compositions.

"Might be water in the lines."

I was overcome with a sense of danger that we were in this small little slab of wood in the middle of this huge body of water—the wind that seemed so gentle and soothing before, was now like a frickin' twister. The gentle flowing tide seemed like the wave that hit the SS Poseidon in that movie where Shirley Temple died trying to swim through the bowels of the ship to save the rest of the passengers.

I was just plain scared—I was a 10-year-old boy and I thought that I was going to drown in Sandy Hook Bay, the Statue of Liberty and the parachute ride at Coney Island off in the distance.

I said, "Dad, there is a buoy back there that looks like it's going to hit us." I know that the words left my mouth because he responded, but it felt as if they were being spoken at a whisper. You know, the kind of whisper that you scream when you are dreaming that there is a murderer in your room in the middle of the night.

The response came quickly and with a cutting hatred, "Jimmy, this fat fucker's engine won't start, and I need some God damn quiet."

I wanted to cry, wanted to scream, wanted to advocate for myself, but, instead, I just sat there watching the huge red channel marker drifting closer and closer as the boat closed ground quickly. About 10 seconds later, we hit the buoy broadside, the grinding of the wood and the steel reminded of the Staten Island Ferry boats as they pounded into the pilings when they were docking.

I reached over to lean into the buoy to ease us around it and the balance of the boat shifted. My dad yelled, "What the fuck are you doing? Why didn't you tell me that we were going to hit the fucking buoy?" When the boat shifted, my dad lost his balance and fell back onto the aft bench seat and hit his head on the engine cover. I retreated into my own head, trying to come to terms with not being heard and avert the oncoming negativity that I would now be enduring for the rest of the day. Here we were on a boat in the middle of a large bay, the engine not running, and the tide drifting us toward the shore with rapidly increasing pace.

My dad removed the carburetor cover and pressed on the floats or some frickin thing—I don't know—10 seconds later the motor sputtered into action and kicked over with a huge belch of blue and black smoke. My dad put the engine cover back into place and clipped the brackets in place to secure it. He reached into the cooler and grabbed a beer to take the edge off and off we traveled back toward our original fishing spot.

It was 9:00 AM, we should have gone back to the marina and gotten another engine—I mean, at my current age, I understand that stuff happens and that it is not something to take personally—just go back, tell Frank that we needed another engine and off we would go. Did he really want to rent out a boat that didn't run well? His entire business was based on repeat customers and his reputation, and he had told us about the rain last night.

My dad kept the engine idling this time and we dropped another can of corn into the water. My dad had swallowed the whole beer and poked three holes in the bottom of the can and sunk it. I got a nibble, then a full bite and reeled in a sea robin. My dad pulled it from the hook, made a derogatory comment about how sea robins were like the lowest form of human (in his opinion) and smashed it against the engine cover. The fish careened off the side of the outboard and hit the water completely knocked out cold. Dad said, "That's what I'd like to do to that son of a bitch Frank."

The idling engine started to hesitate a bit and we could both hear that it was not going to continue to run. My dad reached down and gunned the throttle. I wasn't ready for the thrust forward and fell with one knee into the side of the styrofoam cooler. The cooler broke into two or three pieces, like a thin sheet of ice dropped to the concrete from four feet above. The engine was running, but our lunch and drinks and ice cubes were floating in the couple of inches of water that had collected on the deck of the boat. My dad, completely red in the face, said, "That fat motherfucker, I'm going to kill that fat prick."

We fished for another hour or so, but the tension got the better of my dad's experience and we decided to head in around 11:00 am. I was so happy to be heading back to dry land, even though I told my dad that I wanted to fish. I was thinking that he would feel better if I told him that I wanted to fish, but I didn't count on that fueling his fire even further. He saw my desire to fish combined with the unruly engine, as a lost day and he took it very personally and didn't say a word the entire ride back to the marina.

I sat on the front bench seat, holding on with both hands gripped around the front of the seat, my knuckles white with the flexing of my hands and my knees were bouncing up and down with nervousness. As usual, my stomach was hurting, and I felt the need to expel diarrhea from my bowels. I literally thought I was going to shit my pants with anxiety. It had happened many times before. I was only hoping that I could hold it long enough to get to shore and run through the fishy doughnut smelling coffee shop to the lone toilet with the broken toilet seat and take a crap. I was so scared, yet, I didn't have any voice to speak or communicate my fear, my frustration, my loneliness.

The dock was coming closer and closer, and I could literally smell the inside of the bathroom as my feet slapped against the water-covered deck. My stomach was gurgling, and gas was leaving my body ever so gently so that my bowels didn't get the full green light to let go.

There he was, standing with the sun at his back, the hulking figure of Frank the marina owner. I couldn't see his face because of the sun, it was like looking up at a lunar eclipse as his huge melon blocked out all light. My dad was yelling, "This piece of shit didn't run all day, I want my fucking money back." Frank said, "Slow down, you're going to damage the dock." The tide had gone out and the floating dock was a good ten feet below the marina now, I could see the mussels and the barnacles and the seaweed as it clung to the pilings that the marina was built on.

Dad: "I want a fucking refund, the whole day was ruined because of your God damned boat."

Frank, "I have another engine that we can put on and you can go right back out—it's only 11:30."

Dad: "You fat fuck, I'm not taking any of your shitty boats out."

All I can think of is that I need to get off the boat to use the bathroom. The argument continued with these two ego-driven idiots and I was frozen with fear and anxiety. I couldn't take it any longer and just let it go—I could feel my underwear filling up with shit and sensed that the situation wasn't going to end well. The smell was unmistakable, and it was unbearable, and everyone knew what had happened by the dripping fluid from the bench seat below me.

My dad reached down to the two butterfly bolts that held the outboard motor onto the transom of the boat. He started unscrewing them with both hands as Frank watched. Frank was no idiot, he had seen his share of poor customers over the years—he stood back and said, "That engine hits the water, and you own it, I'm calling the police."

Dad had been completely emasculated as his 11-year-old son sat there in his own feces and he was being threatened with arrest. He did what he always did when confronted with the feelings of emotional pain and anger that he couldn't control. He ran.

Dad said, "Meet me in the car."

He climbed up the ladder to the parking lot, grabbed the fishing rods as I passed them up to him and he walked away, his sneakers crunching against the crushed oyster shells and dirt.

Frank looked at me and said, "There is a bathroom at the back of the building that my employees use, you can go in there, so you don't have to walk through the bait shop."

I cleaned myself up as best I could, threw my underwear in the garbage and walked to the car. My dad was furiously smoking a Marlboro with the windows open. He had placed an old piece of indoor/outdoor carpeting on the seat of his Lincoln Mark IV, and I eased in. We drove back to his apartment without saying a word to each other. I felt like I had let him down, that I was the most disappointing person that had ever come into his life. It was not an unknown feeling for me, and I wallowed in it like a pig wallows in the cool mud on an August day.

He cooked me a steak for dinner and said that he and his neighbor were going out for a few drinks that night. He said that he'd be back late and that I should just watch some TV and go to bed.

I sat on the couch, feeling very refreshed after a nice hot shower, and I was also feeling very relieved that my dad was gone.

His apartment was a one-bedroom garden apartment in Colonia, New Jersey. He had lived in this apartment for as long as I could remember, he moved there when he left my mother nine years earlier. It was on the second floor of a two-story building and was small. It had wall-to-wall shag carpeting that was brown. He said, "The brown keeps it from looking dirty." Yeah, that's because it resembles the shit that was running down my leg earlier that day! Not only did it keep the dirt down, but it also soaked up the odor and the tar and nicotine from the four packs of Marlboros that my dad had inhaled every day since he was a teenager. It was like sitting in a fucking ash tray. I hated that apartment as much as I feared my father.

I watched television for a few hours and climbed into bed around 11:00 pm or so. There was only one bed in the apartment. Yes, I could have and should have slept on the couch or somewhere else; it wasn't appropriate for me to be in that bed with my dad. I didn't possess the strength to tell him that I couldn't sleep there, that I was afraid that I had been awakened more than once while he masturbated next to me. I couldn't tell him because I was afraid that he wouldn't love me anymore or that he would do what he always did, run. I fell asleep with the TV on.

I awoke at 2:30 in the morning, saw the flickering of lights in the room, but didn't see my dad. I moved slowly in the bed because I didn't want him to hear me if he was home from some drunken night out with whoever he was out with. More likely, he was probably out alone. I could sense that he wasn't there and leaned over to the window and separated the metal blinds to see where the flickering lights were coming from. My dad was stooped over in front of a police car talking with a couple cops. He was stumbling a bit and waving his arms. I stood there with my fingers separating the blinds ever so slightly, so I wouldn't be seen and the anxiety that I had felt earlier in the day returned. I ran to the bathroom and vomited. I went back to bed and covered myself up to my chin with the sheets and hid my face in the pillow, the sweat was beading on my upper lip, and I could taste the vomit bile on my teeth and tongue.

Within a few minutes, my dad dropped into bed, smoked a cigarette, and started to jerk off. I lay there as still as I could, feeling the urge to vomit again, and I prayed that he would just fall asleep. He cleaned himself and within minutes was snoring like a lawnmower.

I climbed out of bed and went into the bathroom to brush my teeth. I stood in the bathroom for a half hour or so and decided that I had had enough of this anxiety and fear. I decided that my dad needed to be out of my life—for good.

I tiptoed into the walk-in closet opposite the bathroom, eased the door closed and pulled the cotton string chain that switched on the light. I found the black Samsonite case and opened it up, and there they were, two handguns. The smaller pistol was a .38 caliber detective special and the larger one was a .22 barrel that resembled a German Luger. I didn't know much about guns but had fired both of these guns at target practice with my dad on a couple of occasions. How hard could it be? You just put the magazine into the .22, point and pull the trigger. The .38 was even easier; it had a hair-trigger and I just needed to load the firing chambers, point, and barely touch the trigger. My head was spinning. Was I actually going to do this? Would they put a 10-year-old in prison? I hated my father for putting me in this situation, for making me feel such fear and anxiety all the time. It was a confusing set of feelings—on the one hand, I loved and idolized him, on the other—I hated his fat fucking guts. He was supposed to be my protector, my role model; unfortunately, he was my role model in many negative ways.

The tears welled in my eyes, and I was having a hard time seeing. Then I heard the silence, the snoring had stopped.

"Shit!"

He never stopped snoring, unless he was awake, or preferably, dead. I heard his footsteps creaking the floor as he crossed the brown cigarette ash-soaked shag carpet to the bathroom. The seat went up and the toilet flushed. I saw his shadow as he came toward the closet. The doorknob started to twist, and I leaned back into the pile of stuff that was between me and the wall. He reached in, pulled the cotton string and turned off the light and made his drunken way back to bed. I sat there in the dark for hours, just sobbing.

The next morning, he drove me to Penn Station in New York City, walked me in to get my ticket, and kissed me goodbye. I walked slowly down the stairs after my track was announced and got on the train back to Long Island. Please keep in mind that I was a 10-year-old little boy and had absolutely no business wading my way through Penn Station in 1975, and I definitely should not have been riding the Long Island Railroad back and forth to Baldwin alone.

CHAPTER 14

CONFRONTING
THE FATHER RELATIONSHIP

I hated those Penn Station drop-offs, which went on for many years, until I was old enough to drive back and forth to New Jersey to visit my father. The next time that I remember being dropped off at Penn to take the train back to Long Island was a pivotal moment in the destructive relationship that my father and I lived.

Many years later, at the still very ripe young age of 23, I had finally mustered up the strength to face my dad in a way that I had never done before. Life had pulled me away from his daily psychological manipulations and I was starting to become my own person, at least a little bit. I was married to an incredibly strong and wisdom-filled woman, I had a great job earning more money than both my parents combined, and felt a strong desire to begin to stand on my own as it related to my dad.

The memory of the night, debating with myself about shooting my dad while he lay in a drunken stupor, had been repressed, but the emotional anguish had permeated my being in ways that I didn't consciously understand. I always had this innate desire to separate myself from my dad's being, and I was driven to talk with him about it.

I invited him to meet me for dinner in Hoboken, New Jersey at a local steak house called Arthur's. The location was picked specifically for a couple of reasons. One, my dad lived in New Jersey and I was working in downtown Manhattan on

Fulton and Broadway, just north of Wall Street, which made for a short train ride for me, and two, we both loved steak and I thought it would be a common ground environment for us to share something fun, while we embarked on the journey of a challenging conversation.

I remember things about that night that seem quite obscure now. The smell of the cigar-filled bar as I walked through the front door wearing my tan Burberry raincoat, collar popped to keep the rain off the collars of my blue Ralph Lauren pinstriped suit and custom Egyptian cotton shirt. The rain carried the odor of the snow that would soon follow it as I shook it off of my coat. There was a 20-something year-old guy smoking a pipe—a fucking pipe, I mean, that's just going too far!—in the corner of the bar under the TV screen. The bar was filled with men, mostly white males in their late 20s/early 30s. Among the cacophony of yuppy guys with their hair slicked back, there were several women, but at this time of the early evening on a Tuesday night, most patrons were men who just got off the Path train from New York to down a few beers and eat an enormous slab of meat. The smell of meat being pan-fried, grilled, and oven baked was overpowering all of the other odors that have stuck with me all these years.

That smell will always remind me of the last meaningful conversation that I ever had with my father.

I grabbed a pint of beer at the bar and stood there replaying exactly what I was going to say when we sat down for what was building for me as the last supper. My wife and I had discussed the need that I had for confronting my father, the anger that was bubbling within my being, and the carefully chosen words that would allow for my father to hear what I was saying and provide me with answers as opposed to feeling attacked and immediately becoming defensive.

I was nervous.

To this point in my life, I had swallowed up every single thing that my father had sent my way. All of his behavior, all of it—without question—without protecting myself—without saying NO! This conversation was an opportunity for me to say no, and more importantly, to get some answers about the "whys" that had been plaguing my nightmares for many years.

I turned toward the wood-framed windows that looked out onto the main drag of downtown Hoboken and saw my dad's hefty and sullen figure as it cut a path across the street. His post-Korean War shrapnel-riddled knee was causing him to limp—it was always worse when it was damp and cold outside —and it caused him to move more slowly, more ominously.

Now, I was scared.

He moved into the restaurant, glancing at the hostess as if to say, "I don't need to talk to you. I'm beyond your ability to help."

My dad didn't respect anybody that he perceived to be intellectually beneath him and hostesses at restaurants were definitely not on his list of people to pay any attention to. I had seen him treat "the help" with such disdain over the years and it was another thing that I hated about his DNA being in my veins.

The thing that I never understood about this aspect of my dad's personality is that he was extremely unsuccessful from all measures of American success. He rarely held a job for more than a few years, never had any money, and lived in a shitty one-bedroom apartment in Colonia, New Jersey, forever. I understand now that he was treating people the way that he believed he deserved to be treated, but, at the time, it just pissed me off.

One day while he and I were having lunch at a McDonald's in North Baldwin, a guy was mopping the floor. We had gotten there a little early on our way to go somewhere and I was so excited to be having a Big Mac—it was a huge treat in the '70s. I was like eight or nine years old, and the smell of the Big Mac was making me even hungrier. I bit into it and the euphoric taste was filling my mouth as I heard, "What the fuck, we're eating here!"

I looked up to see that my father had reached over from our plastic booth to grab the worker's mop handle—the grip reddened his hand, and he was staring the guy down like he was going to break the mop in half and beat him over the head with it.

The guy was scared and stumbled into the mop bucket as he moved away, spilling some of the water on the floor. My dad, seeing a weak prey, immediately stood up as if the water had been dumped on our table and was heading for his lap and yelled, "Jesus Christ, how the fuck can we have our lunch now!? You just ruined my meal!"

My stomach lurched and I could feel the diarrhea making its way through the small intestines toward the bowels. My burger, saggy and limp in both hands, had lost all appeal and I just wanted to cry.

My dad walked toward the now scurrying manager and said, "You should fire this guy, my son is upset and the whole place smells like dirty mop water."

The manager, "I'm sorry sir, your lunch is on me."

My dad walked back to our table, stuffing the bills back in his front pants pocket and looked at me as a tear fell down my cheek. Then, he said, "Why are you upset? It's over."

I didn't say anything or move.

My dad said, "I'm going to take you home."

That was his weekly visit. We spent 20 minutes together. 20 minutes that ended in his being pissed off at me for not wanting to eat my food after he berated a guy making $1.85 an hour and just trying to clean the floor of a fucking McDonald's! It wasn't the Rainbow Room—it was a fucking McDonald's.

The anger that had become as familiar to me as the blue tattered security blanket that I carried around until I was five years old, was covering me from head to toe.

Back in Hoboken, I smelled his Marlboro coated being as he embraced me in front of the mahogany bar.

"Hey Dad, what are you drinking? It's on me."

"Dewar's on the rocks."

I turned to the bartender as the heat of the moment started to fill my head like mercury climbing up the gradings of a thermometer.

Drinks in hand, we walked to the hostess, and I said, "Hi, table for two please."

We sat catching up on the usual bullshit that gets bantered about when people are completely superficial and having a relationship that is about an inch deep. Work, my wife, the weather, the train ride out here, my sisters, and a few other inane topics.

I had three scotches inside of me and was feeling strong enough to start reading the script from my mind. It was time— I was 23 years into a dysfunctional relationship with the person whose DNA was attacking my emotional being like leprosy, it was time to have a reckoning.

I had so many questions that I needed answers to.

Why did you leave us?

Why haven't you sent mom money?

Why didn't you pay your taxes and left mom to deal with the IRS for so many years?

Did your dad abuse you?

Why are you alone?

Why am I afraid of you?

...and the list went on.

The steaks were placed on the table on big white plates between a huge fork and a large wooden-handled serrated knife. Two two-pound T-Bones, rare, with sides of onions, mushrooms and baked potatoes. I had switched over to beer and he was drinking red wine.

"Dad, I asked you to meet me for dinner because I would like to talk with you about some stuff that has been bothering me and I'd like to get through it because it has been on my mind for a few years, and I finally have my head cleared enough to know what I want to say."

Dad: "Ok."

"The thing is, I don't really like you very much, I mean, I love you—you're my father, but I don't like you as a person and I really want to try and understand you so that maybe the dislike will go away."

I know, I know, I shouldn't have started off by dropping a missile on the table by telling him that I didn't like him, but the scotch had taken over my filters and I was getting angrier by the second. Looking at this man, was at times, like looking in the mirror. Our facial features were similar, but far deeper, I could see the negative aspects of him within myself—and I hated myself for not being strong enough to keep that down, to push it away like someone trying to bully me.

Dad: "I don't know what I did wrong."

Me: "It's not that you did anything wrong, I'm trying to understand why you did the things you did."

Dad: "If I did something wrong just tell me, I don't know what I did wrong."

I realize now that I was talking to the little boy inside of my father, the little boy that had been physically and psychologically abused. The little boy that only wanted to please his father and never got the satisfaction of living that experience.

In that moment though, I was not getting what I needed, and it was pissing me off that my father was making this about him—THIS ISN'T ABOUT YOU—I wanted to scream.

"Why did you leave us with no food, no money, and not come back?"

"Are you in therapy?" Dad asked.

"No, I'm not in therapy—why?"

"Just curious."

"Can you give me any answers?"

"I just don't understand what I did wrong and now that I know that you hate me, we don't have much to talk about."

And so it goes with a manic-depressive narcissist. It is and always will be about them—and they will refuse to see and/or accept any responsibility for their actions. It's not that they don't want to, it's just that they don't know what they don't know.

I felt so angry at this point and at the same time my learned desire to please my father was making me feel guilty about even raising the issue. The power of psychological manipulation is strong, like the gravitational pull of the earth. You just cannot get away from it without moving to a completely different atmosphere, which is ultimately what I decided to do.

"I'll drive you to Penn Station."

"Uhm, ok—let me just pay the check."

I didn't have the ability to repel the gravitational pull and found myself blindly walking to the passenger side of his Lincoln Continental. My stomach was swirling, and I was afraid I was going to let my entire meal loose onto the tan floor mat as we drove toward the Lincoln Tunnel. As I stared out the window, the toll booth of the tunnel directly in front of us, I regretted getting into this car with this person that I hated with every fiber of my being.

The anger, instead of projecting outward, was clearly being placed in the one place where I could control it and the one place where that kind of anger felt good and normal for me—on myself.

My hands were sweating, and I just wanted to get the fuck out of that car. I hated myself for allowing him to control me again. I was such a pussy and I felt like a three-year-old not getting his way. It was humiliating.

We pulled up to the huge U.S. Post Office on 8th Avenue and he said, "I love you, take care."

We shook hands and I got out of the car across from Madison Square Garden and joined the other people crossing the street to enter the escalators down to the bowels of Penn Station, for the Long Island Railroad ride out to Woodmere.

I mindlessly moved through the throng of commuters, shoppers and homeless people that littered the dirty floors like thrown away candy wrappers. My track was being announced over the loudspeaker, "Far Rockaway, 8:01 to Far Rockaway now boarding, making stops in Jamaica, Valley Stream, Hewlett, Woodmere..."

I couldn't do it.

I couldn't get on that train like I did when I was 10. I didn't want to repeat that experience again—feeling like I had just prostituted myself for my father. I had forsaken my own needs and feelings for a person that only cared about himself.

Earlier in the night I had received a message on my cell phone from a coworker who was going to take a client for sushi over on 44th and Lexington, one of our favorite sushi spots. It was still early and so I decided to jump a cab over there and meet them for a few drinks.

I turned around and went up the escalator, leaving the noise and misery behind me—I hit the open air and hailed a cab.

The cabbie dropped me off at 41st and Lex so I could hit an ATM to get some cash for a night of binge-drinking. There was always something that felt great about having crisp 20s to fold into my Coach leather money clip.

If I didn't find my buddy and our client, it wouldn't matter, I wasn't going to hang out with them anyway—I was just looking for a place where I could escape the feverish anger that was immolating me.

I took $200 out of the bank and walked up Lexington.

I didn't see him in time. A guy had popped out of the vestibule of a deli. It was he and I staring at each other, but only one of us had a knife. There was a very empty look in his eyes, and it occurred to me that he was definitely capable of sticking the knife into me without thinking twice and he told me to give him the cash that I just took out of the bank. I noticed that the knife was very similar to the one that I had just used to cut through my T-Bone at Arthur's—big brown handle, about a seven-inch blade, serrated for three inches at the tip.

It all happened so quickly, and I didn't think very clearly, and I was a little drunk. So, I did what I had done five years earlier when the four Black guys attacked me a block from my house—I handed him the money still folded so nice and neat in my money clip, and I also gave him the money clip. He grabbed it with the fingers of his dirty left hand and bolted across the street, and was gone up 40th, behind the Newsday building.

I walked into Hatsuhana, had a glass of Crown Royal on the rocks with a wedge of lemon and tried to forget the events of the last two hours. At 11:30, we walked out onto the street, and I called for three cars from a NYC livery service that catered to picking up drunk executives all over the city and shuttled them to their bedroom communities out in the suburbs.

My ride, a black Lincoln Town Car, showed up five minutes later and I told the driver where I was headed. The 35-minute drive to Woodmere was uneventful—the thoughts in my head, well, they were not uneventful. I was furious that destiny had granted me the pain of a father that had been abused and turned into an abuser. I was pissed that I had been robbed and my money had been taken from me, without my protest. I was angry that my wife was home waiting for me, not really knowing where I was or what I was doing—once again, I was letting her down and leading her down my self-possessed path of destruction, loneliness and dishonesty.

I decided, as we cruised at 50 MPH down Peninsula Boulevard toward the five towns area of Nassau County, that I was going to take a piece of myself back.

When we pulled up in front of our apartment at 37 Woodmere Boulevard, I signed the voucher for the driver, grabbed my briefcase and walked across the street to our Honda Accord. I opened the door, got in, put the key in the ignition and drove back to Manhattan.

Yes, I drove my drunk and revenge-seeking ass back to Manhattan!

The words of a former college lacrosse teammate rang in my head, "Somebody's got to pay!"

As I drove down the bumpy and pothole-pocked hill on the LIE toward the well-lit Midtown tunnel, I could feel the effects of the alcohol dissipating. I was operating on sober faculties and was making a conscious decision to exact pain on the one person that I could exact pain on from the earlier events of the evening.

I took the first right out of the tunnel and drove up the one-way street to the base of the rear façade of the Newsday building. There, to my right, as if the light of Satan was illuminating him for me, on the corner of 41st and 3rd, was the guy that stole my money.

I pulled the car around the corner, heading north on 3rd and parked in front of McFadden's, a sport's bar that I frequented with friends many times. I got out to walk a block back to where he stood.

I approached him in a very aggressive and fast way, thinking that I would catch him off guard as he had done to me. The tables had been turned and this time, knife or no knife, I was going to show this guy what it meant to really hurt somebody. In my mind, being stabbed to death at this point would have been a welcome relief.

I said, "Hey, remember me?"

He looked at me and said, "Should I?"

I grabbed him by the lapels of the old tan and dirt-colored raincoat that he probably stole from another guy just like me. I pushed his feather-weight body toward the edge of the building on the corner and, just as I had learned while bouncing at the Limelight, I thrust his head into the black stone corner. People's heads are very vulnerable to pain, and it disorients them quickly.

He tried to wheel on me with the knife in his pocket. Too late!

I said, "You picked the wrong guy on the wrong day, when you took my money at knife-point."

I was prepared for him to pull the knife out and as he turned his head to the left to bring his right arm around to strike me, I punched him in his left cheek.

The thrust of my fist coming down from my extended shoulder was powerful. I put my entire 215-pound frame behind that punch. He stumbled and dropped to one knee.

I could feel the blinding pain and misery that was the memory of my discussion with my father. I had left myself.

I pulled him down the street a little bit, away from the light, and I punched him again and again and again, until I was too tired to punch anymore.

I left that miserable prick in a rumpled heap, laying in the doorway of a loading dock behind the Newsday building. I also left my money in his pocket, there was some quick rationalization that he needed it more than I did. I wasn't there for the money, I was there to cause physical pain.

I walked back to my car, got in and started it. It was then, with my hands gripping the blue steering wheel, that I saw the bloody knuckles that I would have to explain to my wife when I got home.

It was 1:00 in the morning as I went through the toll booth at the eastern mouth of the Midtown tunnel. I pulled up the hill on the LIE, leaving the god-forsaken island of Manhattan behind me, and drove home like I had just had a rough day at the office.

I unlocked the door of our apartment, threw my suit into the dry-cleaning pile, took a quick shower to wash off the sweat and grime of the day, and climbed into bed. As with many other nights where I walked in without notice of being out late, my wife awoke and demanded to know where I was.

This was one of those moments when Chris would threaten to leave—she probably should have—and I would explain that I just didn't know who the hell I was, and we would have a protracted argument about life. I explained the discussion with my father, the robbery, and the return to NYC to get revenge.

I said, "I couldn't come home knowing that this guy had violated me, I couldn't let him get away with it."

She said, "Your father?"

Wow, that was a great question. The answer was obvious, but I didn't know it yet.

We eventually got to bed—Chris feeling extremely unsafe with this bloody-knuckled man that she loved, lying next to her. Her own head reeling from the life that she found herself in.

Me? I would spend the next year in and out of deep depressive bouts, laced with much thought about the only solution that I could think of to end the never-ending pain... suicide. This pattern of going back to suicide, as a plan to end my internal suffering, was a continued thought that began on that boat in my yard when I was 12. It wasn't with me all of the time, but, when I felt that I could no longer endure the pain, I would endeavor to just fucking kill myself and the pain along with me.

CHAPTER 15

FINDING & EXTERMINATING THE TERMITES

The life that we create for ourselves, and make no mistake, we create it for our "selves," is like building a house. We build that house as we would any dwelling that we would live in. I have built a couple houses in my life, and have renovated a couple more, and speak with some experience on this topic.

You start with plans and locations, map out the sighting of the structure and then go through hundreds of choices: room locations and sizes, flooring material, wall color, paint, wallpaper, cabinetry materials and facing, choices of exterior materials and colors, plantings, stair rails, decking, electrical outlet locations, entertainment speakers, cable TV jacks, built-in shelving, whirlpool tub, shower, steam shower, sauna, window load, driveway construction, is it paved, loose stone, curved, straight, crescent, circular, wooden clapboard or vinyl siding, fencing, roofing materials, electrical load, and the list goes on.

Those are just some of the decisions that you will ponder and decide on to frame out this whole project, this house for you and your family. Then, you are faced with all the nitty-gritty details: molding in each room, door knob shape, color, material, brass, ceramic, wood, and should each knob match to the outer room and have a different knob for the inner room, closet location and interior organization, knobs for the kitchen cabinets, shelving in the laundry room, shelving in the garage, garage door openers, should they be remote and programmable and should there be a keyless entry panel outside the house. What about security, does this make the house easier to rob, what about an entire security system? The list of details are endless and each choice has an impact on the overall home that results and the life that you will live in that home.

Lots of choices, lots of directions to go in, and if you are present and you have thought about your feelings in every detail, it will become a reflection of who you are, and how you want to live your life.

Your new home is built. It's beautiful and you and your family move in with all the excited expectations of a new life, a new beginning, a new chapter, and everything is brand spankin' new!

You move in with a big family and it's a smashing success. Your friends and family are there to celebrate you and your choices, your expression...your life.

Time marches on and the natural wear and tear of life occurs, making everything change along with it. The wallpaper starts to fade a bit from the sun shining through the southern exposed windows. The facing on the cabinets starts to lose its luster, the pool requires a lot of work and money to maintain, the yard is covered with leaves and sticks and other types of bramble. These are not "bad" things, this is just life happening around you.

From the outside eye's view, your house "looks" like the American Dream. What is not seen and what is not known about are the termites that have been eating away at your foundation joists for years!

This is a metaphor that was introduced to me by my "life guru" (aka holistic therapist) and is also an example of a real-life situation that happened to somebody that I spoke with while working on this book. This guy was going through something that was similar to what I was going through, except he was dealing with his actual home, I was dealing with the termite-infested home of "self" that I had created.

It struck me as the perfect metaphor for our entire lives.

Suppose you have a seemingly beautiful life from a distance, but still live "out of rhythm" or do not find constant joy in the world around you. In that case, you may have a personal and emotional termite infestation from the things that you have done or not done, feelings you have repressed, and not having reckoned with your past.

You might say, "The past is in the past and that's where I want it to stay."

I would agree with you, however, if you don't have a heartfelt reckoning with that past, the termites will reproduce to ten-fold their current population and they will wreak havoc on your world. It's not a matter of "if," it's a matter of "when."

This chapter, above all others in the book, is about the intense pain and work of my reckoning. That reckoning has been embraced, wrestled, run from, worked through, screamed at, faced with gut-wrenching sobbing, and is the very personal struggle of the work that I have had to do. I must point out here that this part of the story is incredibly personal and that it also involves the lives of other people. While I am telling my story, there are pieces of my story that are deeply intertwined with the lives of others. As an explorer on your journey, it is important to understand the power in maintaining personal "control" over your inner world in the form of creative ideas. The work that must be done is inner work, you would dilute the power of this inner work if you shared it with the world before its time.

Harness the Universal Power

When you have an idea, it germinates from the deepest part of your being. At that point, your idea is in full power and the Universe is now drawing all of the resources available to bring this to fruition. This is the concept that what we put in the world will come back to us like the most powerful magnet ever produced. This has been made popular through several books and movies; *The Secret* being the one that I am most familiar with. I have seen this in action and it is amazing to watch how something can be brought to life by a single thought or the action of writing it down.

A quick example of drawing your desire to you based on the power of intention: At 10, my son was into technology and the creative pursuits of digital animation, video game development, and movie making. At the time, he wanted to duplicate the effects that he saw in multi-million-dollar movie productions, like explosions, buildings collapsing, and other graphics driven CGI-type stuff. He wanted a software that would allow him to do this kind of work; the problem was that he was ten and didn't have a reliable source of income—

beyond his parents! We had just watched *The Secret* and suggested that he write down his top 10 intentions on a piece of paper, being very specific about what he wanted. He pushed back on us hard, saying that it would never work, he just needed us to buy him the software and then his life would be "perfect." You know how that discussion goes.

His mom and I told him, "Just try it and let's see what happens."

He reluctantly agreed and hung this little piece of paper on the wall next to his bed. On the piece of paper, it said, "I would like to own Final Cut Express for my Mac so that I can create special FX for my movies."

We forgot about it and went on with our busy lives. But, every day, James looked at that piece of paper and read his goals.

About six months later, I was coaching a lacrosse game at a high school in Massachusetts and needed a videographer to capture footage of the game for my team so that I could watch the play and use it as a teaching tool for the players. It was very cool to see my son (who volunteered) on top of the press box at this gorgeous new facility that the school had built for its athletic program. He was joined on top of that press box by the home team's own videographer/sports information director and they started to talk about "stuff." The guy was very interested in James's level of knowledge around technology and couldn't believe how focused this kid was on getting better at what he was producing and the level of expertise that he had on technology in general.

He asked James, "What are you using for graphic effects?"

"Right now, I create what I can by going onto shareware sites and YouTube, but, I'm saving my money to buy Final Cut Express."

As the day progressed, the game was played, it was a nightmare for me as my team got a serious drubbing and two hours later I sat on the bus completely baffled by how badly we were outplayed and outcoached. Simultaneously, James sat on the bus with a huge smile on his face and I asked him what he and the other guy were talking about.

James filled me in and then said, "He left at halftime and came back 20 minutes later and gave me this."

James held out a new version of Final Cut Express!

He put out his intention and the Universe delivered it, free of charge.

That story amazes me every time I think about it, and it is just an affirmation of the power of our own beings to create our world.

I believe that the power of thought is at its apex when it is held in the light of your own being, only shared with people who fully support who you are as a person. That sharing must be protected because as you share with others, the power is diluted exponentially as it is spread through the world. There are thoughts and ideas that, when shared, develop a mushroom effect and blossom through their universally accepted power. Think Martin Luther King Jr., Jesus, Buddha, John Lennon, etc.

However, most thoughts are just diluted through social judgment and lack of understanding or ignorance. As I went through my reckoning, it was the talk therapy sessions where my wife and I would be retching in emotional pain, sobbing, screaming, and loving each other through the traumatic effects of childhood trauma and the loving understanding that we needed to find. These were the private moments of people in serious pain and at the same time, experiencing serious healing. We did not know where we were going or where we would end up, as people, as parents, and as a couple.

The power of that healing remains undiluted because of our diligent approach to the privacy and intimacy that we share as people. Sharing the specifics of this piece of our journey would completely dilute that power and would not, no, "could not", be understood by anyone other than us, because we lived it in real time and in real context. We were on our journey, a personal evolution through life that is completely ours.

I recently spoke with a group of about 60 people and I was talking about exterminating the termites and the following great question was asked, "How do you know if you have a termite infestation?"

The answer to this question required me to walk through the questions that were asked of me throughout my process of "extermination," which is really another way of saying that I embraced my termites and then released them.

Here are those questions:

1) Do you feel a sense of dread or anxiety in your life?

2) Do you approach situations with anger and aggression?

3) Are you experiencing the love that your partner, friends, and others have to offer?

4) Do you love yourself? (Seriously, you're asking me this, seriously? My answer, "Are you fucking kidding me?!")

5) Do you understand the true meaning of personal connection?

6) Have you lied?

7) Have you been dishonest about your needs?

If you have answered yes or maybe to any of the questions above, you have termite infestation within your life. Termites destroy the foundation and eat away at the interior in places where they cannot be seen. That internal destruction is gasoline poured on the fire of anxiety and depression.

The next question that was asked during this speaking engagement was, "What if it isn't a huge infestation, what if I just have a few termites crawling around?"

Again, a great question and I couldn't have paid her to tee up better softballs for me to hit out of the park!

Therein lies the problem with termites; one is too many and a few are a complete infestation.

As we go through our lives, the presence of dishonest behavior will permeate everything that we do. We carry with us the energy vibration of our actions and behaviors. If that energy vibration is "muddied" with actions that are not in rhythm with our soul's intention, we will carry the vibration everywhere we go and share it with those around us.

Let me explain this further with a real-life example from my own experiences and destructive behavior.

I have talked about my life as a New York City businessman quite often. As a young up and coming 25 to 30-year-old hustling my way through corporate America, I pretty much did what I thought I had to do to get ahead. This included catching 5:30 am trains from Long Island or from Westchester, where we lived during that point in my career, to Wall Street. When I got on that train, I compartmentalized my life to a point where I believed that there was a complete separation between who I was with a blue suit and red tie on and who I was when I was home with my wife and my family.

I was hunting to bring home bounty for my tribe, and if that required me to entertain a client until 3:00 in the morning, well, that's what hunters do. They chase the prey until it is dead. In my case, the prey was dead when they were happy and signed a contract to hire my firm to provide insurance products for their company.

It was a male-dominated business environment where nothing positive happens at 3:00 in the morning. In fact, nothing positive happens after about 8:00 pm, because that is really when the scotch-on-the-rocks kicks in. Bottom line; if you can't see that being home with your family is really where you want to be, the termites are having a field day. If you sit and think about it and can honestly say that you would rather be out having a drink at a bar than being home, that's ok too. That's your truth. Then, you need to question whether living within the family that you have created is the right life choice for you. I have spoken with dozens of people like myself and when we get down to the granularity of that question, the answer is always the same...I want to be home, but I don't know how to get there.

How I was conducting myself was not in rhythm with the life I wanted for my family and me. However, due to my poor self-image, lack of confidence, self-loathing, and depressive episodes that resulted from my DNA that were then fueled further by several childhood traumas, my behavior was extraordinarily destructive. Of course, the ongoing negative behavior (whatever that is for you) creates a death spiral of toxicity, and it feeds upon itself until you are just the passenger in the very backseat of the vehicle that is careening out of control.

I would also point out that while behavior is relative, the destruction is not.

The outcome in dishonesty is the same, whether you steal a million dollars or a candy bar. I know that this is a difficult concept to wrap your head around, however, rationalizing "levels" of dishonesty are just that—rationalizations.

You might ask, "Why did you continue if you knew that this behavior was not in rhythm with who you were?"

A great question!

It's a question that I couldn't have answered at that point in time.

If asked, I would have said something like:

"Get the fuck out of my way or you'll get run over on my way to the bank," or "What are you—some kind of a pussy? It's a dog-eat-dog world and I'm going to eat as many fucking dogs as I can in order to reach my goals!," or, "This is all I know —everybody else is trying to compete and this is what they are doing."

The list of rationalizations and misguided thinking patterns and habits goes on and on and on.

Believe me, there isn't a rationalization that you could utter that is going to work in your life.

I get it, I really do. I've been there, and I've done it a thousand times if I've done it once.

It will not work.

I didn't realize that I was lugging this baggage around like a steamer trunk full of negative energy. Have you heard of Pandora's box? The contents of that box are an infestation of termites within the house of "YOU."

Meeting the "Old" Me

I reconnected with an old friend over the past few months. He was one of my closest friends for the years when I worked in Manhattan, somebody that I spent a tremendous amount of time with. He had heard from a friend that had attended one of my speaking engagements with a group of business professionals in Fairfield, Connecticut and that my discussion was about the pain of depression, misguided behavior, and being honest about who you really are. Thankfully, the positive feedback that he received from his friend pushed him to pick up the phone and call me.

As I sat in a booth in the well-lit and chrome shining diner, I watched him cross the parking lot from his brand-new car. It had been five years since we had seen each other and at least 12 since we had had any meaningful discussion. In short, much time had passed since my friend and I had been friends.

My heart sank as I witnessed the "me" of time gone by. He had gained weight and his shoulders seemed bowed by the life he had chosen. He moved, in his nice suit, white shirt, and red tie, with the energy that says, "Shit, I'm exhausted and something's gotta give."

We embraced, initially, in the way that men tend to embrace, the handshake followed by a quick back slap and a "Hey, how ya doin?" Then, our souls remembered the unspoken importance of a connection that we once had 20 years ago, and the magic that can occur between two soul beings occurred, and we really hugged. It was a momentary acknowledgement of two men that had loved each other at a time in our lives when we were hurtling down our paths to self-destruction and didn't have the tools to be real with each other.

It was one of those moments in this physical life when you feel the healing chill of your soul's desire to connect in a real way with the other souls that we share the world with. That healing chill is something that happens when you are connected and present with yourself, and honoring it takes awareness and practice.

My friend sat across the black and white speckled table, omelets and buttered toast sat on the plates, hot coffee produced swirls of steam that encircled our cups, and he talked with me about his own battles with depression, lack of fulfillment from a highly successful career, and suicidal thoughts.

I thought to myself and later told him that I was sad that he and I had spent so much time together and neither of us ever said to the other, "You know, I'm depressed—I don't know why—but, I just don't get this world."

Admitting that kind of vulnerability is virtually impossible in our society, especially for men.

At the end of a long hunting trip a few thousand years ago, a hunter would return to his tent or cave with his kill and with all the cuts, bruises and blood-stained clothes and hands that go along with flaying and bleeding out fresh animal innards.

Out in the world of business suits, French cuffs, braces, Italian shoes, car services, and airplanes, you don't bring home blood-stained hands that are easy to wash in the local water source. You bring home a blood-stained energy rhythm that cannot be washed away in the cold running mountain water from the creek out back.

Those stains that coat your being are rubbed off on those that you love, it happens subconsciously and silently, and you don't even know that it is occurring.

I have two daughters who could feel my poor energy vibrations and soaked them in whenever I returned from a day at the office. They absorbed energy vibrations such as: fear, anxiety, aggression, anger, pain, loneliness, dishonesty, and greed.

They also absorbed energy vibrations such as the love and affection that I held deeply for each of them.

Unfortunately, the negative energy far outweighed the positive energy and the confusion of these opposing energies created a dramatic sense of fear and caution. This has resulted in my needing to rebuild their houses with me. Rebuild "our house," together, from the ground up. Basically, they developed a termite infestation from yours truly and they didn't even know it. Yes, children, as with everybody else, are on their own path of destiny. They will establish their own sources of termites and difficulties. I don't presume to believe that I am the sole source of their "issues," I am not that "god" arrogant.

However, I don't want to add to the karmic stuff that they are destined to deal with in their path through their own Universe.

Since they are my children and I have them in my daily life, this has become a practice for me, like journaling or brushing my teeth. Every single day, I am looking for ways to continue the rebuilding and am trying to heal their confusion around that energy flow. As I am now conscious of these energies, I can see how it has affected them and how it has shaped their own fears and interpersonal relationships with their friends and family.

Unlike a house with structural issues, this is not something that you can just go in and rip down and rebuild. You need to meet the child where the child is. This is important advice for any relationship that you might try to rebuild in your life. Everyone brings his or her own emotional stuff, good or bad, into every relationship interaction. Especially with children, it is critical to go slow and be consistent.

One of the best quotes I've read about the energy of positive vs. negative came from a simple kid born in a log cabin in Kentucky.

"When I do good, I feel good; when I do bad, I feel bad,

and that is my religion."

- Abraham Lincoln

When I was in Silver Hill, I met a young woman who was 19 years old and had been admitted for attempted suicide, bipolar disorder and cutting. She was intelligent, beautiful, and looked like the typical American teenager. After spending a few days in group therapy sessions with her and sharing meals and other social time, I started to see her as one of my daughters—only a few years older. And that is why, I believe, the Universe put her in my path in the common room at the hospital.

She was living in an affluent town in southwestern Connecticut, in a 7,000-square-foot house with her father and stepmother. She had everything that society says that we want—a new car, fancy clothes, a cell phone, a horse, money, a boyfriend and some other "stuff". She also had what society says you shouldn't want: a clear sense that she didn't want what she had. The more that she acquired, the less she wanted.

As I got to know Maria, we talked a lot about her dad and their relationship. She idolized her father, felt that he was there for her physically, to take care of her and to make sure that she was safe. But, as Maria talked with me about her dad, the man that she had come to love, a sadness came over her that was deep and dark. As it was happening, that sadness grabbed me by the head and smashed my face into the Formica table that we were eating our morning fruit at.

In those conversations with Maria, I had started to see the pain that I had caused my own children through my disconnection and the unintended consequences of my depressive episodes.

Maria was not seeking advice or asking me any questions, she was just removing feelings that had stalked her for years. As I looked at her, I wanted to fix it and tell her that her father was doing the best that he could with the limited tools he had. I wanted to apologize for him, and I wanted to apologize for "me."

Then, my shame and guilt kicked in and I just felt like shit as I looked at my own daughters' experience of the negative energy of my dishonesty, my excessive drinking, my time away from them to pursue money. Yes, I would tell myself that it was for them that I pursued that success, but kids don't need money, they need their parents to be themselves and provide love.

There are no accidents!

Maria had given me a prophetic gift that I wouldn't fully recognize for a couple of years and one that I will never forget.

It is important here to take a brief pause and talk about guilt. There can be no healing while guilt is present. Guilt is a termite. So, while I was experiencing some revelations while hearing Maria's thoughts about her father, I was in no way prepared to really heal, because guilt was kicking my ass up and down the hallway.

To drop guilt, it's important to understand that it is holding you back like a tether to the ego. It will stretch a bit as you try to pull away to freedom, but in the end, you will recoil back into the ego driven abyss. How to drop guilt? Let it go...literally, just let it go.

Letting Go Exercise

Grab a pencil or pen, hold it out in front of you as tight as you can—so tight that your knuckles turn red and then white from the lack of circulation. Squeeze it like you've never squeezed anything in your life. That's your guilt-driven feeling. Feel the strength of that grip, how your arm starts to shake a little and pay attention to the tingling moving up your arm toward your elbow. Really feel your way through that physical reaction to the grip on that object. Now, go to the less noticeable physical reactions; perspiration on your palm, increased heart beating, perhaps your breath is getting a little shortened. You are stressing your body to the point of discomfort. The physical stress will start to create emotional feelings of discomfort...embrace those feelings, sense them and notice what is happening so that you can recognize it later as it happens in life.

Squeeze tighter!

Now, close your eyes, gently breathe in and as you exhale, say, "I release you" and drop the pencil. Listen for the "tick-tick-tick" as it hits the ground.

That pencil was not helping you, it was creating distress, discomfort, and had you firmly rooted in where you were in that physical position.

It is the same with guilt. Drop it and listen for the "tick-tick-tick" as you release it and move to more productive thoughts and feelings. After you have done this several times, in some cases it will be more, in some cases less, you will recognize guilt as it is coming up and when you get present with your world, you won't find yourself reaching for that "guilt-pencil" anymore.

CHAPTER 16

SLEEPING IN THE CLOSET

I took my life, my relationship with the one person in my life that had given me nothing but love, and I threw a huge scud missile into the center of it.

Actually, I didn't throw it, I mounted it like Harry Potter's Nimbus 2000 and rode it into my living room, holding on as tight as I could while it exploded and spread carnage and body parts all over the house.

As you may have gathered in reading this far into my story, I believe in honesty, at every level, and in granular ways that you probably didn't think were important.

I have said, over and over again, "It all matters."

Everything that we do matters. The smallest gesture, phrase, feeling, look, expression—all of it. It all matters.

With that said, I do believe that there are "degrees" of dishonesty. While I believe now that even the smallest of degrees is destructive over time, I think that we all understand the difference of the consequences of telling someone that you weigh 200 pounds when you really weigh 230 pounds versus telling your partner that you were at the gym, when you were out at a bar throwing back shots of scotch and a few pints.

However, I believe that both situations are as destructive as the next. It all serves to create distance from our true selves, which creates distance between us and those we are here to share our intimate lives with.

My dishonesty was off the charts, and there is no barometer for the level of how dishonest I could be. Think cartoon thermometer where the red mercury blows through the top, shattering the glass and shooting up about 150 feet in the air. I had become so dishonest that I really didn't know where the truth fell or where the dishonesty started. That is the way that it is when you bullshit your way through your life.

That is the way of addiction and depression; being dishonest becomes a way of life. There is a familiar warmth in the personal disgust felt with each lie and each behavior that is counter to who you are. I believed with all that I was, that I deserved that disgust, that that was all I was suitable for, and it was punishment for shit that happened to me when I was a child, at a time when I had no control to make it stop. I owned that self-loathing, it was normal, and without it I felt as if I was undeserving of life. Without it—that would mean a life of happiness, and that was not an option for me.

A full 18 months after my attempted suicide, through my journey of self-analysis and reckoning, I was learning with each passing day that I was carrying around the infestation of termites that my dishonesty had created. The only way to exterminate those termites was to go in and release them to the world. It was time to finally eliminate the termites that were living in my foundation. Termites are a tricky plague, and as you go through one room, searching all of the beams and boards for signs of bugs, you will find one stray bug that you didn't think was a "big deal." It took me that long to face the fact that the only way that I was going to rid myself of all of these damn bugs was to put it all out there in the open and stomp on them one at a time.

I had decided on New Year's Eve of 2007, that I was never going to lie again, and more importantly, I was going to embrace the truth. To embrace everything that I am and that I feel, and that I think.

That was the toughest life decision that I had ever made and the most important. It was also something that I had dreaded for most of my life, as telling the truth was a completely foreign concept.

My dishonesty was well forged in a childhood growing up in a broken home, where my father would come and visit us on Saturdays. I found myself waiting at the front door or on the red brick stoop, just hoping that he would come again. Typically, he arrived several hours later than he said he would, only to be met by my mother's request for money to put food on the table. On many days, my father would lose his patience and storm out the nearest door, only to disappear until the following weekend. The sound of the rear screen door of our house slamming against the wood frame was a haunting reminder of those moments when the reality of unhappiness, rage, and some semblance of love would leave the building.

I had learned to keep things nice and happy, always. So, the truth wasn't a possibility, the only possibility was doing and saying whatever was necessary to keep everybody happy and pleasant.

Through my talk therapy sessions, the impact of being a liar was becoming clear to me. I had been telling my deepest secrets to another person, peeling back the layers of the onion that was my soul, to try and find who I was beneath the layers of shit that I had covered "me" up with. With each new layer, I uncovered another area that was infested with termites, and as painful as it was, it felt cathartic. I was jolted into reality by looking at the impact that my lies were having on others.

I had to tell the truth despite the consequences. I accepted the fact that the outcome was not my responsibility. The only responsibility I had was to be honest and loving. I could not control or manipulate another person's reaction to my honesty, that was on them.

The most important piece of being dishonest, especially within the context of a relationship with a significant other, is that it takes the other person's power away. Life is a conglomeration of the choices that we make in our lives. If you are making choices without the full scope of information available to you, you are operating at a significant disadvantage. My wife had made many decisions in the course of being in a relationship with me. Those decisions were based on what she thought was a certain set of facts as presented to her. Her decisions would have been significantly different had she known all that she needed and deserved to know.

As a liar, I was seeking control of the outcome. That manipulation is where the destruction begins, and where taking another's power to decide is like stealing a piece of their soul.

You might read that and say, "Dude, we all learn when we're in kindergarten that lying is wrong and you shouldn't do it."

As I said earlier, there are degrees of dishonesty, but all dishonesty, no matter how benign you might feel that it is, is as destructive as another. Set aside the judgment and look honestly at your own behavior and understand that if you tell one lie, to anyone, it will echo throughout your life in ways that you cannot possibly control.

Again, it all matters.

Here's a simple and fictional illustration of this concept. You're on your way home from work on a beautiful sunny Thursday afternoon when you get a phone call from a buddy who says, "Dude, I'm sitting at Joe's Bar, and I'm drinking the tallest, coldest beer I've ever had. You gotta come by."

You know that your wife is home with the kids, and she's expecting you by 6:30 pm. But, it's only 4:30 pm because you left the office early—so, you've got a two-hour cushion—plenty of time to down a couple brews with your best friend, maybe a chicken wing or two—chew some gum to freshen your breath and you're home on time. Shit, you earned that beer with your friend, you're a man, you're the king of your castle, you deserve it. You text your wife and tell her that you're finishing up some stuff at the office and you'll be on time. She writes back, "Thanks, I love you." Man, this plan is getting better all the time.

You show up at Joe's and the place is just starting to hop with a great Thursday happy hour, guys with suits on, their ties hanging loose to the second button on their now rumpled Egyptian cotton shirts, women in skirts and heels with freshly applied makeup. There's your buddy sitting at the bar and he's already gotten you a beer and, what's that, a shot? Sure! You get the picture.

You high-five your buddy and snap towels with him, and at 6:15 pm, amble across the parking lot to your car, admiring your life, the life that you are the master of. That's the alcohol coursing through your veins, feeding your ego about how cool you are. Ten minutes later you pull into your driveway, walk into the house, the kids run to you and love and hugs are shared all around. You give your wife a kiss and a hug. It's all good.

Three weeks later, you're sitting in your office at 10:00 in the morning and you pick up your phone as it rings. It's your lovely wife calling you after her Pilates class.

"I just had my 8:30 class and I ran into Janice, we hadn't seen each other for a while and stopped to chat and catch up for a bit."

"Cool."

"She was telling me about how she heard that our vacation to the shore was so much fun and that our house renovation was going so well."

"How'd she hear that—man, the rumor mill in town is such a pain in the ass. Don't these people have anything better to do?"

"She said that she heard it from you—at Joe's Bar and Grill—two Thursdays ago!"

You: "Yeah, I stopped in there to use the bathroom and she was getting sloshed at the bar..."

Ok, so you've now lied again and you're in complete panic mode. Your veins are now filled with cortisol which is our body's protection against imminent danger. It is a chemical that is released by the adrenal gland in response to stress. There are lots of physiological effects of cortisol secretion and it can be a good thing in the right situation. However, your body doesn't know the difference between stress responses, like, is this a life-threatening situation or is this something that I've created from being a bullshit artist? The results are the same. There are no degrees of dishonesty that your body is sorting through to select the appropriate response.

It's all the same and it all matters.

Your blood pressure has elevated, your immune system has been compromised, your insulin levels have increased, in short, you are no longer the physical being that you were before the phone rang at 10:00 am.

"Really? She said that you talked for an hour or so and then you had to leave to get home by 6:30—right after one more shot. She said that you were so funny."

Your ego is now in full control of your thoughts and words.

"You know what? I'm working my ass off and if I want to stop at the local pub and have a beer with my buddy, I think I deserve that—I mean, really, what am I—a child? I don't need your permission every time I want to take a leak...."

You and your wife have just entered the abyss that is the ego-driven relationship argument. Once you step into that abyss, it is difficult to meander your way back to reality and it can be painful. That's just the 10% of the iceberg that is floating above the sea's surface; the 90% that you cannot see is where the biggest damage is happening.

You both know that you are lying, and you're continuing to disrespect her as you try to dance your way

171

through a myriad of stories, preventing a real connection in the future. Once that trust has been compromised, it is impossible for you both to share in the connection that your soul is seeking on the trip in this physical world. The wedge that has been created will exist between you forever, until you face your wife and say something like this:

"You know, I am sorry for lying to you. I was at Joe's—I didn't want you to think that I was blowing off my responsibilities as a husband and father by choosing to go there instead of coming home early. I felt guilty about it and thought that you'd be pissed off at me. There is a part of me that needs to have friendships outside of our family—like my relationship with Steve, and that's why I met him for a beer."

That will be the start of the honesty that needs to exist. Very simple and honest communication that isn't tainted by fear, guilt, shame, bravado and a desire to have a secretive approach to life.

Here is what they don't teach you when you get married: your spouse loves you, and because of that love, he or she wants you to be happy in your life. So if you want something that will bring you happiness, they will want that for you. As with trying to manipulate my parents by keeping things even-keeled, I chose the same approach with my wife and the other relationships in my life.

Now, if your need for something is destructive to the relationship, then he or she might choose not to be in that relationship. That is their choice to make; it is not your choice to control the information that will lead them to a choice.

Make sense?

The upgrade to the above illustration would have been to let your partner know that you were on your way home early and your buddy called and you're going to meet him for a beer or two. Again, if that doesn't work for your partner, the conversation will go where it needs to go, but now you both have all of the information you need to have an open discussion and make a decision.

The days that followed my decision to open the flood gates of honesty were like riding the world's largest and fastest roller coaster, without being strapped into your seat. The questions became the "click-click" ascent up to the peaks—you know, that anxiety-ridden time right before you know that the cars are going to race straight down. The answers were the descents. When you're not strapped in, those descents can be harrowing and you really don't have any idea how you're possibly going to survive. This feeling was made more difficult for me because I realized that my wife wasn't strapped in on the first race down from the peak of the ride to the trough below. I had to keep her from flying off the ride onto the concrete pathways below, knowing that I was the reason why she was on the ride in the first place.

When you finally decide that honesty is how you choose to live, you also have to accept that the people you are being honest with have the ability to make their own choices. All you can do is put yourself out there, what they choose to do with it is their business.

Living with someone that is deeply depressed over a long period of time is like living with an alcoholic or a drug addict. It is an addiction in many ways.

My wife sacrificed a lot by sticking with me and my lack of functionality. She had faith that I was with her and that I was a cooperative partner in our relationship.

When you look into your partner's eyes and say, "Despite having you in my life, I have wanted to kill myself for much of the duration of our relationship," the pain and suffering that can ensue is incredibly intense. It is the ultimate betrayal of trust to tell someone that despite your relationship and love, that you have obsessed about suicide for 30 years. It's a slap in the face, at best. At worst, it is a level of dishonesty that cannot be explained, and rightly so.

Chris met my statement with a strong sense of compassion and sadness for the pain that I had endured in my life. As I said, all you can do is be honest and then make space for the other person's needs.

In our case, my wife's choice was clearly a simple one and she said, "Jim, now that you are safe from harming yourself, I cannot put myself at risk any longer and while I love you, you need to pack your stuff and we need to move on separately and not as a couple."

It seemed straightforward to both of us.

However, when you have created a 20-year life together, including having three additional lives that have been interwoven into the fabric that has become our world, those decisions are not as cut and dry.

This was occurring within our relationship, while we were in therapy, separately and together, and I must say here that without the help of a very objective third party, an amazing professional therapist that employed a very holistic approach to our work, we never would have made it through the first day. My best advice to anyone is to find somebody that can work with you, both of you, to navigate the perils and the joys of honesty. This is where the real work occurred, the private moments of fear, the snot-gushing and red swollen eyes that accompanied our bodies contorting on the floor in heaps of sorrow and pain.

It is not for those that are weak in spirit or lack the desired goal of peace and grace.

My wife and I mutually decided to separate from our relationship as a first step to deciding where to go in the long term. We both understood that we were on a path, walking through a forest that was completely overgrown with bramble, thorns, insanely thick branching, and some wild fucking animals that were trying to eat us with every step.

The bottom line is that we didn't know where we would end up, and that was a complete letting go and letting God. Having faith in some force that the Universe would provide and deliver us to where we needed to be.

We created a separation within our home to try and minimize the negative impact that event would have on our children. That separation required some logistical as well as emotional management. We needed physical space that provided for some alone time and we also needed time to take breaks or time-outs from the raw conversations that we were having. The first thing that we did was to create the "CZ"—the Couple's Zone, which was our private space that our kids could not go into—unless the house was burning down.

In our home, the largest bedroom suite consists of three separate rooms and two walk-in closets. Chris took the room where our bed is and I was to take the other room where we had a good-sized daybed. This was not out of punishment; it just seemed like the right way to divide up the space. Additionally, we agreed that we would switch if I needed to sleep in the bed for a few nights. The third room was the bathroom, which we just used as needed.

I was laying on the daybed one night staring at the ceiling trying to calm my heart from jumping through my chest and splattering all over the eggshell white paint, and I got up and walked into the closet off the bathroom. I stood there looking at the racks of clothes; a dozen business suits, 30 well-starched shirts, 50 pairs of shoes, both of ours, and dozens of dresses in every color imaginable, and I realized that the space was incredibly cozy. It just looked warm and safe.

I walked down the hall, tiptoeing my way across the creaky oak flooring so I wouldn't wake the kids and the dogs, and grabbed every blanket that was folded and stuffed in the hallway linen closet. I then made my way back to the bedroom closet, covered the brown Berber carpet with a fluffy pile of blankets and pillows, and laid down. The closet was small and felt like a cocoon of safety. I could hear Chris behind all of her beautiful dresses, on the other side of the wall, sobbing uncontrollably.

I started to cry as I realized what I had created came down on me like hot asphalt pouring out of the back of a yellow D.O.T. truck.

It had been three days since I started sleeping alone on the daybed and for the first time that week, I slept through the night.

The closet became my space and so I made it homier with each passing day. I rolled out two yoga mats under the blankets for some needed firmness and plugged in a small reading lamp. Lastly, I surrounded my makeshift bed with a dozen books. A few of those books became my reference pieces for healing myself and for dissecting the mess that my marital relationship had become. Two books, *Keeping The Love You Find* and *Getting The Love You Want*, by Harville Hendrix, became my bibles.

Dr. Hendrix outlines relationship creation and nurturing using the intellectual understanding of what he calls Imago Theory. The Imago Theory is based on the belief and understanding that, in relationships, whether a partner or some other close connection, we are attracted to people who force us to face our past experiences. The "work" that we need to do to become fully evolved beings in this experience. I read the first 20 pages of Hendrix's words at midnight on the fourth night in my closet. When I put the book down, the sun was shining through the small window in the corner of my hovel, and I was only about halfway through the few hundred pages of the whole book.

As I read each page, I reread it several times. It was as if Dr. Hendrix had written this book for my wife and me, like he was in my closet lecturing me on the confrontation, with my father's ability to make me feel like complete shit.

That morning, after I folded my blankets and rolled up the yoga mats, I actually felt that we would survive the post-scud missile carnage. I had hoped that my instinct about telling the truth had been correct and that despite the initial pain, we would be far better off connecting in real ways.

As I said, there were two of us living through this. While I was feeling a little better that morning, Chris was firmly ensconced in the position that I should be flailed and skinned alive in the town square.

You don't realize how much negative messaging we receive in our daily lives around the relationship that exists between a husband and wife. Because we were battling for our lives as a couple, we were extremely sensitive to that messaging, and it was everywhere.

Every time we made a little progress, our egos would kick in and tell us to fight back, tell Chris that I was never going to be worth trusting, and that my suicidal tendencies would resurface, and then we would be back at ground zero again. Again, it was a miserable roller coaster ride, but the work had to be done in order to break through.

CHAPTER 17

GOING DEEPER

Prior to our separation, we had booked a trip to a favorite romantic resort on the west coast of Florida. The trip was booked and paid for and would go to waste if we didn't use it. At some point in the healing process, we decided that we needed to get away from our lives for even a few days and we took a major risk and got on the plane together to Ft. Lauderdale, Florida.

It was a huge risk because a visit to a place where we had shared some special times together during periods of time when I was not being honest, or when I was extremely depressed and hiding my suicidal tendencies, would certainly dredge up memories. Facing those memories and all the questions that ensued about what was real and what wasn't could completely derail the entire situation.

We spent four days walking on the beach, laying on large poolside outdoor beds, and listening to music on our iPods, each song carrying some special message about what our lives are all about. Oh, yeah, and sobbing together.

It was raw and incredibly intense.

We completely immersed ourselves in the "Jim and Chris" that met in 1985 and we stared into the teeth of the dragon, holding each others hands in a show of solidarity and connection that said, "Don't fuck with us, we are one, and we will fight for what we have built, despite any demons that have arisen."

Despite all the anguish, pain, and dishonesty, we discovered that we had a strong foundation of love. We still loved each other and despite not knowing where we were headed as a couple, we knew that our love for each other was a good start.

On that trip, Chris shared a visual that would serve as a powerful metaphor for my understanding of what she was going through. To paraphrase: "I feel like we have been walking in a forest together for years, you carrying me on your back at times, but, when you get sick and disappear and isolate yourself, you put me down on the forest bed and tell me, 'Stay here, I'll be right back.' And, most of the time, you just put me down and don't say anything—you just leave me there—in the dark, not knowing where I am or what you're doing. I have no idea when you're coming back and I'm left to fight off all kinds of wild animals and nature's fury, by myself. To fight and protect myself and our life. I want to be carried through the forest, never put down, I want to feel safe, I need to know that I am safe and that you are not going to leave me alone in the forest, ever again. I need you to carry me, carry all of us, to safety on the other side of the forest, only then, will I know that this is real. I am too tired to do anymore carrying or fighting off the animals, you need to do the fighting now."

On the plane, returning from this healing trip together, I wrote the following to my wife and myself.

Contract of Commitments
1/26/08

I. **Honesty:** I vow to be honest about feelings, what I want and need to do, where I am going and where I have been.

II. **Truth:** I vow to be true to my feelings and communicate what those are and to be honest about the truth.

III. **Faith:** I vow to be faithful to you, to me, and to "the couple." This is not only faithful to the physical part of the commitment, this is a faithful commitment to you as a woman that includes respectful talk and intention to that "womanly" spirit.

IV. **Honor:** I will honor you and me, and will stay with myself. If I feel that I am "not Jim" at any time during the day, I vow to contact one of my guides to get back to me.

V. **Real:** I vow to be real.

VI. **Health:** I vow to take care of and respect my body, to continue to live a healthy lifestyle.

VII. **Safe:** I vow to live a life that will give you a feeling of safety and security.

VIII. **Self:** I vow to be myself, if I feel "not Jim" coming forward, I will be conscious of that which is not me and bring me back.

IX. **Intention:** I will live a life of intention to be a husband, friend, father, and a strong and confident soul.

X. **Communication:** I will keep myself open to speaking my feelings and to listen to your feelings, and to discussing how those impact our needs.

XI. **Present:** I vow to be present and in the current moment.

XII. **Exits:** I will block my exits.

XIII. **Growth:** I will grow, and as I grow, I will leave myself open to all possibilities and will share my feelings with you so that growth can be shared, if possible. My additional commitments will be additive to this initial draft and as I develop new commitments I will share them as part of that growth.

XIV. **Needs:** I have a need for you to read this and ask any questions, seek clarification, and acknowledge that you are receiving this gift of love.

XV. I have a need for you to keep this and refer me to specific areas for work and improvement as we live our lives.

Signed..... "your loving spiritual match"

I wrote these commitments from the most honest place that I have ever been in, and I own them. I feel strong and confident when I look at this expression of who I am and who I want to be. It is the road map for the "who" I choose to live.

After a couple of years of hard work, my wife has forgiven me for putting her in danger. We continue to work intensely and with intent to achieve a deep level of understanding of each other's deepest beings and release the schmutz.

However, forgiveness and trust are two completely different things and the latter is something that I will always strive to earn.

Depression can lead to addictive behaviors and the demons of addiction are strong forces that weasel their way back into the fabric of our daily lives. If we didn't have children, Chris would have left or dislodged me from her world a long time ago. This would have been unfortunate, because as Dr. Hendrix has taught me, Imago shows us that we would repeat these relationship patterns again until they are healed.

When you add children into a relationship, things are changed because of the responsibility of creating a life for these people that were not given a choice of which parents they were to be living with on this journey. Through no fault of their own, they received me as their father, an unfortunate result in some ways, a very fortunate result in others. As parents, we have had to walk the fine line of doing the "right" thing for our children while trying to maintain our own sanity and self-respect.

One of those things that are difficult to get past is our own ability to beat ourselves up with feelings of guilt. We were both raised as Roman Catholic. The Roman Catholic Church has the market cornered on creating guilt and shame. You know, the whole God will punish you and you'll go to hell thing. I find the church to be too structured and limiting for the life that I choose to live. I find it far too judgmental and limited in belief, and the approach to punishment and reward is so dark ages. However, the faith and community of being a member of a larger entity can be a great safety zone for many people.

Here is a great quote about guilt that I think outlines it well:

"All blame (and therefore, guilt) is a waste of time. No matter how much fault you find with another, and regardless of how much you blame him, it will not change you. The only thing blame does is to keep the focus off you when you are looking for external reasons to explain your unhappiness or frustration. You may succeed in making another feel guilty about something by blaming him, but you won't succeed in changing whatever it is about you that is making you unhappy."
- Wayne Dyer

The thing about living in honesty and eliminating termites is that you must be vigilant in your intention. Old habits die hard. I find myself, at times, actually listening to words as they leave my mouth and thinking, *Wait a second big man, that's simply not true.* At those moments, I have found that it is easy to apologize to the person I am talking to and explain that what I just said isn't true. That feeling of immediate release of an untruth is the working out of an emotional muscle that I didn't know that I had and that has gotten stronger with each passing day.

Living honestly and eliminating those termites is not a matter of what you say, it is driven by how you live and the choices that you make about everything that your life is.

"The best sermon is a good example."
-Benjamin Franklin

This is the building of the house that you are choosing to live in. Choices that include your job/career, your house, nutrition, exercise routines, the city you live in, who you live with, what you drive, the clothes you wear, everything that you do, it all matters, and it is a reflection of whether you are living within your soul's rhythm. In the next chapter, I will talk about the changes that I needed to make in my life so that I could live honestly within my rhythm as a person and manage the disease of my depression.

My Daughters & Their Reckoning

In addition to the work that my wife and I have done with respect to our relationship, I have also had to work intensely and with intent on reconnecting the damaged connections with my children. My dishonesty and negative energy had affected them since birth and my attempted suicide drove a tremendous wedge of distrust and fear between us. This was especially true for my daughters, because Ashley and Lyndsay were 12 and 10 when I went into the hospital.

I caution you to be very careful about how you communicate with your children around mental health issues, because after all, they are children and are not emotionally developed enough to understand. You really need a professional support system that has the expertise to work with you and your children in developing a solid road map for handling these very serious issues. I was blessed to be working with such a person and it was a gift that the Universe provided me at a time when I really needed it. The process was a three-year journey and culminated in an opportunity for me to ask for and receive forgiveness from my girls in a way that had them feeling safe and secure.

On a summer weekend, the three of us traveled to Monhegan Island, Maine, to participate in a family therapy retreat. The retreat was created and managed by our family's therapist, who had a strong background and understanding of what we were all living through. She also has had many years of experience working with teens, adults with depression, and holistic family issues. One of the reasons for the timing of this program was that my oldest daughter was getting ready to go to college and we felt that this healing needed to happen before she left to go out into the world. Therapeutically, it was a risk—albeit a calculated one.

Monhegan is a special place, located 10 miles off mainland Maine. It has a small population of full-time residents and is only 4.5 square miles in area. It is secluded and the kind of place where you go to connect with nature in a way that you would be hard pressed to do in many places. The hiking trails that traverse the island are circuitous and provide opportunities for Atlantic Ocean vistas that are just breathtaking.

This was a very private and intimate event for all of us and I will not divulge the intimate details of the therapeutic event that occurred, after all, this is not just about me. However, I will share the gift that my daughters gave me on that four-day trip and some insight that I gained that is pertinent to the extermination of termites.

On the second day on the island, the sun was shining through the large colonial saltbox windows as we sat in an old one-room schoolhouse, and the wind was gently flowing in from the ocean about 100 yards down a rocky crag. There were 11 of us attending this very carefully designed retreat and we were sitting in a circle around a symbolic "fire" of connection.

The request from the moderator was simple, "Please share why you are here, what you hope to gain from the next few days, and anything else that you would like to share with the group."

A few people spoke and it was evident that we were all there to put in the work necessary to accomplish our individual goals. The environment was safe and nurturing and that energy permeated through the participants, which allowed for us all to feel open.

I tearfully and openly shared with the group. "A few years ago, I was completely consumed by a depressive episode that I couldn't control and I wanted to eliminate myself from my family's world so that I wouldn't continue to cause damage to them all—especially to my daughters who were living with a father who was not a good example of the kind of man that I want to see them partner with in their lives. I didn't want to be their model for the partners that they choose to share their world with in the future. I am here to apologize to my daughters for living such a disconnected life and to try and heal that disconnection."

I felt relieved to have been able to be so honest with these people, especially my daughters. It was the first time that I really had a chance to explain to them that I was vulnerable, afraid, and yet courageous enough to let them know that I was working with every ounce of my being to live a better life, for and with them.

As I have said previously, all that you are responsible for is your own honesty about what you feel. You cannot be responsible for and have absolutely no control over what others will feel about what you are sharing with them. That is part of letting go and realizing that you cannot control anything or anybody. At the end, everyone will be better able to attain a real and loving connection, one that includes the nonjudgmental love that our souls crave.

With that said, I was not prepared for what my daughters said, one after another, to this intimate gathering of people trying to learn and evolve. With tremendous intention, strength, and the impact of any spiritual prophet that I have ever read, they each shared their innermost fears, pains and anger! Lots of anger. I was both proud and devastated at the same time.

Here's a summary of their combined sharing with the group: "When my dad went into the hospital I was scared, really scared that he was sick and that he wasn't coming home. When I understood why he was in the hospital I got really pissed that he would leave us—then I got mad when I realized that I had inherited his depression. I have been sad in my life too—uncontrollably sad—and I didn't know that it was something that could be hereditary. It would have been helpful to know that. I don't think that I'll ever trust him again. I don't think I'll ever trust anybody—ever again. He told us that he loved us—how can you love somebody and then die by suicide —that's gotta be the most selfish thing that anybody could do. I hated my father for putting us through this. I still don't think that this can ever be explained."

The brutally honest and heartfelt feedback continued for what seemed like three hours. It was actually only about three or four minutes for each of them.

My ego was screaming to be heard, to defend, to fight back, to demand respect and to scold.

My skin was itchy, my stomach was in severe pain and my palms were sweating profusely. It was all happening at the same time, all of the familiar physical signs of the anxiety that I lived for so many years. I felt as if I was going to pass out right there on the oak floor.

I heard the voice of Thich Nhat Hanh from a meditation series that had become a useful tool in managing my anxiety and depression, and in helping me to stay as present as possible.

"Breathing in - I know that I am breathing in -
Breathing out - I know that I am breathing out."
-Thich Nhat Hanh

Then, I was brought back to my days in the hospital when we met with a group of survivors, children whose parents had suicided. The room of 24 patients in a semi-circle, sitting on couches, easy chairs, backwards on cafeteria style seats and on the floor—all listening with rapt attention as the four people talked of their mothers and fathers who had taken their lives. One of the gentlemen struck me with the force of a hurricane when he spoke of his father "checking out," as he put it. He spoke of his father's aftershave, his dutiful involvement in World War II, his devotion to his wife and children, the uncontrolled drinking, how he smelled after he smoked a cigarette while working on an old Chevy Camaro in the garage behind the house, and how, when his father died, he couldn't go near the Camaro and they ultimately gave the car away to get it out of their lives. It was too painful a memory. He shared intimate and finite details of his father, a man that he came to hate through the years that followed his death. A man that he spent a lot of time not respecting, not understanding, yet, never forgetting.

He said that his dad had been dead for over 40 years!

This guy was in his 60s and the pain was as fresh as it had been the day after it happened. That was the message that this very helpful group was delivering, from people that had lived what my children could have lived. The pain never ends, the questions persist forever, and the feelings of loss continue until your last breath.

I swallowed hard as my youngest daughter echoed her sister's feelings, but with her own take on how it affected her. She was eloquent, concise, and very much afraid of what could have happened and whether it would happen again.

My job during this session was to be present to hear it all and to open my heart enough to provide as much space for whatever it was that they needed to say.

All that I could muster when they were finished was, "I hear you and thank you."

That night, with the windows open to the ocean breeze, I didn't sleep much as I lay thinking about what I had created for my children. I cried for hours that night, eventually falling asleep out of pure emotional exhaustion.

The next morning, after a check-in with the entire group, the three of us set out to hike around the island. The trails are well marked and provide some intermediate level hiking from ocean front rock covered beaches to rocky precipices that disappear into the clouds which hover over the evergreens that overlook the blue Atlantic.

We thought that it would be a one-hour walk around this very small island that is nothing more than a dot off the coast of Maine. Two and a half hours into our exploration, we had only made it about half-way around the island. We decided to take a rest on a beach that was little more than a 50 foot expanse of rocks that lay there as the ocean pounded incessantly onto the land. We sat on a large flat black slab of something that looked like it had landed there from outer space after an asteroid exploded.

It was a moment that I had been working toward since I was released from the hospital and an opportunity that had been created by their opening up the night before. I started to cry uncontrollably as I told my daughters what they had waited three years to hear.

"I want to thank you for sharing yourselves with me yesterday, I had no idea how you felt. I want you both to know that I am so sorry that I squandered our love and that I disrespected each of you by wanting to leave this world. I really thought that you would be better off not having me around. I believed with all that I was that you would stop suffering if I left. I am sorry for your pain, I understand your anger, and I hope that we can work together to help us all heal. Lastly, at some point, when you feel that you can do it, I would like your forgiveness. I am human just like you and I make mistakes. This was a huge mistake and I will need your forgiveness to get to the place of peace that we all want."

They sat quietly for some time as we watched some seagulls forage for clams and crabs in the shallow tide pools that had formed in and around the rocks.

My oldest daughter spoke first, with the amazing confidence of someone that knows exactly how she feels.

"Dad, I forgive you."

My youngest, as a follow up to her sister, said, "I still have some anger and some fear, but I understand how painful your life has been at times and I forgive you too."

This was another victory for truth and honesty, another step toward peace, and a deep connection with people that I had deeply hurt.

We talked on "rock beach" for another 20 minutes picking up some cool rocks that we could bring home to make some cairns and to have as memories of this day, which was a rebirth for a father and his girls.

I still carry one of those rocks around in my pocket with me on most days to serve as a touchstone for who I strive to be.

The three of us were able to live this gift of connection, unlike the relationship that I experienced with my parents, especially my father. Neither of us were equipped to have the connection that was needed to experience a soul healing. It took my experiences to break the cycle of disconnection.

That is a glimpse into the extermination of the termites that existed within my marital and family relationships. That was, by far, the largest infestation that existed in my world and it has taken years to clean it all out.

My "life house" was infested in every room and so I have had to kill termites and fumigate the rest of it. This fumigation includes lots of people that I have interacted with over the years: family, friends, and casual connections. I have done my best to approach these relationships with the intention of requesting forgiveness and clearing the way for honest connection. Again, all I can do is my part. I cannot control what others might feel or not feel and some of those relationships remain distant. You have to meet people where they are and hope for the best outcome.

CHAPTER 18

SELF-FORGIVENESS MUST BE A CONSCIOUS GIFT

Of all the work that I have done in trying to recapture the real me, to rescue the child that lives inside, and really get to the core of who I am, forgiveness is the toughest piece I have had to face. It requires muscles, emotional and mental, that society just doesn't honor enough, and for me, these are muscles that were completely atrophied.

Webster's definition of "atrophy": "Decrease in size or wasting away of a body part or tissue; also: arrested development or loss of a part or organ incidental to the normal development or life of an animal or plant."

This is the perfect description of my personal emotional "muscles" and the arrested development of those muscles since childhood.

I have been asked by many people how I have been able to get past my traumas, my emotional distance, and the abuse that I rendered on myself, my wife, my family, and friends. The best description that I have come up with is...

Forgiveness is really fucking hard.

There is no other way to say it that would effectively provide the enormity of the task of letting yourself accept that you were victimized. As a result, you acted out in ways that were unhealthy. You did, and you made choices, some consciously and some unconsciously, that were stupid, uncaring, selfish, boorish, negative, irresponsible, dangerous, and generally "not you." I don't mean this to say that I "wasn't there" in those experiences and so, they are excused. What I am saying is that I was there, I acknowledge my behavior and I understand that others mistreated me. However, in my conscious child-self, that is not the behavior of my soul being or the soul beings of others.

I created defensive walls and it was the "not me" that I allowed to consume my actions, choices and general outward being for the world to interact with.

At an early age, I trained myself to self-blame. That lack of compassion begins at an early age when we are children, and we think that we are responsible for everything that happens to us. I personally carried that blame until I was almost 44 years old! I was a child, I was innocent, I couldn't say "no," or "you're crazy," or "I'm moving out." You don't get that option as a child.

So, instead, what do we do? We feed the monster that continues to shame us, and we continue to self-judge so that we remain stuck in those feelings of self-loathing and self-doubt that have plagued us from our early childhood. It is so important to take responsibility without the guilt and shame that we have become so accustomed to. This chapter is about owning those feelings, honoring the events that created them, facing the choices that we have made, and moving through it all, which starts with self-forgiveness.

One of the most difficult tasks of healing yourself in this life is allowing yourself the gift of forgiveness.

The goal is to get to a place where you can let go of the judgment you carry about yourself and just give yourself a break. For me, I can forgive anyone just about anything, and I have. However, when it comes to me—no frickin' way. I have struggled with letting go of the guilt and self-punishment. It is a habit that is so comfortable that I wear it like an old ugly stretched out sweater, but it keeps me warm and brings me back to days of old.

> *"You have to grow from the inside out. None can teach you, none can make you spiritual. There is no other teacher but your own soul."*
> - Swami Vivekanandra (1890)

When it comes to habits, we go to the things that we have become comfortable with, things in our toy box of where we go when we are children. It doesn't matter whether those things are positive or negative; they just become those habitual things that we do.

One of the best visuals that I have been given over the years is that of the mental index card catalog that rests in the back of my head. When an event triggers a specific feeling, the feeling has been cataloged as a specific reaction, for example, card number 15.

So, let's say card number 15 is fear of abandonment.

When something happens in life, it doesn't matter who is involved, where it occurs, why, or the impetus, the triggered feeling is fear. I reach into my head, and pull out card number 15, and it has been mapped in my body as "get defensive, be irritable, be nasty, and be afraid."

The catalog has only 20 or 30 cards in it, and there are a thousand different things that could and do happen to trigger a specific card. I have learned that the reactions are limited, and it is interesting that the causes are infinite. Also, as I have seen over the past several years of being present and in observing others, I can see that all of our card catalogs are pretty much the same. I will expand on the concept of "remapping" your behavioral responses later on in the book.

As you have probably figured out by now, my wife is an absolute gift from the Universe, a saint that is walking the earth. I don't mean this in the way that many people use the term "saint." I think that the term has been overused and it has become a description that lends itself to the "niceness" of someone.

I don't mean it in that way.

I mean it in the literal sense of the word. I believe that she was sent to this physical experience as a saint that has been assigned to help me heal. I believe that our souls made a deal or pact of healing on another plane and we are here to fulfill that deal for each other.

As we have learned, ironically, I have been sent here to be her saint and to help her heal. Yes, believe it or not, my purpose is to help her heal as well. This speaks to the Imago relationship work that I mentioned in a previous chapter.

The reality is that now that I have become a more present and functionally positive force in her life, she has been given the "green light" to be weaker and learn about her own needs for healing. One of the habits that we created in our relationship together is that I was always the identified patient and the "needy" one. Now that I am healing, my wife has been able to let herself go and start to experience her own issues, shortcomings, emotional trauma, etc...

Ask and the Universe Delivers

As we have gone through this incredibly difficult journey together, it was imperative for her to forgive me my trespasses. When we started the dissection of our relationship, we weren't sure whether we would survive the process as a couple and we just knew that the process would take us down a path, and we didn't know where that path would take us. It has been a path with many twists and turns and we've even had to lay a few new bricks to create a completely different path to walk on.

So, whether we were to stay together or not, the fact remained that in order for Chris to get through her own healing, she needed to forgive me.

Asking for forgiveness was very painful and very difficult for me. I hurt the one person in my life that only gave me love and support through the entire duration of our relationship. The "not knowing" of whether we would or could survive this healing continues to be a work in progress, but, the only way to truly experience the closeness of a soulmate connection is just to be completely honest about anything and everything. Allowing your partner the space that he/she needs to be completely honest will require forgiveness, unconditionally.

Think about a child that has just done the unthinkable. For example, they have taken a permanent marker and ran the entire length of your home covering the new wallpaper with a thick black line of freshly smelling and permanent ink.

Holy shit!

Well, what do you do? You might yell a little, you might stomp and fret, shake your head like a wild animal that doesn't know what to do with the energy that is flowing through every fiber of its being. You might call your spouse and rant and rave about all the stress that you have to endure. The thing is, you just have this negative energy running through you, and you think you might explode.

Ultimately, no matter how bad what your child has done, you will forgive them.

Right?

That's what we do, we love them, regardless of the poor choices or mistakes they have made. That is the degree of forgiveness that you need to seek with your partner, spouse, and eventually yourself.

All of my children were left with an incredible sense of fear, because the life that they had known just simply vanished. However, at 12 years old, Ashley was the one that really knew the details of what was happening around her. It was as if she was watching the house burn down from the street and she was helpless to move or call out. She was hit with the fear that everything that had been presented to her about her world was a complete and utter lie.

Over the next decade of work and healing, one of the areas that I had chosen to spend much energy and love was with the relationships that I had broken with my children. It took years for me to re-build their trust and to establish myself as the father that would protect and love them for all the days that we are on this earth together.

The first step in asking for forgiveness is communication. Once you have communicated your feelings about something, asking for forgiveness is easy!

I would like to share a letter with you, a letter that I have written to my oldest daughter, the one that was most aware of what was happening on the day that I tried to commit suicide. I am providing it to you to give you a sense of the level of communication, love, and understanding that must exist for a fundamental level of trust to exist.

February 2011

Dear Ashley,

I am writing to make a request. Before I do that, I need to provide a little background and insight into why I am making this request, not with the hope that it will provide you with the impetus to say yes, but, more, to provide you with the presence and caring with which I am making this request. It has been 10 years since I ran the NY Marathon, for the second time, and I am now prepared to run it again with you in nine short months. You see, I know the physical and mental commitment to running 26.2 miles, and there is something that you haven't heard me discuss and I really want to share it with you. When I ran the race in November of 2001, the country was still numb from the terrorist attacks on our world, and New York City was the central image for all the hatred that our attackers had for the US and its residents. Walking through Ground Zero, the neighborhood where I worked for years, was extremely upsetting and provided me with a lot of incentive to run the race as a metaphor for toughness, honor, a memorial for friends lost, and for being a proud American. The theme for the race was actually "United We Run."

What I have come to understand about my running and the reason why I stopped running for a few years is that I was actually running away from myself. While I do have some great memories of the two marathons that I ran, especially the 2001 race, because of the United We Run experience following the 9/11 attacks, living an examined life has shown me that my running was not me running with me, for me, and as a fulfilling experience. I ran to "run," to get away from all the shit that had been swirling around in my head for so long. I also ran to give myself some physical abuse, kind of like a self-punishment for not living a life of honesty and strong character. It was an ego-driven statement to tell people, "Hey, I'm running the NY Marathon," and that had its place in helping me to feel some level of satisfaction about myself. However, at the end of the day, I was trying to get away and that is what it felt like and it left me feeling a little bit empty.

Having lived through the examination of self over the last six years, I now have a deeper understanding of all that I feel and have felt in the past. During that period of breaking myself down and looking at all the parts, I pretty much stopped running. I tried to run, and it was such a chore. My body just didn't feel the "mojo" that you need to really get out there and push yourself, to soak up the experience. So, I replaced running with other physical pursuits: yoga, lifting weights, and hiking. It was enough to keep my body in some semblance of shape, but I had lost my connection to the thrill of achieving that "runner's high" that I have experienced many times in the past. When you and I talked about running the marathon together, I saw a genuine opportunity to get that back and to connect with you in a way that will bond us even more deeply than we are today and we will share something that very few people ever get to share—running 26.2 miles. I embraced our decision to run together with optimism, hope and a lot of fear.

This past weekend, when you and I were in Middlebury, Vermont for the lacrosse tournament, I woke up on Sunday morning with a feeling that I hadn't had for years, I wanted to run. I wanted to go outside in the 45-degree rain and see the town, smell the rain, see the ice that was floating in the river, look at shops and businesses as I slogged through the half-frozen puddles that fill the streets while the ice and snow melted around me. And, that is exactly what I did—I put on my rain pants and jacket and went running.

I immediately felt a bounce in my step, the cold air flowing into my lungs was like an incredible swirling light that permeated my entire being and burst out of every pore in my body. I felt like a newborn gazelle bounding through the savannah—I'm sure I looked more like a Clydesdale or buffalo as I slowly meandered my way down Route 7 toward the center of town. It's been 10 years since I ran my last marathon and my pace has slowed considerably, which is a bit humbling, but the awe-inspiring feeling of connecting with my body and nature has overtaken anything else that I am feeling. As I turned on Cross Street and went across the bridge, I started to cry and I stopped in the middle of the bridge to take in the view of town, the ice flow of the river, and the light tapping of the rain falling on the concrete sidewalk where I stood. I feel like God entered my heart at that moment, touching me ever so gently and telling me that I needed to forgive myself completely for all of my transgressions and to let them go. It hit me, right there on that rain-soaked bridge in Middlebury; I had not completely forgiven myself for all the pain that I have caused my family and friends and the separation that I created in those relationships as a result.

I put my hands on the black steel railing and looked down at the water below. It was an ironic moment because several years ago I would have felt like jumping off that bridge to end my pain and suffering, and I am sure that it must have looked like I was getting ready to jump to anybody driving by—not today! That bridge was now a metaphor for carrying me across the chasm from pain to joy, from "dis"ease to wellness.

I took a deep breath and said, "Jim, I forgive you, you are great, and I love you very much. It's time to let go of your self-judgment and give yourself a break."

I turned and started to run again and felt like 100 pounds had been lifted from my shoulders! It was exhilarating! I understood that I had not been able to run during my period of self-discovery because the habit of running from myself didn't feel in rhythm with who I wanted to be and what I wanted to experience. This past Sunday, I ran with myself for the first time in many, many years and it was wonderful.

So, back to my request, it's a big one. I ask this of you knowing that you may not say yes, and that is great. I am asking because it is something that I need for myself, not because I think that you need it. If you should choose not to give it to me, that is as it should be. I am thrilled that I have identified something that I actually need and can verbalize it from a place of genuine love and caring.

I feel that I need to cross the finish line of the 2011 NYC marathon holding your hand. This goal is going to require a lot of patience from you; you could probably run the marathon "today" at the pace that we will run. After all, I am 46, 25 pounds overweight and my knees are doing their best to operate after years of athletic abuse. Is that something that you can give to me?

Please let me know what you think. I love you very much, am so proud of the person that you are and I am happy to be here in life with you, in complete presence.

Love, Dad

Much to my surprise, as it always is with my kids, Ashley wrote back to me and enclosed a picture of the two of us that was taken on Easter Sunday when she was seven years old. Her response was a resounding *YES* to finishing the marathon together and she agreed that this would be an amazing journey and that we would hold hands and finish it together. She felt that it would be a great metaphor for the work that we had all done to heal our emotional and mental health scars. I realized in that moment that the disaster of my hospitalization and all the fear and work that followed, was all part of breaking the cycle that needed to occur for our entire family.

Unfortunately, I injured my leg and needed to have a torn ACL repaired and could not run the marathon with Ashley. She ran it, finished it, and was on her own journey. I was sad to have missed that race with her, but the gift of our connection with the communication and intention that we shared was a great gift that I hold in my heart.

The message here is simple: If you really want to forgive yourself and live a life of connection with the souls in your life, this is the level of honest communication that needs to exist.

In order for you to see that self-forgiveness is holding you back, when you push yourself to uncomfortable levels of explaining your fears, hopes, love...you will sense that there is something keeping you from completely letting go. That is the feeling of the need to attend to your self-forgiveness.

When you are at that point, you will require a conscious intention to say to yourself, *I forgive you. Although you have done wrong, lived poorly, judged others, abused alcohol, screamed, cursed, made bad decisions, you are forgiven. You are human and as a human, you will make mistakes, it's ok, you are loved. You will have these things inside of you as part of your past, but not "who you are." It's OK, you are loved. I love you.*

You can put in any wording that you choose and I recommend writing this down and reading it to yourself several times a day for 30 days. That will allow your consciousness to accept that this is real and from the heart.

Once you've accomplished this forgiveness, you will see your world open with opportunities you never thought possible. People will embrace you, and you will feel it, your body will experience a "healing chill" that will tell you that you are open to all the love that exists.

Now, please don't confuse my self-forgiveness with a lack of acceptance of responsibility for my actions.

I am not saying, "Hey, what I did to you, the way that I treated you doesn't matter, because I forgive myself."

What I have been saying is that you must confront those poor actions and behaviors with the people in your life. When you have achieved that level of responsibility with the people that were wronged, you are then free to pursue your inner forgiveness. The people that you mistreated may not forgive you, that's their own work to do. However, you can and must forgive yourself.

What has your behavior done to you?

Your behavior has betrayed the inner self, the one being that you need to love to be happy and at peace in this world. If you betray yourself, you cannot achieve peace because you will always feel some angst in your world. That duplicity with which you have acted is actually a dishonesty that you have perpetrated on yourself.

I can hear you right now, you're saying, "What the heck are you talking about?"

This is what we are not taught, in fact, some of us are taught quite the opposite of what I am saying here. You should take care of everybody else first, and then you can worry about yourself.

You need to think like you're on a plane where those oxygen masks are dropping in front of you. Put your mask on first, then help those around you. Same concept.

This is a very foreign concept for some of us. The best way to explain the importance of you focusing on you is this: If you are not completely and utterly yourself, the people in your life, your partner, children, friends, neighbors, the woman at the counter at the local coffee shop, will not get to experience "you." They will experience some version of you or what I like to call "not you."

We create the "not you" at a young age to cope with the socialization that occurs from our parents, siblings, aunts, uncles, cousins, neighbors, and everyone that we come in contact with. That socialization takes us away from the perfect being that we are born into and as the morphing takes place, we need to be able to deal with it in a way that is tantamount to the survival of "you."

In order to survive, you create a second being within yourself, not an alter ego, but, this second being becomes the person that the world sees and interacts with. I have met people in my life, not many, but some, who have been able to stay with themselves without creating the "not you" being.

Visualization Concept

Take a piece of paper and draw a heart on it, then inside the heart, draw a stick figure. This is you, so, underneath that stick figure write "me."

Now, draw a thick line to the right of the heart from the top of the paper to the bottom. Label this line "attacks of socialization." You can also write some words along the line, like, fear, anxiety, discomfort, confusion, abuse, screaming, arguments, hiding. Write whatever feels right about what would cause you to want to protect yourself from pain or perceived attack.

To the right of the line, draw an exact mirror image stick figure to the one on the left—except, do not put this one inside a heart. Draw a large arrow from the top of the heart arcing over the line to the "look alike you" on the right of the line of socialization. This line is kind of like your personal demilitarized zone or what I call the "area of neutrality" (AON).

On one side of the line is peace and tranquility. You cross the AON and enter the battle to guard your "you" from perceived attacks as life happens. You then become your alternative person, and to the world, you look exactly like you, but, you have left "you" inside the safety of the heart and you have started to at from a place of ego, protection, fear, anger, judgment, deceit, dishonesty, and all of the actions that we partake in throughout our days.

Again, this isn't a way to explain away the poor way that you have acted or will act out in the future. It is a helpful illustration so that you may be able to have a stronger understanding of this in the future. A helpful exercise with the goal of understanding this follows below.

Exercise

Take one piece of paper and fold it into a pants pocket sized sheet that you can comfortably carry in your front pocket. When you are prepared for your day, stare into a mirror and say hello to yourself, the real you.

Then, go on about your day interacting with your world and the people in it, and ask yourself these questions:

What would the real me do?

What does the real me want?

Am I still being me?

Throughout the next two hours, take out that piece of paper and note your feelings and experiences as they relate to those questions and your actions.

Then, add the following question:

Is that how "I" really feel and want to act?

Write down the answers to those questions. Remember, the work requires discipline and intention.

I suggest two hours because it doesn't take long for your "not self" to take over. It is a habitual behavior that we are unconscious of. I don't want it to be an overwhelming all-day project. It's like going to the gym and starting an exercise program for the first time in 20 years. You wouldn't go to the elliptical machine and ride it for an hour or you might awaken on the hard rubber floor to find yourself getting mouth to mouth from some staff member. No, you'd start with an advisable 15-minute duration and then stretch and get some water. Over time, 15 minutes could become 60 minutes, and it would take you a couple weeks to get there. It is the same concept with emotional muscles that we haven't used for a long time, for many of us, those emotional muscles were never used.

Unlike physical muscle development, where you can feel the aches and pains of expanding muscle growth, emotional muscles don't give you that kind of tangible feedback. The feedback is much more subtle and hidden in ego driven reactions to our Universe. You might find yourself getting irritable, feeling tired, craving carbs or sugar, panicky, or a general feeling of being threatened. This is the ego feedback that you need to look for and be aware of. Look for it, see it, feel it, and write it down.

Later, after you've gotten home from your day, sit quietly and do a five-minute relaxation in a quiet place. Just sit for five minutes and listen to yourself breathe. (I will discuss meditation later in the chapter.) Then, take out the sheet of paper where you have written down your two-hour emotional workout. Read each comment and think of yourself in those moments. It is imperative that you have complete silence when you are doing this.

Then, ask yourself the questions again. Write down your answers and honestly feel inside yourself. Remember, there is nobody else there to see your answers or to sit in judgment. It's just you and your personal god.

As you get better at this exercise, expand from two hours to four hours to a whole day to weeks, etc... After two months, it will become part of who you are and the real you will be more present than not. When that is the case, you will see things open up in your world like you've never experienced before. There will be a lightness of being, a happy feeling of energy coursing through your body, an intention for life, and a general feeling of purpose that is driving your actions and behaviors.

The next phase of this exercise series is much more difficult. I told you that self-forgiveness was difficult. You think I just wrote that to keep you reading? Remember, honesty is required—there is peace in truth!

When you have a couple of months of emotional muscle training under your belt, tell a friend, spouse, partner, or someone you are close with, that you would like to review some thoughts and feelings about specific situations.

My first word of caution here is simple. When you are in a relationship with someone, you bring all of your life: baggage, impressions, judgment, and socialization of you into the relationship. Correct? Well, they are doing the same thing, they're bringing all their "stuff" with them. In most cases, they will not have had the benefit of working out their emotional muscles for the last two months. So please consciously understand this and that you need to put on your "big boy tighty-whities" and listen to what they are saying, accept it as their thought, their reaction, their stuff, and smile and say thank you.

As you begin this discussion, ask them if they can give you the gift of listening until you have finished. Here is how that conversation would be beneficial.

You might start by saying, "I am doing some work on understanding myself and trying to evolve. I love and respect you, and value you in my life. I'd like to share some thoughts with you."

They've probably already jumped in with a statement such as, "Me too," or "What is it, you're scaring me," or "Cool, do you want to watch the news?" The list of interruptions is infinite as people will typically not listen to hear, they will be thinking about what they want to say next. This is part of the learned habitual behavior of the ego.

It is your work, so you need to steer this conversation to have you receive what you need, which is an honest sharing.

Remember, you are trying to get to 60 minutes on the metaphorical elliptical trainer, so far, you've gotten to 30 minutes.

While being as calm and gentle as possible, with eye contact, you could say, "I would like to go through some things, and would ask that you wait to speak until I say, "That is all", can you give that to me?"

If they agree, then you can say, "Thank you for giving me that, sometimes it is hard for me to focus on what I am feeling and because our relationship is so important to me, I want to make sure that I say what I mean."

Now that the table is set and they are waiting for you to "serve dinner," begin with an overview of a specific situation and walk through how you would have handled this situation two months ago. Then, walk through how you feel about it today. This will show some of the contrast between who you are and the projection you have portrayed for all these years on the other side of the AON.

When you have completed saying what you need to say, then, as you said you would, please say, "That's all, I'm finished."

Now, they've given you the opportunity to speak without interruption, and no matter how intense the feeling is to react to what they will say, it's important for you to sit and let their words flow. Don't just shut them off. These are additions to the words that you have written on your pieces of paper over the last two months and this is the food that your emotional muscles needs to grow and expand beyond your wildest dreams.

I would suggest putting a time limit on this conversation. As with exercising, after two months, you will feel like you can ride the elliptical for 90 minutes. While you probably could do it, you will open yourself up for the possibility of injury and severe strain. No pain, no gain, is not a description that should be used for stretching emotional muscles. Suppose you limit the conversation to 30 or 40 minutes, followed by sharing a cup of tea or coffee. In that case, you will have gotten an amazing workout and provided a relationship honoring with your partner that will feel true to your soul. As time goes by, these conversations will become more common and eventually become the deeper interaction that you are seeking in your life.

The feedback you receive in your interaction will be difficult to hear and your desire to fight back and defend yourself will be strong. Do not allow your ego to take you over the AON to allow your false self to take over. Thank your partner and get to a quiet space.

Meditation has been critical to my goals of self-forgiveness and in managing my anxiety and, ultimately, my depression.

This is not sitting on a mountain top at some ashram in Tibet with your legs crossed as you calmly stare off into the abyss of your soul, searching your inner being for 20 years. We're in a life here, we are not Tibetan monks. Tibetan monks are pursuing a life of spirituality and understanding of that spirituality and that's their way of life, their "job," and they are good at it.

Meditation is simple and by the way, you can call it whatever you want: quiet time, rest, peace, study, whatever you want to call it. It is a time that you are going to devote to yourself to connect with you in the heart.

Meditation Exercise

Find a quiet spot, sit or lay back as comfortably as possible. Some people do not recommend laying back, but I am a proponent of doing what works for your physical body. Some people have a hard time sitting up for any length of time. I am going to walk you through a sitting meditation that I like to do, and feel free to insert laying down where necessary.

Sit in a comfortable chair, back supported well against the chair, your head should be aligned to be balanced over your neck and spine, with your feet flat on the floor. Place your hands on your thighs, gently, palms facing up. Then, place your thumb and forefinger together, gently, as if you were holding a thin and fragile feather between them. The finger connection is a way for your energy to connect and flow through your body and it also provides an intention in the action that you are undertaking for yourself. You are telling your brain that this is different than anything that you have ever done—you are remapping your brain's reaction to your actions.

Gently close your eyes. Feel your heart beating as you slow your breathing. Now, listen.

What do you hear? What is the most present thing that exists within our body? It is our breath. We don't make it happen, it just does. And, it is happening, in the here and now, the absolute present.

Sometimes I play some background music during my meditation and sometimes I meditate by the water and listen to the gentle flow of the waves, and sometimes in the forest and listen to the wind blowing through the leaves, and sometimes, in complete silence with the sound of my breath flowing through the back of my throat. Do whatever works for you.

For this exercise, please play some music, here is a suggestion that I have found on YouTube and also from a Spotify playlist that I use: *"Breathing Space, Sacred Earth, Call to the Divine."* This is an eight-minute session and the music will serve as the timer for your session.

As you quiet your mind and listen to your breath, hit "play" and then allow your mind to go where it will go. There is no possibility of shutting off thought. Follow wherever your mind takes you and if you find yourself focusing on "to-dos" or "what I should be doing instead of this," take a long and deep breath in, slowly release that breath through your nose and go back to focusing on the breath moving through your nose and throat. Remember, you are now teaching your mind that you are in charge and you are going to build out that muscle over time. It is an intention.

Follow that process for the duration of this eight-minute song and when the song has stopped playing, I like to end my meditation with three cleansing breaths.

1. Breathe in through your mouth...say out loud or to yourself, "I am grateful for this day," and breathe out slowly through your nose.

2. Breathe in through your mouth, "I am grateful for this day," and breathe out slowly.

3. Breathe in through your mouth, "I am grateful for this day," breathe out slowly. Open your eyes and you are ready to go.

I try to meditate everyday and sometimes two or three times a day. Again, it doesn't need to be a formal process. Sometimes, I pull my car over when I am out and about and sit quietly with my eyes shut for a few minutes and then I am off.

As with many things in our world, we tend to overcomplicate the simplest of gifts. Meditation, practiced regularly, is one of the most powerful and simplest gifts you can give yourself.

A Navajo Prayer: A lovely way to start your day.

Happily may I walk
May it be beautiful before me
May it be beautiful behind me
May it be beautiful below me
May it be beautiful above me
May it be beautiful all around me
In beauty, it is finished

I have added my own words to this:
"Beauty surrounds me in all that I am and all that I do!"

CHAPTER 19

THE EGO IS NOT
THE CEO OF YOU

Peace doesn't just happen. You don't wake up one day and say to yourself, "OK, it's now time to be happy," and it magically occurs. It also won't happen if somebody tells you to stop being depressed and be happy. Altering our mindset requires a diligent practice of the things you find that work for you to achieve the peace and happiness you seek. This chapter will cover some of the reminders that we all need to help us stay on track and I want to discuss one of the critical points in managing our reaction to the world and that is the ego.

The fact is that knowing what you need to do for happiness or having the intellectual understanding of best practices around living in rhythm do not mean anything unless you actually "practice." If you've ever played on a sports team and experienced the end of a practice where the coach is running you through sprints and you feel like you're just about to die, like your lungs are collapsing and the searing pain in your thighs is never going to end, then you know that practice requires discipline and perhaps some discomfort. Then, when practice is over, you've survived, and you feel great. You might be a little sore and tired, but the feeling of accomplishment and the physical strength that you are developing is so wonderful that you forget about the pain of that moment.

With physical exercise or training, it is easy to identify why you would be in pain and why your brain would be begging you to stop. In an emotional situation, it is not that easy. We don't identify the trials of emotional work as being "tiring" or as producing "pain." However, it is the same thing. The emotional muscles of the mind need to be worked out just as we work the physical muscles in exercising our bodies. If you work out physically when you are younger, your body reaps the benefits for years to come. If you work out the emotional muscles, again, you reap the benefits for years to come, in your ability to be honest, live in rhythm and to love yourself.

On the contrary, if you decide one day at the age of 45, that you are going to start working out and you join a gym, the pain can be excruciating. Your body has no friggin' idea what you are doing and tells your mind to stop. Your body says, *"Hey, we're in danger here. This has never happened before. What the hell?!"* If, in your 40s, you decide that your life is missing something and you want to start to work on those missing pieces, and that you want to start working out your emotional muscles, the result will be the same. Your mind will tell you, *"Hey, we can't share this stuff. We've never shared this stuff. We're in danger here. This has never happened before. What the hell?!"*

What does it mean to practice? Well, it's just like being a good athlete or piano player. You don't sit down and tickle the ivories, you start with a disciplined practice plan, right? First you play scales, then arpeggios, then specific tunes that help you warm up your hands, and you follow a practice plan. The discipline that it requires to learn to play the piano is the kind of discipline that flexing your emotional muscles will require, it is a steady and consistent use of those muscles that will bring rhythm and peace to your life.

The Ego is Not the CEO of "YOU"

The ego is within us for many reasons, self-reflection, to protect, and to defend what it believes are threats against us. Through the years of our lives, as we grow older, the ego, if unchecked or misunderstood, gains stronger control over our thoughts and feelings. It gets to the point of thinking that it is the Chief Executive Officer, or CEO, of "you."

To find a place of peace in life, to get that ego in check, the ego must learn and accept that you are the CEO of you and the ego is merely an employee. Freud, commonly identified as the father of psychoanalysis, explains the ego, super-ego, and the id as the "psycho apparatus" and provides great detail of the roles and responsibilities of each. To have a catch-all word that is easily understood, I will use the word ego as the overall structure of the interaction of the three parts that Freud described in his work. In recent years, much of Freud's work has been disproven or updated to reflect what is now better understood, but his work was the foundation for those that followed, and he described the inner workings of the ego in a very easy to grasp way. He described the interaction between the id and the ego as a horse and rider respectively, with the horse sometimes becoming too much to control. Again, the employee wants to be the CEO.

Like a typical employee, the ego is an integral part of the success of the organization and must feel that way. It is imperative for the feelings and thoughts that are developed from the ego, to be recognized and reflected upon. This provides a feeling of satisfaction that there is value in those thoughts and feelings. Employees are much more productive and satisfied if they feel that they are being seen and heard. The difficulty that I have had about understanding and accepting that the ego must be addressed is centered on the fact that the ego is not a separate entity. It's not a person and it took time for my mind to compute that, while it is not a person, it has developed into a powerful and uncontrolled being.

Just like a typical employee, from time to time, the ego will also get pissed off and threaten to quit or take over or strike! Your job as CEO is to recognize when the employee needs some attention, some stroking, some education, a vacation, or self-empowerment, and to gain an understanding of what the trigger points are for those needs.

I recently faced a difficult situation at work, where my ego had gone into the fully blown "pissed off" mode, going absolutely bat shit crazy. A friend that I work with, someone I have known for almost 30 years, someone I considered a close friend, acted in a way that left me feeling like I needed to fight back. In situations where the person is closer to me, I find myself having a much higher stake in emotional damage and therefore, dig my heels in even further. As this is someone that I've known for a long time, he has lived through the earlier years of my career, going from lackey to leader and ultimately his boss. In this current job however, we are peers. So, my ego sees this person who was an employee, making me look bad. That is essentially the internal feeling and here is the conversation that ensues.

"Jimmy, you look bad here, we gotta fight, we gotta kick some fucking ass—RIGHT NOW! You cannot let this happen, you will not let this happen, get in there and beat him like a rented mule. C'mon!"

Do any of those words sound familiar to you? I'm sure they do. That internal conversation gives me the sense of being backed into a corner that I need to fight my way out of. I learned at an early age that if you're in a bar fight, you hit first, hit hard, and keep hitting until the owner throws you out or the cops show up. As a more highly evolved person, I understand that these are just feelings, that it is OK to feel like you need to fight, but not actually throw a punch. However, in this situation with my friend and co-worker, I needed to extricate myself from the office and clear my head. I was hurt and feeling that I had been wronged and belittled, that I had been disregarded. Bottom line, I was sad that my relationship with this individual had been reduced to some financial decisions on his part that were taking me out of some business opportunities that I was working toward. In short, my feelings were hurt.

What do I do when faced with that type of conflict? I ask myself a couple of questions, questions that I require my ego to listen to and understand. It shows my mind that I am in control, that I am the CEO, and that the ego is an employee. Byron Katie explains these questions in-depth and very well in her book, *Who Would You Be Without Your Story*. She breaks the questioning of the mind down to four essential questions.

For purposes of my world, essentially, I am asking myself the same four questions, but they are expanded into very many internal and external (conversations with my wife and friends, maybe) discussions.

1. *Why did Joe do this to me?*

2. *Did Joe, in fact, do this to me?*

3. *Why am I assuming that I have a frickin' clue why Joe did what he did?*

4. *Chris, I can't believe that this prick did this to me, can you fucking believe that he did this?*

   a. Chris replied, *"Jim, maybe he is focusing on his own family's needs and doesn't see another option"* or *"maybe you are just being paranoid, and he wasn't considering you at all in his decision, you've been friends a long time, maybe you are wrong. Is that possible?"*

5. *Here are some expanded questions I ask myself when I am trying to ground myself in the present moment:*
    a. *What if my attitude and my actions suggested to Joe that I did not want to be part of his world?*
    b. *What is my responsibility in this?*
    c. *How do I feel right now?*
    d. *Is this a good feeling?*
    e. *Am I at peace?*
    f. *Do I want to feel this way?*
    g. *When I feel this way is it productive to me, or anybody else?*

In any given situation, the list of questions varies from a couple, in simple issues of the ego, to extensive when the ego is really pushed to the limit. I find that the more my ego is injured in "public," meaning that somebody else witnesses my embarrassment or belittling, (remember this isn't real stuff, it's just the mind telling us that it is real) the questions and resulting mood are intense. A reminder, one of the best bumper stickers that I've ever seen on the back of a car said, "Don't believe everything you think!"

Journaling Exercise

When you wake up tomorrow morning, I want you to write in a journal, every thought that comes into your head. Just take about the first 30 minutes of your day and write every single thing that pops into your head. Everything!

Here is what it looked like for me today:

Thank you, Universe.
Damn, I hate waking up in the dark (it was 4:30 in the morning.)
Man, I'd love to sleep another 45 minutes.
The flight is leaving at 7:40, if I don't get on the road by 5:00, I'm not going to make it through security in time to get on the plane.
I hope that my shirt fits well.

Chris is so beautiful when she sleeps, and she smells great.
Did I buy gas last night?
I wonder if it's going to rain.
Shit, I'm behind schedule.
What's the weather doing—wonder if the Ravens beat the Browns last night—need to take my vitamins today, it's going to be a long one.
Those pricks at the firm I just left are going to wish they had me still on board.
The house is so quiet in the morning.

Those were the thoughts that I wrote down in the first two minutes of my day. As you can see and as you know intellectually as you review this morning, there's a lot of shit going on in our brains. That is the job of the mind, right? It's a computer whose job is to process information; as long as you are awake, it will continue to process non-stop. Given the opportunity to run free, your mind will never stop. It will make your head so noisy that you will have confusion and muddled thoughts throughout your day. The monks of the eastern cultures devote their entire lives to meditation to calm their minds to reach true peace and enlightenment. They practice focusing their minds on no thought. They believe that true peace can only be attained by turning off the uncontrolled thoughts of the thinking mind. When this is accomplished, they will then be ready to hear the words of the Buddha or God.

I have learned to calm my mind and ego by questioning my mind and meditating for the answers. If you ask the questions of your mind, the mind, given the opportunity to answer, will seek the answer. I don't know about you, but I am a puzzle freak. I love crosswords, word jumbles, and mind exercises. I relish Sunday mornings when I can sit with my wife and start the Sunday New York Times crossword puzzle. My mind is incredibly inquisitive and will not allow me to stop working on it until it is finished. That doesn't mean that I sit and bang it out in one sitting, but over the period of the next couple days I will pick it up and put it down a half dozen times. Each time, I add more answers, and with my wife and me working together, we finish most of them. Again, given questions, the mind will not stop until it has the answer. However, providing the right answers on a crossword puzzle is easy compared to the ever-changing permutations we weave in our brains when the ego is threatened. In a crossword, there is only one answer that fits the puzzle. In the puzzle of the ego, there are many questions and many answers. If we allow the ego to ask ego-driven questions and answer with ego-driven answers, we are not gaining the proper ground to calm the mind.

Providing the answers that will calm the mind and put you in rhythm, requires thoughtful meditation. I know that I am being honest and "non-ego driven" when I feel that I am in rhythm. When the answer that I have arrived at gives me a feeling of complete flow and calm. This may result in my realizing that I created the problem, or I was the "asshole" in a given situation and it's not the others, I'm just the last one to know that I am just wrong.

In June of 2001, I was at a youth lacrosse tournament in New Haven at the Yale University athletic fields. It was a beautiful day, just the perfect day for a lacrosse game, the kind of day that makes a kid want to be a lax gladiator. The sun was high in the sky, and it was hot and very bright. I was there as a coach of a group of 14- and 15-year-old boys that were representing our town's youth lacrosse program in six games, playing against teams from all over the northeast. In between our games, I typically staked a great spot on the grass to sit and watch other teams play. The spirit of the game of lacrosse is so alive when there are 1,000 or so kids running around like the Native Americans did for hundreds of years.

I sat on the sideline of a game that was bet- ween two competitive teams and the score was close. At first, I didn't see the father that would alter this day for hundreds of people, I only heard him. I heard him "coaching" his son very aggressively as he stalked the sideline at the end of the field where his 14-year-old was playing attack. Attack players are charged with creating offense and scoring goals, and as such, tend to be a big focus of the game, especially when the game is competitive, everybody looks to the attackmen to get to the goal.

Every time the ball made its way to the offensive end of the field for "team blue," this father would start yelling at his son, "Go get it, attack the ball, get low, go around that kid, come on, cut to the goal, gotta have the ball, cradle hard, shoot, shoot, shoot!"

As someone who has been coaching youth sports for 30 years, I have seen and heard it all, and sometimes it ain't pretty! However, on this particular day I was about to witness the "seen it all" part of that statement. It is very difficult for kids that are playing sports to hear what their coaches are saying to them, especially when they put helmets on and people are cheering and their teammates are calling them, etc... When you add the verbal abuse of a parent or fan that is hurled at you incessantly, everything else is just noise and that tends to be all you hear. The boy was becoming visibly agitated by his dad's comments and was starting to "wave him off" with a hand gesture that I thought was actually respectful. He was saying, *Dad, please leave me alone, I'm trying my best.*

As the game went on, the dad was becoming more and verbally aggressive and people on the sidelines were distancing themselves from his space. I watched the boy on the field with intensive focus; I had been there, I had experienced the kind of "coaching" that he was experiencing and the feelings of embarrassment and shame that go along with it. The game was tied with 30 seconds to go, it was a very exciting moment in the battle between these two really good teams of young boys. The son got the ball around the midpoint of the field, about 10 yards from the sideline nearest the dad. The dad yelled, "This is it; this is your shot to win this game—do it, get it done!"

As the words left his lips, the defender from the other team drove his stick down over the boy's stick and dislodged the ball. The ball skirted to the side and there was a melee for it and the clock ticked down to zero. As this was a "friendly" tournament, there would be no overtime and the game would end in a tie. Because of the way the game finished, with all the cheering, I lost track of the berating dad and his son. I was watching the boys gather in the center of the field for the handshake and exchange high fives and words of "nice game." Out of the corner of my eye I could see a large male figure walking aggressively toward the pack of players that had gathered at midfield.

The first thing the dad said was, "What the hell is wrong with you, you had the game on your stick, all you had to do was get to the goal and score—it would have been over." The son tried to ignore him and join the line of boys to shake hands with the other team, but the dad didn't want to be ignored. I could see his ego going into full defensive mode. It was telling him, "You are looking pretty stupid here, 'you' are in danger of being wrong—by having a little boy make you look like a fool. You need to defend 'us!'"

The father did what I was hoping he wouldn't, he grabbed the son by the facemask of his helmet and yanked him to the side of the line of boys, and said, "Get your stuff, we're going home."

I could hear the boy pleading, "Dad, let go, leave the field, Dad..."

I didn't see her coming, but the boy's mom was on top of the father as the boy was prying the dad's hands from his helmet and she swung at him with her bare hand as hard as she could. Her ego, and correctly so, was telling her that one of hers was in terrible danger and that she needed to act with extreme urgency and force, that this was a matter of life and death. As such, she came to her child's defense.

As in any situation in life, we have choices to make that will ultimately tell the story of our lives. Everything matters. In this volatile situation, the father would have a choice to make, in a split second, which would tell his story for some time. At this point, he could have realized his misdirection and ego-driven response to his feelings about his son's play on the field and how it was making him feel. He could have realized that his egoic reaction was not based in reality, for anyone but for himself, and he could have walked away. It would have been simple for him to walk away, albeit emotionally bruised and battered. On the other hand, not having a grip on his ego, not realizing that his ego is the employee acting in the CEO role, he chose a different path, the path that we all choose at one time or another, sometimes much more than we should.

The father squared his shoulders to the mother and punched her in the face! It was sickening to watch, and it took me weeks to get my head around what I had witnessed. As I started to run toward the father, I watched in horror as the son lifted his lacrosse stick and smashed his dad in the back of the head with a stunning blow that brought him to his knees. As the boy was reaching his arms and his stick above his head for another downward blow, his mom, with blood dripping down her face, had the presence of mind to get between her son and his father and yelled, "ENOUGH!"

The police were called, and the dad was led away in handcuffs while the rest of us were interviewed about the incident. When I got to my car after that game, I cried as I tried to contemplate the violence that exists in all of us. I felt so sorry for that little boy, and I saw myself in him as he tried to manage a situation with a father that was a narcissist and completely ego-driven and out of control. It was not until years later that I would learn the power of the ego to drive our behavior in ways that prevent our peace and happiness.

Put your ego on notice immediately, take a page from the mother of the story that I have just told you. "Enough ego boy or girl, I need you *and* you are demoted to the rank-and-file employee status that you were meant to work in."

How do we accomplish the demotion of the ego? Acknowledging your ego and the role that it plays can help. I've found the following tools helpful.

Writing Prompts and Journaling

Some ways to explore this:

1) Write down on a piece of paper the instances in the last day when you felt that your ego was in play and what happened.

2) Write down how you reacted, what you said.

3) Write how you would change that reaction and read it out loud with the following words in front: "Ego, in the future, I will...""Ego, the next time that this occurs, this is what we will do..." "Ego, I am in charge."

Roleplay with a Friend, Spouse, Partner or in Your Journal

Write a script for a real event that happened at work or on the highway when you were driving or a conversation with a colleague or family member.

Have your partner in this role-play be you and you be the person that you engaged within an ego-driven way.

Put yourself in the other person's position. (For example, as I discussed earlier, I asked myself the questions around the issue with my coworker and friend and as I put myself in his position, I realized that I was inventing stories for all of us.)

Try to Eliminate the Words "Should," "Has To," "Must," and "Needs To", as they Relate to Other's Actions

For example, I was driving on the highway on Thanksgiving night, and I was making a beeline for home from a full day in New York City with my family. It was Thanksgiving night, the road was clear of traffic, but it had been a long day, and I could just feel my freshly made bed beneath my tired body. Ahead, in the left lane, I saw a car with New Hampshire license plates traveling around 60 MPH. I said out loud to nobody, but since my wife was sitting next to me, she heads it, "That guy shouldn't be in the left lane, he has to move over, don't they teach people in New Hampshire about the left lane courtesy...?" My wife, knowing the reaction of the ego, said, "How do you know what he has to do?"

Stop Telling Yourself the Answers to Everybody's Actions

The fact of the matter is, that regardless of history, we have no idea what someone will do, say, feel, etc... Based on our history with that person and our observations, we may have a strong feeling about how things might go. However, anybody who knew me 15 years ago would not know the person that I am today. Important point: people can change, people can get their ego to be an employee.

Give Up the Need to be Right

If you feel that you need to be "right" and that everyone needs to accept and know that you are right, you will never find peace. The CEO ego must be right and every person involved (and some who aren't) needs to know that you're right and you're not going to let anybody forget it.

This is a death spiral. Nobody is right all the time, and the reality is that everybody" can be right all the time. Others may not agree that he/she is right, and if they believe it, then it really doesn't matter. You could say to a teacher who just marked your answer on a test incorrect, "Hey Teach, that answer that I put down is correct—I know it is!"

She might say, "Well I am glad that you know that, but that is not the answer I was looking for." In that situation, you get the answer wrong as it relates to the teacher's grade, but if you choose to believe that you are right and that works for you, then go ahead and take that with you.

Take Some Time to React

The ego takes a split second to take in data and decide whether it is life threatening, then it drives us to an action immediately. When you see a lion coming out of the weeds and he's got blood dripping from his chin, you need an immediate reaction to run like a frickin' lion is chasing you. However, when you're talking to your mom about how your sister is a pain in the ass because she won't commit to making apple crisp for Christmas dessert, you can take some time before your ego tells you that this is life threatening and requires an immediate verbal burst of return fire.

There is no time limit on your need to react in most situations. Yes, if you're a doctor or an airplane pilot or cop or army demolitions expert, this doesn't apply. For the rest of us walking around in our everyday lives though, there is no immediacy to our actions. Relax and take some time to think and feel your way through a situation. When you feel some rhythm in your thoughts, then you will know that it is time to act.

Upgrade Your Actions

As you are eliminating "should haves" or "needs to" or "musts" from your lexicon, you will experience feelings of guilt and anger that you acted the way that you did in a given situation. This is destructive to your growth and will not allow your ego the ability to climb out of the hole it's been demoted to. Be gentle with yourself and use the language of "upgrades."

Upgrade Examples

- In the situation with my co-worker, my upgrade was to talk with him about what I observed and what I felt in that observation. When I heard his explanation of what he observed, I quickly understood that it was just a misunderstanding.

- The dad at the lacrosse game could have used the time during the game to make notes for his son for when they got home. A great upgrade would have been to just cheer for the boys and then have some time later to teach. He could have upgraded throughout the incident, at any point, by saying, "You know what, I'm sorry, I lost it." You might be thinking, *Yeah, right Jimmy, give me a break, the guy's a psycho.* I would submit that we are all psychos, judgment is not for any of us to contemplate.

- Last summer, I was driving in a very dense traffic jam with my family in the car. It was following the local 4th of July parade and people were merging from side streets onto Route 1, the main street in town. I was on a side street trying to make a right-hand turn and I saw the car that I was supposed to merge in front of inch up closer to the bumper of the car in front of him. Immediately, my ego said to me, *Dude, you going to let him box you out?* My mind immediately took me to a place of fight for being wronged or challenged. Instead of reacting, I took a breath, and waited for the opportunity to merge. The reality, in that situation, is that it was not my time to merge, for whatever reason. Waiting for your time to merge can be helpful in slowing yourself down before you let the ego driven decision rule the moment.

This work around ego is critical in breaking down the walls that we create to "defend" ourselves from whatever our minds deem as an attack. As I have said before, I believe that we are here to connect with each other with every fiber of my soul. If you are not present and cannot recognize your ego's desire to be the CEO, you will be prevented from true connection. This is a conscious practice that requires time and intention. I was completely blind to my ego's CEO role, and it caused me to be numb in my life for a very long time, and as a result, I was prevented from connecting in a real way with most of the people that passed through my life.

Here is a quote that I came across recently that I thought nails the idea of managing the ego:

"Getting your shit together requires a level of honesty that you cannot imagine. There's nothing easy about realizing that you are the one that's been holding you back this whole time."
-Brad Pitt

When I was learning about the ego and its role, I was excited to do the work to demote mine to employee because it was a change that was in my control. There are a lot of things about my depression that are less controllable and knowing that I can manage this makes it a lot easier for me to confront and change.

Here's my additional thought to Brad Pitt's quote:

It's all you—always has been and always will be.
When you are ready to change, you need the disciplined approach of a world-class athlete.

As a formerly successful athlete, and someone that grew up being lauded for my physical capability, I learned at a very young age that I could be recognized by people that I considered to be role models as being "special." This fed my ego and proved to me that my worth was in my physical abilities. This is an epidemic in our society in all youth sports today. It also creates ego-driven habits that are hard to break and carry far into adulthood and impact everything that we do. I see direct parallels with athletic prowess and success in making money in the business world. They are both false boosts to the ego and are also lauded by society as we all chase the dream. This ongoing cycle continues and gets worse over time as our egos take over as CEO.

CHAPTER 20

BE THE HERO

Ancestral Healing is a concept that comes from many indigenous cultures where there is a firm belief and understanding that we are echoes of our ancestral family events, memories, emotional issues, trauma, and celebrations. This is especially true of Native American tribes, and I think that this is why my tie to the spirit of the game of lacrosse is strong. Lacrosse is also a Native American cultural event that held strong ties to the circle of life. Ancestral Healers believe that you can heal your collective soul seven generations in the past and seven generations into the future. An ancestor is any person from whom one is descended, so, in doing your work, you are not only healing yourself; you are healing seven generations going forward.

Essentially, ancestral healing allows for the repair of the connections between you and your ancestors, and you are removing the destructive patterns going forward for those who will follow.

I can tell you that this is something that I fully believe in, and it is something that I am hopeful does exist. To me, this is a noble goal and the thought of being able to heal your ancestry is just amazing and a goal worth chasing. I have spoken with hundreds of people who have struggled with depression or who live with someone that is struggling from depression and high levels of anxiety. Everyone has their own motivation for wanting to heal and some are not ready to do the work that needs to be done. They need a reason to justify or to motivate themselves into that work. For some, it can be their partner, or their children. These relationships were and continue to be strong motivations for me to want to be in health and to have better relationships for those connections in my life.

From the beginning of my breakthrough healing journey, I have felt that I was breaking the cycle of disease that I inherited from my parents and that they inherited from their parents. I didn't want to pass this cycle on to my children, and to their children. I had a strong desire to put an end to that dysfunction while I was still alive. That's ironic, after wanting to kill myself for so many years. Of course, this realization didn't occur until I was deeper into my therapeutic process and the rebirth that I experienced as a result.

I would add this concept of ancestral healing to my list of motivations and suggest that if you are seeking a reason to do the work to heal, add this to the list. I mean, can there be a goal with a bigger impact than the idea of being able to heal your generational wounds?

You can be the chosen one, the leader that your ancestors and your future generation will cheer for, the individual soul that stands up for all those that came before and couldn't find that strength, "The Hero."

As I have said, breaking through to being that hero requires time, patience, strength, discipline, and, at times, a lot of tears. It is not an easy road, although the payoff is absolute magic. To achieve the magic, to live your heaven, here on earth, requires a solid understanding of what the illness is and it needs to be a topic that is open for discussion.

Depression, Anxiety, Suicide: A Much Needed Conversation

I believe that we need to have a conversation about depression, anxiety, and suicide. Suicide, which often results from anxiety and depression, is something that people are uncomfortable speaking about. I get it, death is a difficult topic. We're talking about the finality of a life, and that is scary. However, avoidance is not working.

Here are some statistics from the Centers for Disease Control and the World Health Organization:

- 48,000 people a year die by suicide in the United States (135 people per day).
- There is one death in the US by suicide every 11 minutes.
- There is one death by suicide for every 25 attempts.
- Depression affects 25% of the adult population (some statistics say that this number could be as high as 40%).
- Only half of the people experiencing a major bout of depression seek and/or receive treatment.
- Globally, someone dies by suicide every 40 seconds.
- Suicide is the second leading cause of death, globally, for those from ages 15 to 24.
- Depression is the leading cause of disability worldwide.

And a very positive statistic:

- 80%-90% of those that seek treatment for depression are treated successfully using medications and/or therapy.

The numbers are staggering, and we are living in an epidemic of tragedy for something that can be addressed and save lives. The fact that treatment is so successful underscores the need for dialogue.

I was fortunate to be introduced, through a mutual friend, to John Trautwein. John played professional baseball for the Boston Red Sox. He and his wife Susie live in the Atlanta area. They experienced one of the worst nightmares that a parent can experience; their son Will died by suicide when he was 15. Following this incredible tragedy, John did, I believe, what needs to be done. He devoted his life to teen suicide awareness and through the Will-To-Live Foundation he speaks to high school students about his son and what their family and friends have endured. His goal is to raise awareness and spread love so that everyone knows that they matter. I highly recommend   reading the book that John wrote about his family's experience, *My Living Will*.[4]

John is the hero of his ancestral healing.

Here's the thing about Will's decision to die by suicide; he wasn't showing any signs of anxiety, depression, or unease about life. There was no warning, and the Trautwein's were living the American Dream life that we all strive for. That is why depression can be a silent killer and I think that the stigma and vulnerability attached to admitting that you need help is a strong reason for this silence. I know that I lived that stigma, in my mind, for a very long time. I also didn't want to be labeled and I didn't want to be on medication for the rest of my life.

This is why I believe that we need regular conversations with those in our lives about how we feel. Let's expose ourselves with those that we love and are connected with. Let's open the curtains and the windows and let the spring sunshine come blazing in, let the fresh air breeze into the room to eliminate the darkness and the dank, in every corner.

It's simple really. Not easy, but simple.

Here are a couple conversation examples for you to see the simplicity.

Me talking with my son (actual conversation):

Me: "Hey buddy, how are things going?"

James: "Good."

Me: "Man, I have had a stressful day. One of my clients wasn't happy with the contract that I sent him to review and he friggin' yelled at me that his patience was wearing thin and that he needed what he asked for...yesterday!"

James: "That sucks."

Me: "Yeah, I went outside and laid on the grass and stared at the clouds for a bit to calm down."

James: "Did it work?"

---

[4] To learn more go to to the foundation's website: https://will-to-live.org/

Me: "Yes, and I was able to see where we miscommunicated."

James: "Cool."

Me: "How about you—how are you feeling today?"

James: "Pretty good."

Me: "Cool. Is there more?"

James: "Well, I don't feel like things are going right. I feel like I'm making a mistake about my career and my path, and I have this project that is due, and I think it is terrible. I didn't sleep last night, and now I'm tired, I'm nervous, and shit is just going to hell in a hand-basket."

Me: "OK, do you want to talk about it? Do you want my advice, do you want me to just listen? What is your nervousness causing you to feel?"

James: "I don't want your opinion, if I can just tell you what's going on, that'd work."

Me: "OK—go for it."

As a person in a relationship with another person that I would like to "check-in" with, I may need to just shut up and listen. I have been teaching people in the business world how to "listen to hear" and not "listen to respond." In this short conversation, I have drawn my son into a discussion about his feelings and he is about to tell me his inner thoughts, fears and feelings. I want him to understand that he can do that without judgment, without comment on my part, and without having to worry about what I am going to say. Seems simple, right? It is and it is not easy.

Learning to work through the practice of non-judgment and "listening to hear" requires your commitment not to comment, and at the end of the other person's thoughts, I have found that the following question is the way to close the loop on the discussion:

Me: "Is there more?"

James: "No, that's it."

Me: "OK, thanks for sharing."

The practice in this relationship interaction is doing what you have said that you will do, and that is finishing with that. There is no further engagement around that topic, and letting go of outcome expectations can empower both people. When there is ongoing trust between two people that this is going to happen, that is when the floodgates of communication will open, and the stronger connection and bond in the relationship can flourish.

My path to peace and health has not been linear. At times, working through the journey, has been a fucking trek through Mordor, and at other times it has been like riding on a cloud in a deep blue sky looking down on a world with infinite possibilities. During those periods of work where it has felt like a trek, it felt like crawling over broken glass. The jagged shards dug into the cuts in my hands and knees, the blood and pus oozed out over my body. Sometimes, I just wanted to lay down and give up. I had this intuition that there would be something better on the other side of the broken glass.

At a speaking engagement a few years ago, somebody asked me, "How many broken glass paths did you have to cross to get to the other side of that path?"

My answer, "As many as it takes."

My response was deliberate in that the work continues, and when you choose to live an examined life, the magic of that work doesn't stop. Just as the guard in the *Wizard of Oz* says, "Nobody gets in to see the wizard, not nobody, not no-how!" That work doesn't stop, not ever, not no-how. You can get in to see the Wizard, when you have achieved the goal of releasing fear and living in love—then, only then, do you get to see the Wizard.

I am here despite all attempts to sabotage myself. I understand the pain of it all. The pain of the world, how we've been given this gift, this opportunity to connect with each other at the highest end of the animal kingdom, and we continue to fuck it up. I feel the desperate pain of feeling useless in the face of just not understanding why the world is as it is. I feel the frustration. I get it. All of it. The bottom line, that feeling of pain and frustration, in what appears to be a view of how fucked up the world is, is really just the turmoil that exists inside of ourselves. That turmoil may have resulted from being abandoned, abused, molested, or ignored, or all of the above.

When you reckon with that trauma, you can gain control over those feelings of pain and frustration. Unrecognized trauma brings more trauma, which brings more trauma. It's a never-ending cycle until you embrace that and those which bring you pain, hold it as closely as you can. Cry with it. Yell at it. Scream at it. Jump up and down in anger. Write about it. Meditate through it. Then, let it go. It is not serving you, and you do not need to continue to victimize yourself. One of the greatest pandemics of the human condition is the habitual behavior of living in the past. Be the hero of you and of your family and of your ancestors and future generations, and let it go.[5]

This doesn't mean that the world still isn't fucked up, in many ways, it is. What it allows is for you to create the space to see that it is not you, you are not your pain, and you are pure love. When you are pure love, you can change the world, your world.

I have learned why we are here, and this is the thing that gives me joy. That "why" is the connection to the people that we meet in our world. We are here to connect. Everything else is white noise and window dressing.

My story is not uncommon, and my approach to healing is.

Time & Intention

The practice of my personal health evolved over a period of three years of intensive focus. I was in a dangerous and disease-ridden situation and chose to seek life and joy for myself and my family. That was the choice that I made to work toward healing, and as soon as possible. It was not easy, and it certainly did not happen quickly. This writing has been 15 years since my hospitalization, and I continue to do the practice and the work that I have discussed.

It is important to understand that there is no magic pill that can be taken, and no one thing will solve the issue of anxiety or depression. For me, it is a collective road map to health that I developed over a long period of time with the intention to heal and live in peace and joy. I spent many days being discouraged and elated and sad and angry and

---

[5] Try the "Letting Go Exercise" on page 165 for support.

encouraged and pissed off and happy and everything in between. Thankfully, those feelings didn't all occur in one day, and when feelings do come up, I believe that it is important to feel through them. It's important to understand that each person's illness and journey to health are unique and require a little tweak here and there. As the Hero of your story, your mission is to determine which tweaks work for you and which do not.

I talked about the medication coma that I was put in early in the process so that I didn't hurt myself. I continued to take medication for my depression and anxiety for eight years after my hospitalization. I was terrified when I started because I didn't want to be on medication for the rest of my life, and I also didn't want to be labeled as someone that needed meds to live. However, I quickly learned that medication was necessary for my body to produce the chemicals I needed to manage the mood swings that can be driven by anxiety and lead to a depressive episode. I describe this as taking something that allowed my brain to control its balance so that I would not experience the dramatic highs and lows that go along with my illness. It provided gates that would close to swing in either direction.

Medication was a gift that I am very thankful for, and multiple people closely monitored me while we learned what worked and what didn't. As important, I was doing the therapeutic work very diligently while I was on medication to take advantage of the balance that was being helped along with the meds. Drugs can be helpful if taken under the supervision of professionals and are also involved in your ongoing path to health.

I have met many people over the years that are diagnosed with depression and their doctor prescribed some medication to help with that. They have taken the pills and waited for change. To me, that's like giving someone a helicopter and assuming that they can now fly themselves around without taking any lessons about being an expert helicopter pilot. In short, I wouldn't advise it. Whether you are flying a helicopter without lessons or taking medication without consistent therapy and medication management, the results are the same... you crash and burn.

I came to a point where I felt like I would like to stop taking medication for many reasons, the physical side effects and the unknown of the long-term impact were just a few. The decision to stop was something that was a collective decision between me, my therapist, and my family. After all, we are all in this together. It is critically important to wean yourself off of medication just as you started, with close monitoring of your behavior, health, mood and thoughts, sleeping patterns, diet, and many other factors that only a skilled professional should manage with you.

The first time that I tried to wean off of the meds, I became violently ill and I was terrified and went back to my original dosage. We waited three months and then tried again. Your body becomes attached to something that it has relied on for so long and it takes time to train it that it's OK not to be there any longer. My best advice is to be patient and drink a shit ton of water.

I have been meds-free for eight years, give or take, and I feel great. I have mood swings from time to time, and I can typically figure out what is causing me to feel like I am slipping into a depressive episode within a couple of days. I will say that I have had bouts of depression over the past 15 years—it is something that will never leave me. I have also been suicidal a few times. What? Really? Yes, I am a human that suffers from severe anxiety and depression. That's OK. It is not who I am, it is part of my experience. I have a genetic predisposition to this disease, and I have lived through some trauma (as we all have), and occasionally these things crop up and try to bring me back down the rabbit hole.

It is in those moments when I am tested to bring my practice forward and let the disease and the ego know that they are not the CEO.

As I have lived an examined life, and as I have become the Hero of my ancestral line, I have learned to love myself and to love my parents, and to love the people that attacked me, and to love everyone who has ever fucked with me. I have learned to be grateful for all that I am, and I love the present moment. I have also learned to apologize for mistakes that I have made and will continue to make. I have asked for forgiveness, and I have granted it. I have learned to "drop the pencil", it does not serve me.

It Does Not Serve You

In 2010, I was sitting in a glass-windowed office in the tallest office building in Hartford, Connecticut. My high-backed executive leather chair was swiveled away from the internal office and I was staring out the floor to ceiling window, watching a bird soar above the Connecticut River off in the distance. In my mind, I was thinking about the therapy session I had the night before where I was screaming into a pillow about my father and how absolutely terrified I was of that man that I loved. I sat there, the sun was coming through the window and it was hot against my cheeks and I could feel sweat beading up on my eye brows and the back of my neck.

I felt a hand on my shoulder and I turned to see that no one was there. It felt as real as anything I've ever felt and I turned to watch the bird and it was closer to the building than it had been and I felt a cool breeze float across my face as if the bird's wings had created a little wind to cool me.

The hand was still on my shoulder and I heard a voice say, "Jimmy, let it go. Your father loved you as best he could. Let it go. Your anger does not serve you. Let it go, it does not serve you."

I felt an immediate relief and lightness of my being, and that was the day when I started the journey of healing that relationship. It's the quiet times where the work sinks in and allows you to speed up your healing. Getting quiet and slowing down are two things that I was never taught, and they are two parts of the practice that are incredibly powerful. I tell the athletes and the executives that I coach to "slow down to speed up." When you slow down and feel, you generate your most creative, intelligent, and real thoughts. That is where your magic is.

So, a part of the practice has been and continues to be, being in a state of engagement in life and with others where I am sharing all of who I am, and I am being who I want to be. I require myself to talk with people about what I am feeling, the good, the bad, the fear, the sadness, the happiness, the remorse, the anxiety, the hope, the optimism, and the love. For someone that grew up in a state of fear about self, a home filled with silence and lack of sharing, and with an athletic background where emotion is considered weak, I have had to learn to believe that I am a great person.

I have had to look in the mirror, tell myself, "I love you", and believe it with all of my heart and soul. It is not enough to look in the mirror and say, "I love you." It must be heard, understood, and believed. That is critical. Otherwise, you are not doing the work, you are just bullshitting your way through it. That is not sustainable and will not work—your ego is too smart for that.

It starts with talking. You don't have to have a psychoanalytical guru or expensive therapist, although talk therapy with a trained professional can be very helpful and important. This is where my work began and continues today. Having a person that is objective, trained in varied treatments and philosophies, and accessible, will provide you with the support system that you will need to break through your trauma. Talking will start working out the emotional muscles that are feeble and atrophied from years of not being used. It becomes the stretching before a workout and then morphs into the heavy lifting that you have to do at the squat rack to build the foundation muscles to support your entire being.

I caution you that the process of finding a therapist can be quite difficult and extremely frustrating. Due to great need and demand, the mental health system is taxed to the point where, in many geographic areas, there is a huge shortage of qualified people that are able to take on new patients. Please try to be patient as you seek out the right person. When you have found someone, go into the session with the attitude that you are interviewing them as much as they are interviewing you. Just as some shoes don't fit some feet, all therapists and clients do not fit each other either. There must be a "fit" for the process to be beneficial.

This is a person with whom you are going to establish a trusting bond. That relationship can only begin with true chemistry between the therapist and the client. Now, I'm not talking about the kind of chemistry that you seek with a friend or romantic partner. This is a chemistry of personality, philosophy, intelligence, and approach. A good therapist will meet the client where the client is, so, in many cases, the chemistry happens right away. In some situations, a particular therapist may be the right fit for the time being, but as you grow and evolve, you may outgrow your therapist's ability to help you.

This did happen with a therapist that I was seeing right after I was released from the hospital. He was a very caring and very strong professional who I was referred to by the hospital. We had a chemistry in treatment from the start, but after a year of sessions, we had reached a plateau. It was apparent to both of us that for me to go further, which was something that

I wanted to do, I was going to need to find another person to take me to the next level.

How do I find a therapist? Start working out your emotional muscles a little and ask friends, relatives, your doctor, and anybody else that you come in contact with during your day. If you have an insurance program, chances are that program includes an Employee Assistance Program or a mental health management component that you can call and talk with someone that will provide a referral to a professional within your benefit program. You find people by connecting with people.

"But, Jimmy, I don't have the money to pay a therapist." That is understandable and in a lot of cases, people don't seek the help that they need because they feel that it is unaffordable and they just cannot stretch their budget any further. I would submit to you that there is no more important expense than talk therapy. You cannot be your whole self without achieving a level of rhythm and peace. But, I also understand the stress that squeezing another expense item into the budget can create. Find a religious leader—a priest, rabbi, minister, etc.—that you can talk with. There are also public advocate therapists in some cities who work with clients as part of their study and learn how to be better at what they do. You can also find a friend that may be willing to provide you with a helpful ear. This can be difficult though, because you really need the objectivity of someone that is not emotionally engaged in your life.

There are resources out there, and the Universe always delivers what you need, when you are ready to accept the help and hear it, and are ready to heal. That is a universal fact and I urge you to go be the Hero of your story.

"This above all to thine own self be true, and it must follow, as the night the day, thou canst not then be false to any man."
-William Shakespeare

Translated to:
There is peace in truth.

CHAPTER 21

THE FIRST TRAUMA

In many ways, this is the most difficult chapter to write. I have thought about this for many months and have sat to write something meaningful at least 15 times. I came up with a blank sheet of paper every single fucking time. Anguish, fear, shame, embarrassment, and emptiness all seem like the right terms to describe the feelings that I experienced as I worked through this experience in my life. I was sexually abused a couple of times by the same person starting when I was a six-year-old little boy and then again when I was an 11-year-old.

There, I said it, and it's the event of my first trauma.

However, that is not the reason that I couldn't write about it. I lived it, I have relived it, and I have lost many nights of sleep over this trauma. I have discussed it with my therapist, my life partner, and my children. That is not the reason for the difficulty in writing about it as part of my story. The problem is that I don't know what to say that hasn't been said by countless victims. I want to have something meaningful to add to the conversation and to bring it into the light of day. I know that it is much more common than people think and there are thousands of men out there, just like me, who have experienced some form of sexual abuse. They are afraid to admit that level of vulnerability, or they don't want to face the pain and shame, or they just don't fucking remember.

I can attest to the following: there are things that occur in our lives that we have the ability to block out entirely and trauma, all trauma, affects us at a cellular level. To me, that means that it puts an imprint on your body that requires the most gentle and diligent and disciplined cleansing to find it and reckon with it. Then, and only then, can it be released into the Universe. And, that is the goal.

The goal is not retribution or some form of vengeance that gets played out in a movie scene where the victim boils their abuser in a vat of hot oil. While that romantic notion of payback can be alluring to some, in the end, you are still in the same place that you were in, and the scars of that trauma will continue to be embedded in the deepest reaches of your heart, mind, and body.

Here's the thing about trauma, it is not about the specifics. If I've said it once, I've said it a thousand times: TRAUMA IS FUCKING TRAUMA. It is about energy and feeling and what it leaves behind. It's not about what happened to one person being worse than what happened to another. It is about what each person experiences as a result of being victimized. The resulting pain will be etched inside of you regardless of the depths of the actions that you are experiencing.

Let me explain a little. I have lived my share of trauma in life and those events have created deep-seated pain and suffering and have led to deep depression and high levels of anxiety. If I had only experienced one trauma, say, the brutal assault when I was 17, the result would have been the same. I would have lived in fear. If I had only been exposed to a father who was ill and wasn't aware of his destructive actions, I would have lived in fear.

My point here is that if you are reflecting on your life, there may be traumatic events that you have blocked or have diminished in your mind, thinking that it's one small event and I'm lucky that I wasn't molested, psychologically abused, mugged, and riddled with depression. The fear that was created from whatever that event was for you, is real and needs to be understood and reckoned with. In short, your trauma and your feelings about your abuser, need a hug. Not a physical hug, obviously, an emotional hug. I am not saying that it is easy to get to that hug, I am saying that once you get to that place, you can be free and happy.

To my point about trauma being trauma, the problem with sexual abuse is that it is not about the physical act that created problems for me. In fact, physically, it was exciting and some of it felt good. It's the emotional trauma that creates the anguish and the fear that just controls you over and over and over and over again.

My abuser used language to describe my body, negative and toxic words about my physical features, that played like a fucking echo chamber in my head for decades. I was a six and 11-year-old boy. I was hairless. I hadn't reached puberty, so my genitals were not developed, and I had some areas of baby fat in my midsection. All normal and perfectly healthy things about a little boy. All the perfection of the human body and the innocence of a child. I was a fucking child and the reality is that I didn't reach puberty until I was in college, when I grew four inches from a tall high school kid of six feet, to a man of 6-feet 4-inches in my freshman year. The reality is that I believed those caustic words that were being said to me.

They were said to me by somebody that was in my life, someone I saw as a role model, and those words were cutting. More than that, they enveloped me in a suit of fear, shame and helplessness for much of the rest of my life. I cannot put into words the pain and suffering that I lived, and lived again, and lived again, over the course of the 30 years that followed. I had blocked out the events, but the feelings were imprinted on a cellular level. While my mind put these events in a very small box and buried it somewhere in the corner of my brain, my heart, and my cells had already been damaged.

To try and help you understand the peeling back of layers in my process, here is how my memories of those events came back to me.

As a part of my journey, my guru was taking me through several modalities of work, including talk therapy, Reiki and body work, meditation, couples therapy, nutrition education, sleep behavior analysis, journaling, and more. The value of this work being done as a holistic approach was amazing. This person that the Universe delivered into my life was a miracle and yet another sign that there is a force at work beyond this physical world.

My wife and I were doing a 30-day detox program that was monitored daily and included nutritional supplements and very focused food intake. During what I call a nutritional reset, we went for 15 days consuming only liquids and removing all sugar and yeast from our bodies. As I said, this was closely monitored by a professional and I wouldn't recommend doing it any other way.

Removing sugar from the body is an intense exercise and it has the most amazing impact, not only on the physical body, but on the mind as well. In the first couple of days, I experienced jitteriness, headaches, and body aches, like I had never experienced before. I would lay in a hot bath of Epsom salts to calm my body and mind down so that I could continue moving forward to health. Each day, I felt closer and closer to the essence of who I am and I was experiencing revelations in very uplifting and exhilarating feelings.

About a week into this detox, I had a flash of a memory that I knew was not good. It was a feeling of dread, and all I saw was the bedpost of my wooden childhood single bed. After two days of talking about this flash with my guru, she asked me to close my eyes and sit on that bed, and she took me through a guided meditation that was one of the worst nightmares that I had ever seen. I could smell my room, my pillow, the musty rug below my bed in my basement bedroom. I went through that event, feeling my way through a myriad of mental blocks —it was like cutting through the Amazon rainforest with a machete. My mind had created a huge wall of protection, and I was determined to get through it and hug that fucking nightmare into submission.

Timeline check: I was 18 months-ish post-hospital stay at this point in time and had been going to our guru at least once and sometimes twice a week for that period. The nutrition program and detox was the next level of emotional connection, and the toxic shit that we put in our bodies is like any other drug, it prevents us from living our full potential of feelings.

Once I lived the feelings and the memory of this trauma, the first trauma, I went to work on forgiveness. Coming face to face with the farthest reaches of my mind was akin to the worst nightmares that you can conjure. It felt as if I had to walk through a blazing fire with a wet blanket around my body. Each step, the blanket would get hotter and hotter, until it disintegrated and it was just my bare skin being burned inch by inch until the flesh was dripping from my bones. Moving forward was the only way to get through it and getting to the other side of that fire was the healing station to have my wounds cared for so that I could heal.

Applying real tactics: Can you make room in your blue sky for the darkest, largest, and most tumultuous tempest clouds that you have ever seen? I spoke of seeing the vast sky as your peace, with some dark clouds dotting the sky of our lives from time to time. This is where that practice takes you to task.

You might think that forgiving the abuser was the hard part, and it was difficult, but the hardest part was forgiving the victim (me, that little boy). Here I am, as an adult. I am physically large and strong and fucking tough. I had to go back into my six-year-old little body and hold that child and let him know that he was safe and that I would not let anything like that happen ever again. I had to tell him that it was not his fault and that not defending himself was OK and that not telling his mom was also OK. I had to tell that little boy that he was safe and loved for all of who he was and let it go. I forgave myself for being a victim, not telling somebody, and hating myself for letting it happen.

As I experienced this healing, it was evident that a gentle, loving touch was necessary. Not vengeance and anger and retribution. That little boy, sitting on that single bed in the basement of my childhood home was not going to benefit from anger and vengeance. In fact, just the opposite. He needed to know that it was OK to be vulnerable. He needed a gentle voice, an open heart. He needed to be heard, to be held, to be loved in a way that he had never experienced. This underscores, for me, the need for us to teach our little boys to be vulnerable and to be open to love and that it is OK to experience that to the fullest. Those teachings will play out throughout their lives.

This experience of forgiveness didn't happen overnight and it involved lots of screaming into pillows and clawing at the ground on my hands and knees in gut-wrenching blood-curdling crying to the point of complete exhaustion. The hate and self-loathing rushed out of me like a newly sprung oil well, just spewing in all directions out of the ground.

As I was going through this process, I was reflecting on the impact of that trauma. It set fear in my cells like freshly poured concrete had been laid in my veins and hardened up like a pillar under a huge suspension bridge. That fear created a path of victimhood and resulted in lots of future trauma and anxiety and depression.

This specific trauma also had a massive impact on my ability to be sexually intimate in a way that was free and flowing. That connection between the physical experience of sexual intimacy and the emotional love of relationship, had been severed. That was another path of work to pursue and heal and would be work that could be shared in another book.

This experience of healing had opened up a box of guilt, shame, and pain that was buried deeply inside of me. Opening up that box was a fucking miracle and allowed for further understanding of who I am and what life could feel like if I was living in peace and grace.

Thankfully, there are many resources to get support for sexual abuse, here is one that I have recommended: https://www.rainn.org/resources

CHAPTER 22

THE SCREEN DOOR
GENTLY CLOSES

I have a palpable memory of my parents fighting. After all, as you have learned, they were not a match made in heaven, and they were both the products of abusive and traumatic childhoods. It's no wonder that they lived in such pain and fought with each other.

When I was very young, probably five or six, I would sit on the front stoop of our little house every Saturday morning and wait for my father to come for his weekly visit. There were many Saturdays when he didn't show up and when he did show up, he was always late. I would sit out there on the steps, picking at the ants as they dug their holes between the red bricks or I would take a baseball and glove and throw it up against the stoop, practicing my grounders. My dad would pull up into the driveway and throw his lit cigarette onto the lawn, stamp it out with his boot and hand me a big brown paper bag filled with fresh bagels and cream cheese from Brooklyn. He'd give me a hug and kiss my head and tell me that he was sorry he was late, "boy, there was bad traffic on the Belt Parkway today, Jimmy."

We'd walk in the front door together and head to the kitchen where my mom would have a fresh pot of coffee on the stove, and she'd pour my dad a cup. He only drank it black and I thought it was disgusting. My mom would take the bagels into the dining room and put everything out nicely, with plates and serving platters, and she'd put a clean butter knife into the cream cheese, and I just couldn't wait to take a thick sesame bagel and slather it with cream cheese and sink my teeth into it. My sisters and I all sat at the table using our best manners as the food was passed around, and everybody got their special Saturday breakfast buttered and "schmeared" and sliced and whatever they chose.

My dad always sat at the head of the table and my mom would put an ashtray next to the steaming hot cup of coffee, and once everybody had what they needed, she would take a seat. One big "happy" family.

My mom would say, "I need to buy food this week, can you give me some money to buy food?"

Dad would reply, "I'll see what I can do."

"I need to take the kids for their preschool doctor check-ups, and that's going to cost another $50 this week."

Dad: "OK."

Mom: "We got a letter from the State of New York Tax Office and..."

My dad, at the top of his lungs would yell, "Jesus Christ, I haven't even had my coffee yet. I'm not made of money. I have to go."

The kids, all four of us, sitting quietly with tears running down our cheeks, would watch him pound the table with his fleshy fist, grab his pack of Marlboros, a matchbook, and his keys, stand up, aggressively slide his chair back behind his legs and we all watched and heard it as it smacked against the wall. Then, he'd walk around the table to his right, open the back door with a quick push and as he left the room, he would grab the door and slam it loudly. Then, he was gone.

Depending on the degree to which the argument escalated, and how inadequate my father felt, would dictate whether he would return the following week or not. There were no guarantees and we, the kids, always tried to behave to prevent any massive blow ups.

That back door was a heavy pine, painted white, with a four-inch thick panel border, heavy metal screening that had green molding around it. One day, when I was older, I took that door off the hinges and painted it for my mom. It weighed like 50 pounds. It was old school heavy.

That story of my dad leaving happened more often that I like to remember, and that door became a physical and metaphorical symbol of the dysfunction that we all lived in. Later in life, the slamming of that door, as it shook the whole fucking house, was the physical sound of anxiety and depression. I hated that fucking door and I hated that I couldn't get that sound out of my head for many, many years.

From that door slamming, to here and now, my path has been circuitous, and it all happened for a reason. I am painfully aware of the times that I spent thinking about ending my life, contemplating my own inadequacies, believing the stories that were swirling around in my head. Yet, as I moved down the path of an examined life, I came to a place of gratitude and peace through the same discipline and practice that I employed to be an elite athlete.

My Road Map to Health

My Road Map (in no particular order) to health is simple:

1. **Sleep:** At least 7 – 8 hours a night.

2. **Nutrition:** Eat a diet that leaves me feeling good and doesn't have me gaining weight.

3. **Water:** Drink lots of water daily, the goal is 90 oz a day. I am usually around 60 – 70 oz a day.

4. **Meditate:** Establish some daily quiet time.

5. **Journal:** Write it down, whatever it is, write it down.

6. **Connect with People:** Acknowledge those around you.

7. **Exercise:** I run four to five times a week (or as much as my old body will allow).

8. **Gratitude:** I try to be grateful daily, for me, and my life, and those around me.

9. **Stay Present:** Focus on this moment in time and be 100% in that place.

10. **Forgive:** Let it go, forgive yourself and anyone else.

As I said, it's simple...it ain't easy, but it is simple. These are the 10 things that I do to keep my anxiety and depression under control. I do not do every one of them, every day, although I strive to do most of them daily. My Road Map to health has become a part of me like my heart or my arms are a part of me. When I start to slip mentally or emotionally, when I feel myself sliding off into the abyss, I will sit down and look at my last couple days and see where the missing elements of the practice are, and I can get myself back on track quickly.

I have tried to clearly share how I decided in 2005 to end my pain once and for all, and to leave this world.

Having been given the gift to survive that and then to be given the gift of evolving and living an examined life, my life experience, as someone who is present in it, I have lived significant life events.

Three of my children's high school graduations.

I coached my daughter's high school varsity lacrosse team and lived my dream of having a child play Division I lacrosse.

Three of my kid's college graduations.

Two marriage proposals for my daughters.

One wedding (the second will be next year).

Two business school graduations (my daughter and son-in-law graduated from MIT Sloane and Harvard).

My daughter went into business with my wife and they have built a very successful women's clothing business

I was present for a huge celebration of a New Year's Eve in Milan, Italy with the entire family plus spouses and spouses-to-be.

I have traveled all over the world, including Europe a few times, Asia, the Caribbean, Canada, and dozens of cities and states in the United States.

I held my wife's hand as we sipped champagne while we watched the sunset on our little beach in our little town.

I have cooked countless meals for my family, including 16 Thanksgiving feasts.

I have coached hundreds of lacrosse players and played in many games. I achieved a lacrosse milestone in that I played and coached for 40 years!

My son and I got lost in the woods while on a hike during a huge snow storm and it was one of the most peaceful and magical afternoons of my life.

I have had two knee surgeries.

I have laid on the rocks at the beach with my kids, and listened to their thoughts while the water rolled over the shoreline.

I have marveled at the power of true connection with people.

I have helped to build and/or run several companies and have taught many executives how to meditate, that it is an incredible value to be yourself, and it's better for everyone if you bring your authentic self into the boardroom.

I have immersed myself in some amazing entertainment: movies, books, TV programs, live music – including watching Muse perform in Atlanta with my son, and my wife and I danced to U2 in New York City while Bono was about 20 yards away from us, doing what Bono does.

We have been to many Broadway shows and I have stood in awe under the Christmas tree in Rockefeller Center every year since 2005.

I have continued to run and train and push my physical body to do what I love to do. Yes, I'm a little slower and I'm in a little bit of pain from time to time, and I LOVE IT.

I have witnessed my own children work through their own examined lives and develop the tools necessary to manage their inherited anxiety and depressive traits.

I lived through a pandemic.

I have lived!

I am aware of every day's gift to me, my family, and the people in my life. The list above is a short reminder of what I would have missed and the people I love would have missed with me. Life would have continued for everyone, and they would have continued to experience the things that we move through in our lives, and it would not have been as great for anyone, had I not been there. We have all been given a gift through this healing and the breaking of the cycle of destruction that would have continued for us and our ancestors.

A Journaling Exercise

As an exercise of reflection, grab a pen and some paper and write down the things that you did over the past few years, as many things as you can remember. Add the people that were there with you when you lived those experiences. That is a powerful statement of the impact that you have had.

Our family has fought to grow as people. We did the work, and I am grateful for the people around me who supported me to get back to myself. To allow me to go back to the trauma, feel and love through it, and heal.

You see, we all matter. Everything that we do matters, and it has an impact on the people in our lives, and while you may not believe that or be able to feel it, it is fact. You matter. I matter. We all matter, and to think otherwise is just your ego preventing you from living your best self.

Today, I sit in my backyard in the rain. It is a warm mid-August day in New England, the birds are singing, my dogs are walking around the back yard smelling the day as the world wakes up. I sit on the porch steps, feeling my way through a few things happening in my life, and it starts to rain. Steady and cool and the leaves start to patter as the big drops make their way to the ground. I look up into the sky and see the sun breaking through to the east and the gray clouded sky is now alight in one spot with the sun as it bursts through, letting me know that there is a brightness despite the gray over my head. It is a reminder of life's challenges, stresses, and joys.

I think of the sky as a metaphor for the mind's thoughts. The sky, your mind, is vast and filled with clouds, which can represent sadness or anger or a shit storm of bad stuff, and there is clear blue sky which represents happiness, peace, joy, and grace. When I experience a dark cloud in my day, I might be sad or anxious. And, the sky is vast, and the clouds and the clear blue share the same atmosphere. I have expanded the sky in my mind to where it is big enough to hold all of it, and it is comforting to know that despite one cloud in the current moment, my sky is holding clear blue and that it is there for me to behold anytime that I want to see it.

It rains harder, and I am now wet from head to toe, and the dogs are standing next to me and waiting for me to open the door to let them into the dry shelter. A raindrop runs down the front of my wet head, over my nose, and bounces off my top lip, I watch it fall to my leg. I laugh as I think, *There is coffee in the fridge, Jimmy...there is always coffee in the fridge.*

I stand up, walk to our house's back door, open it, and let the dogs in and out of the rain. I stop and look back as the rain falls harder on the wooden planks of the deck. I put my hand on the inside of the door, and gently let the screen close behind me.

EPILOGUE

THE EVOLUTION

The work never stops and therefore, the evolution continues through time. Having anxiety and depression is part of who I am and that will never go away. Managing my anxiety and depression is similar to battling any addiction and the ongoing work is a daily practice. My Road Map for peace and grace described in the previous chapter is something that I follow regularly and I encourage you to create your own Road Map to wellness. Once you have created your Road Map, be gentle with yourself. We all live in the real world and sometimes things do not always happen on schedule. For me, meditation and sleep are the things that I need every day to succeed in being at peace. There are periods of time where I may miss a few days and that's OK. I have learned to accept my flaws as part of what makes my journey my own.

To be totally honest, I never thought that I could live the feeling of pure happiness, and when people ask me how I continued to focus on my work, I tell them that the goal of happiness was always a motivation. My wife modeled happiness for me. I wanted to feel what she felt, and now I do. It is an amazing way to feel, and practicing the elements of my Road Map allows me to be in that state more often than not. If I had given up instead of breaking through, I would not have had the chance to live that.

The journey of forgiveness and gratitude is critical to allowing the grace of life to live within me. I have been able to let go of all the anger and distress. Although, at times, it can bubble up a bit with specific people or events, and those that have caused me trauma have been forgiven and embraced. The essay below was something that I wrote in 2019 to put out into the Universe, a forgiving message to the guys that assaulted me when I was 17. This is part of the work that is important in releasing that type of anger. Writing your feelings down on paper can have the same effect as having a direct conversation with someone; it releases those feelings into the Universe and out of your body. I hope you can see the forgiveness in my words.

An Essay by James Francis

October 2019

I think of you often....

I think of you often; I hope that you did not hurt too many other people on your way to driving the demons out of your body and mind. I wonder if you learned that the pain of childhood cannot be extinguished through passing that pain on to others. I have tried that myself, and in that experience, we are one.

I think of you often; our meeting set me on a path that was not what I was supposed to do with my life. I was meant for other things where I could find outlets for my creativity and express my deep feelings and emotions. That event put me on a harder path of focus on money so that I could escape the poor neighborhood of my childhood which was why I was where I was when I met you and your friends. Trauma causes fear and fear causes walls to go up.

I think of you often; I feel sad that we never really connected. I wonder if the blood that splattered onto you and your friends, my blood, gave you any sense of who I was. I am sure that you are funny or caring or could teach me how to draw or change the oil in my car. I am certain that the events of that night had nothing to do with "you" and who you are. You were a product of a society that isn't fair and is very fucking confusing.

I think of you often; to this day, the smell of blood, the salty metallic odor that covered my head as I ran away in fear of the beating continuing, gives me flashbacks. When my daughter was seven years old, she fell over the handlebars of her bike and as I carried her home, the smell of the blood dripping from her face wafted to my nose, and there you were.

I think of you often; I know that I am better for our meeting and I forgive you. I was a kid. Tall for my age and probably looked like an adult who had just gotten off the Long Island Rail Road train from New York and maybe you thought I had money. It was dark and cold on that Tuesday night in January. I gave you my pay for the week *of working at my high school job. $138. Was it worth it? That was the cheapest life lesson that I ever invested in.*

I think of you often; the anger in the words, "white piece of shit," caused nightmares for years. The dozens of stitches in the back of my head have left me with scars that still hurt on a cold damp day. I grew up in a neighborhood of people that were racists, bigots, anti-Semites, and I never understood the pure anger and fear that existed. That night, the four of you taught me to fear and to be angry. I still saw and felt the difference between "good" people and "bad" people and it didn't matter what color their skin was. There are no "good" and "bad" people. There are only damaged or healed people and I truly hope that you are healed.

I think of you often; the scars on my head, the bones in my hand that never healed properly, the constant awareness of my surroundings, especially at night. That meeting never leaves me and I wonder if you even remember it or if the emotional scars of that night are still with you or if you have been able to heal.

I think of you often; I was alone, and I now understand that you were alone too. Yes, there were four of you, but your loneliness in this world must have been a flash point for your anger. I feel sad that you and I shared that level of loneliness in life.

I think of you often; the recent racially charged events of Ferguson and Charlottesville and the constant undercurrent of racism that seems to continue to permeate our world is a constant reminder of the physical blows of hate that you rained down on my face, my head, and my back. That hatred was palpable and we both know what it was and why it was happening. It was you saying, my life is not fair, I was brought into a society that is unequal and this white boy is a symbol of that unfairness and I am going to kill him with my anger.

I think of you often; I am healed, physically and emotionally and all is forgiven. We met in 1982 and while I have changed, the world around me is still struggling with the same issues and sometimes it feels like nothing has changed. We continue to make the same mistakes and the anger and fear is still as it was on that January night on Long Island. The world needs to do the work to heal, accept, and love.

In Closing

The work can be hard and it can be a long road. On the other side of the work is the magic that you were meant to live.

I hope that you enjoyed reading my story and I leave you with this:

Life is too short to wake up in the morning with regrets.
So, love the people who treat you right,
forgive the ones who don't
and believe that everything happens for a reason.
If you get the chance, take it.
If it changes your life, let it.
Nobody said it would be easy,
they just promised it would be worth it.
- Dr. Seuss

MUSIC AS A HEALING AID

One of the most powerful tools that I have leveraged in my evolution to healing is music. There is a magical resonance to the body, mind and heart's reaction to lyrics and music and melody and harmony and everything that goes into a great song. There are songs that have touched my soul from an early age in life, and when I started to wake up from the numbness of depression, I wanted to devote my time to activities that would nurture my future. As I have discussed, meditation is one of those key activities and I have tied my meditations to music in many cases. I have created a number of playlists on Spotify that include songs that I use when I am meditating. It is a literal combination of life's experiences that I associate with specific songs, and as I wrote this book there were specific songs that jumped off the page at me that I would apply to each chapter. The song for a specific chapter might include one sentence that underscores what I was feeling or thinking during that chapter's events or topics.

Ideally, I would have included those lines of lyrics in the story, however, copyright laws are very strict and prevent that from being a way to illustrate those connections. I think that some brilliant songwriters have provided prophetic advice in their music and below you will find a list of some of the songs that I have found to be helpful and that I would associate with a specific chapter of the book. In most cases, I have also included the section of the song that resonates with the experience of that chapter:

Chapter 1: American Tune, Paul Simon (lyric of note is 1:00 - 1:51)

Chapter 2: Vienna, Billy Joel (lyric of note is 2:19 - 2:25)

Chapter 3: Woke Up This Morning, Alabama3 (lyric of note is 1:52 - 2:07

Chapter 4: Wish You Were Here, Pink Floyd (3:16 - 3:44)

Chapter 5: Don't Give Up, Peter Gabriel (2:52 - 3:20)

Chapter 6: When I Look To The Sky, Train (2:23 - 3:23)

Chapter 7: Fix You, Coldplay (3:32 - 4:46)

Chapter 8: What's Up, 4 Non-Blondes (:57 - 1:24)

Chapter 9: Dark Side, Kelly Clarkson (1:05 - 1:26)

Chapter 10: Redemption Song, Bob Marley (1:14 - 2:11)

Chapter 11: Once in a Lifetime, Talking Heads (:31 - :41)

Chapter 12: Cat's in the Cradle, Harry Chapin (:34 - :50)

Chapter 13: Everybody Hurts, REM (:17 - 2:17)

Chapter 14: Human, Christina Perri (1:13 - 1:37)

Chapter 15: Into the Wild, LP (1:49 - 2:57)

Chapter 16: Power of Two, Indigo Girls (:55 - 1:27)

Chapter 17: Somewhere Over the Rainbow, I. Kamakawawiwo 'ole (1:02 - 1:50)

Chapter 18: The Riddle, Five for Fighting (2:58 - 3:36)

Chapter 19: Forever Young, Alphaville (:45 - 1:26)

Chapter 20: Rocky Mountain High, John Denver (1:33 - 2:19)

ABOUT THE AUTHOR

James Francis, aka Jim Rinere, is an entrepreneur and professional speaker. He has been a successful executive, starting and running several businesses in the wellness and insurance markets.

Through the course of his three-decade career, he has worked closely with private equity and venture capital investors, he has run sales teams for large publicly traded companies, he has been a c-suite executive for six start-ups in the healthcare and well-being space, and he also owned and operated a vintage Good Humor Ice Cream Truck.

He is a 28-year resident of Madison, Connecticut and is a father and husband, and has been practicing mindfulness for 15 years.

GREEN HEART
LIVING
— PRESS —

Green Heart Living Press publishes inspirational books and stories of healing and transformation, making the world a more loving and peaceful place, one book at a time. You can meet Green Heart authors on the Green Heart Living YouTube channel and the Green Heart Living Podcast.

www.greenheartliving.com

Made in the USA
Monee, IL
16 February 2024

53634609R00144